Ric Throssell is the only so

accomplished writer and playwright. His biography of his father, Hugo Throssell, was published in 1989 as *My Father's Son* and was shortlisted for many major literary awards.

By the same author:
Autobiography:
My Father's Son
As Editor:
Straight Left: The articles and addresses of Katharine Susannah Prichard
Tribute: The short stories of Katharine Susannah Prichard
Plays:
Devil Wear Black
The Day Before Tomorrow
For Valour
Legend
The Sweet Sad Story of Elmo and Me
and other plays.

IMPRINT

WILD WEEDS AND WINDFLOWERS

RIC THROSSELL

AN ANGUS & ROBERTSON BOOK

First published in Australia in 1975 by
Angus & Robertson Publishers Australia
This revised edition published in 1990
by Collins/Angus & Robertson Publishers Australia

Collins/Angus & Robertson Publishers Australia
Unit 4, Eden Park, 31 Waterloo Road, North Ryde,
NSW 2113, Australia

Collins/Angus & Robertson Publishers New Zealand
31 View Road, Glenfield, Auckland 10, New Zealand

Angus & Robertson (UK)
16 Golden Square, London W1R 4BN, United Kingdom

National Library of Australia
Cataloguing-in-Publication data

Throssell, Ric, 1922–
Wild weeds and windflowers : the life and letters of Katharine Susannah Prichard.

Bibliography.
Includes index.
ISBN 0 207 16683 8.

1. Prichard, Katharine Susannah, 1883–1969 - Biography.
2. Women authors, Australian - 20th century - Biography.
I. Prichard, Katharine Susannah, 1883–1969. II. Title.

A823.2

Cover photograph of Katharine Susannah Prichard in her workroom in 1945 (courtesy of Ric Throssell).

Printed in Australia by Globe Press, Victoria

5 4 3 2 1
95 94 93 92 91 90

To
the good friends and comrades
of
Katharine Susannah Prichard

CONTENTS

For me — to have made one soul
  The better for my birth:
To have added but one flower
  To the garden of the earth;

To have struck one blow for truth
  In the daily fight with lies,
To have done one deed of right
  In the face of calumnies;

To have sown in the souls of men
  One thought that will not die —
To have been a link in the chain of life,
  Shall be immortality.

FOREWORD

Katharine persuaded herself to write about her own life in sheer self-defence. She always had reservations about the Freudian generalization and was appalled when a student in search of daring new interpretations of the psychological influences upon the writing of Katharine Susannah Prichard attributed her Marxism to a subconscious hostility to her father. It was necessary, she believed, to set the story straight. Even so, she hated the idea of writing her memoirs and found an excuse, whenever she could, to hide behind the aunts, uncles and cousins who surrounded her as a girl and the great persons she had met and interviewed abroad.

The naive young lady of *Child of the Hurricane* was a stranger, completely different from the woman I had come to know since my childhood; although idly exploring the drawers of family photographs I once found a picture of a young woman leaning dreamily against a paper-bark tree in shadowed bushland. I have the picture now, inscribed "sweet-hearting with Jimmy in Ferntree Gully", and the beauty and serenity of it still haunts me.

Katharine felt no obligation to take part in public confession of all the intimate details of her personal life, like a penitent drunk at a Salvation Army street-corner meeting. She set out to recapture the memory of herself as a young woman: attitudes long since left behind, the wonder and joy of youth, her search for answers to "the world's great anguish and its wrong". But the story remained incomplete.

Catherine Duncan understood Katharine's reluctance to reveal herself, when in a recent letter she compared her attitude with the "rage for privacy" that Leon Edel sees in the work of Henry James. Catherine wrote:

> This rage explains why Kattie was incapable of the strip-tease of an autobiography. She could only record events which are the least important aspects of a life. The essential experience had to be exposed indirectly, never in a personal form. We can know much more about her by reading the novels than *Child of the Hurricane.*

There are echoes of herself in some of the novels. They often reflect her own attitudes and occasionally draw directly on personal experiences. Incidents, words and phrases impressed upon her memory in moments of pain or revelation re-echo through the lives of her characters; but none of the novels is autobiographical, except *The Wild Oats of Han,* the story of her childhood in Tasmania. Han, that wild, tender young being, I know: so full of joy in living, so much hurt by the pain of others, so full of wilful determination, perhaps because I see in my own daughter, Karen Han, the image of the young Katharine Susannah.

A sequel to *The Wild Oats of Han,* which Katharine once intended to write and had meant to call *Cuckoo Oats,* for the second, spring sowing of the seed, was never written. *Child of the Hurricane* was first conceived as a novel for which she had made notes long ago. It became instead her reluctant autobiography. The autobiography itself was first meant to be in two parts, but Katharine could not bring herself to spend any more time on the story of her life in the thirty-six years after my father's death. She felt there was more important work to be done and was glad to turn to the novel which she expected to be her last major work.

It is from this point that my story begins, although for the sake of continuity the years of her childhood and youth are briefly retold. There is little that I have been able to add to her own account of that time. Few records of the early years of her life remain. Few who knew her well as a young woman are still living. I have been able to deal more fully with the time during the twenties, when the publication of *Working Bullocks* and *Coonardoo* established her literary reputation and opened new doors for Australian writers.

It was the same "rage for privacy" that led Katharine to insist that all uncompleted work and her private letters should be destroyed after her death. In an interview with Tony Thomas in *The Critic* in December 1967, Katharine was asked if she was going to burn all her drafts and corrected manuscripts. She replied:

> I am dreading having to go through them all. There is a lot more burning to be done. I do not want anything of mine to be published after I am dead that I have not approved of while I have my wits. I do not like to be seen in déshabillé even in manuscript . . .

For years Katharine sorted and sifted through cupboards and cartons of manuscripts and letters accumulated in a lifetime of writing: the old suitcases crammed with photographs, the shelves stacked with books and publications from all over the world, the briefcases and satchels stuffed with notebooks and jottings, quotations from the writers of the past and the eighty-five years of her own life. She destroyed my father's letters, her own father's love letters to her mother, my letters from New Guinea, Moscow and Rio de Janeiro. Long before, Katharine had burnt Hugh McCrae's letters, too, as he had asked, "ritually over a little fire of gum-leaves, seeing them ascend as incense into a blue bush afternoon". Only a few she could not part with. They were kept with his pressed flowers and pretty words, in remembrance of the man she believed she knew.

Most of the work was done when I arrived at Greenmount on 2 October 1969, an hour after she died. The letters which she believed to be of more than personal interest she had put aside. Shortly before her death she at last agreed that these should be preserved. The remaining private papers and unfinished manuscripts were burnt, as she wished.

I think it was her right to know that only completed work would become public; and that her private life would remain private. For years friends had tried to persuade Katharine that all her papers should be preserved for historical and literary research. Katharine could not agree. She hated the idea of being under the literary researchers' magnifying glass, like a bug on a pin. She was shocked when her own letters to friends were released to the public by their heirs and insisted that they should not be used without her permission.

The corrected typescripts of published works were given to the Australian National Library in Canberra, as Katharine had asked, except for *Haxby's Circus*, which she had given to Stephen Murray-Smith shortly after *Overland* was established, and *Subtle Flame*, which I believed belonged in a way to Dr Alec Jolly, whose dedication and medical skill had made it possible for Katharine to complete her last novel. Her notebooks were bequeathed to my daughter, Karen. The manuscripts of completed plays, stories, articles and notes for lectures and broadcasts, letters on literature and political affairs, press cuttings from around the world, I have kept myself. I could not burn her own weekly letters to me; but those, too, will remain mine alone. It is from these that I have drawn in writing of her.

Katharine placed no literary value on her letters. "I'm sure really that my letters have no literary airs and graces," she told me. "I haven't time to make them literary items. Always feel that they can never be exhumed as the letters of some writers are — because they're such dull things, as a matter of fact. Just no'count mumurings to my dear ones about every day happenings, and wanting to know about theirs." Katharine Susannah Prichard's reputation rests on the twenty-four published volumes of her work: novels, short stories, poems and plays, and the translations of the major novels and stories into some fifteen foreign languages. Her letters are Katharine herself.

I had not intended to write about my mother. Only in the course of preparing this biography did I discover that Katharine hoped that I might write the story of her life someday. I cannot attempt a dispassionate study. I can pretend to no cold, academic impartiality. Mine is a personal picture. I make no literary evaluation of my mother's work; no assessment of the rights and wrongs of the political beliefs which were an essential part of her writing and her life. That is for others to do, or for the most impartial observer of all: time

The great events of the world in which she lived — war, depression and revolution — deeply affected Katharine Susannah Prichard. They are part of her own history, as are the labours of the militant political movements in Australia with which she was identified. Her personal triumphs and tragedies were the calendar by which her days were measured. But, sometimes, it is the insignificant events of a past day which leave their trace upon memory. These things, too, have a part in her story.

All the threads of her life were one. Katharine Susannah Prichard, authoress, wife of Captain Hugo Throssell VC, was also Comrade Katharine, foundation member of the Communist Party of Australia. There was no schizophrenic division of her consciousness into that which belonged to life and that which belonged to literature. But in this account I have for the greater part separated the strands to show each one, chapter by chapter, avoiding the fragmentation of a strictly chronological presentation of events. I have been able, generally, to follow the progression of her life; but the arrangement of important activities into a more easily understandable pattern than life itself allows has meant that some events briefly referred to in the introductory chapters are repeated in greater detail later; others are anticipated, appearing before their place in the sequence of actuality.

At several points in the narrative of Katharine's life, I have therefore preserved the random order of reality to suggest more truly the way her days were spent: the intrusion of unrelated events;

the small, unimportant things of daily life; the flow of her attention from one demanding interest to another. Inevitably, much that was at one time significant in her eighty-five years of life has been omitted.

There can, of course, be no mechanical consistency throughout all the years of a human life. Katharine's attitude to her work, her understanding of the role of literature, her feeling about people and places, the world she lived in and the better world that she hoped some day others would enjoy, changed with the circumstances of her life and her society. An interpretation is unnecessary. I prefer to allow Katharine, as far as possible, to tell her own story through letters and articles, broadcasts, lectures and speeches, leaving comment to the replies and asides of her friends and critics. My role will be that of scene-shifter and, occasionally, prompter in the wings.

Where the written record is silent, I will draw upon my own memory and upon the recollections of the many people who have kindly assisted in my research.

I acknowledge with gratitude the assistance of the Commonwealth Literary Fund; the National Library of Australia; the Mitchell Library, Sydney; the Latrobe Library, Melbourne; the Battye Library, Perth; the Australian Broadcasting Commission; the Communist Party of Australia; the *West Australian*; *Meanjin*; *Overland*; her publishers, Jonathan Cape, Angus & Robertson and the Australasian Book Society, the All Union Book Chamber of the USSR, and the many friends of Katharine Susannah Prichard who have kindly made available their private correspondence.

Where the written record is silent, I drew upon my own memory and upon the recollections of the many people who kindly assisted in my research.

In the years since this biography was written, further fragments of Katharine's story have emerged. Research by a new generation of scholars into the growing collections of personal papers in the archives of the Australian National Library and other State collections has revealed some interesting reflections of Katharine Susannah Prichard through the eyes of her contemporaries. Manning Clark recognises in the sixth volume of his *History of Australia* the part that Katharine Susannah Prichard's vision of a new Australia played in the making of his "young tree green". Revived interest in the significant part played by women in Australia's political and cultural birth has also bred some strange interpretive fantasies.

Where new studies give an added dimension to understanding Katharine and her times, I have welcomed them and made my papers freely available. Where in pursuit of original thought a thesis has distorted reality to fit the shape of some grand encompassing philosophy, I have stepped out of my place in the wings to take my part among the players and say: "But that is not how it was".

One damaging misrepresentation of events which played a crucial part in Katharine's life was published widely throughout Australia by both press and radio. In the first edition of *Wild Weeds and Wind Flowers*, I told of my mother's long-hidden fear that my father's suicide in 1933 had been prompted by reading the unfinished manuscript of *Intimate Strangers.* That secret doubt disclosed at the end of her life was seized upon by *The Australian Women's Weekly* in a pre-release review of the 1981 television film of *Intimate Strangers*—and presented as cold established fact. In introducing a reading of the novel on radio, the Australian Broadcasting Commission repeated the same supposition. The less sensational explanation that I had given in this book was ignored. A returned soldier brought to the point of taking his own life by financial disaster, illness and the despair of the Depression years was not newsworthy. Over a hundred suicides had been recorded in Western Australia in the first year of the 'thirties. They had become just one of the tragic symptoms of a sick society that the world preferred not to know about.

By disclosing my mother's fear that she may have been responsible for my father's death, however unlikely that was, it seemed as if I had made it believable. The ABC's television film of *Intimate Strangers* gave its own aura of actuality to the fictional characters. Hoping that it might be possible to restore *Intimate Strangers* to the form that it had before Katharine rewrote the end in 1936, I had agreed that the scriptwriter, Brian Bell, should attempt to reconstruct the original conclusion. On the screen the suicide of Greg Blackwood was all too convincing. The thought that the story reflected my parents' lives was deeply hurtful to those who knew them. I had to find out what really happened, as far as it was possible after fifty years.

The official facts, untraced when I wrote in 1974, emerged from medical histories and legal evidence are not susceptible to subjective interpretation, nor to fanciful invention. My inquiries showed that my father had rewritten his Will on the day before he took his own life, leaving everything he possessed to my mother. From a brief article in *The West Australian* on 14th March 1934, announcing probate of his Will, I learnt that:

> In a Will cancelling all former Wills, and made on the day before he committed suicide last November, Captain H. V. H. Throssell, V.C., late of York Road, Greenmount, appointed Charles Merry, accountant, of Perth, his sole executor, and bequeathed all his estate and effects, real and personal, to his wife, Katharine Susannah Throssell, known in literary circles as Katharine Prichard.
>
> On the back of the Will the deceased had penned a short note, reading: "I have never recovered from my 1914–18 experiences, and, with this in view, I appeal to the State to see that my wife and child get the usual war pension. No man could have a truer mate."
>
> The Will has been lodged for probate.

His army medical records detail his admission to hospitals in England and Egypt for treatment of his wounds, meningitis and "fever". The Department of Veterans Affairs confirmed that H. V. H. Throssell, V.C. had received a 50% pension since the time of his discharge from the Army. The Repatriation Commission had determined after considering all the available evidence on his Service history and medical record that his death would be regarded as "due to War Service".

Both the author of *The Australian Women's Weekly* article and the ABC apologized for their error, but few who saw Hugo Throssell and Katharine in the fictional characters of *Intimate Strangers* knew their private anguish.

Our rich country sees again the futility of unwanted lives and wasted hopes. It may be more comforting to those reluctant to face the problems of the unwanted victims of a faltering economy to accept the romantic fantasy of a war hero dying for disappointed love. It is harder to accept the bitter truth that the sacrifice of my father's life, once offered at Gallipoli, should have become necessary to buy a widow's pension for his wife and son. It was typical of Katharine Susannah Prichard that she should have taken the blame for his self-sacrifice upon herself; but there was no guilt for that one tragedy of universal disaster. There were only the casualties of the time.

Katharine at first disclaimed a pension—but it was her only source of support in the lean years when her own work could not provide a living; until translations and new editions brought her international recognition and a fragile financial independence.

In my autobiography, *My Father's Son*, I tried to come to an understanding of the reasons why my father believed that the only way out of debt, unemployment and his own sense of failure was to destroy himself.

I acknowledge with gratitude the assistance of the Commonwealth Literary Fund; the National Library of Australia; the Mitchell Library, Sydney; the Latrobe Library, Melbourne; the Battye Library, Perth; the Australian Broadcasting Commission; the Communist Party of Australia; *The West Australian*; *Meanjin*; *Overland*; her publishers, Jonathan Cape, Angus & Robertson and the Australasian Book Society; the All Union Book Chamber of the U.S.S.R., and the many friends of Katharine Susannah Prichard who have kindly made available their private correspondence.

I am grateful to the Agent General for Western Australia in London, the Department of Veterans Affairs and the Department of the Army for their sympathetic assistance in retracing the circumstances of the death of H. V. H. Throssell, V.C.

Ric Throssell
Canberra, 1989

CHAPTER 1

KATTIE

Among the dusty albums, gilt-embossed with marvellous curlicues, I found the thick, time-tinted postcard of a solemn, bright-eyed baby in the arms of her Fijian nurse. There were verses, too, in the sweeping flourishes of her father's hand, four words to a line, pouring out across the page his pride in the wilful, tempestuous child, full of laughter and tears and imperious demands, born at the height of the tropical hurricane that devastated Levuka, old capital of Fiji, on 4 December 1883: "Kattie", Katharine Susannah Prichard, his "Luve ni Cava", his child of the hurricane:

Put all her perfections on paper!
I would that my eyes I could shut
To the marvellous metrical caper
My pen is expected to cut.

If virtues alone were commended
The list I could quickly attest;
But where shall the record be ended
Of half the perfections possessed?

The term is employed rather oddly,
For surely the fact must be plain
That characters worldly and godly
May both to perfection attain;
And if anyone carps at my theory
Or strives to convict me of error
I point him at once to our "dearie"
Who ranks as a *perfect* young terror.

Her mandate admits no resistance;
She rules with imperious sway;
She sees but her right of insistence
And deems it your place to obey.
She makes no concession contingent;
She takes no intention on trust:
Her practice is simple but stringent;
No compulsion; but only — "You must".

From the fragments of family history, the short stories and articles, letters, poems and diaries of T. H. Prichard, Editor of the *Fiji Times* and Secretary of the Planters Association; from her mother's tentative watercolours of a bungalow high above blue seas and distant islands, framed by feathery palms; from memories of family folklore and legend, tales lovingly retold of babyhood and a little girl's exploits, Katharine reconstructed the story of her infancy. With detached amusement, as if that "sprite of nature intense" were her own adored grand-daughter, Katharine looked back over eighty years and recounted the adventures of the baby Kattie in the opening chapters of *Child of the Hurricane*, her autobiography and twentieth published work.

She told of N'gardo, the male nurse, so scornful of the idea of a girl baby, who was completely captivated by his "Luve ni Cava"; how he formally presented her to the local chief as custom required; taught the baby the language of the chiefly caste; shepherded his unpredictable small charge from harm:

> There was a long flight of steps, cut in the hillside, which led from our bungalow to the township and the sea. As soon as I could walk, apparently, it was the joy of my life to make for these steps and pelt down them as fast as I could. "Quick, N'gardo," Mother would call. "Kattie's running down the steps." N'gardo trotted after me, picked me up when I sprawled, or joined in my gleeful triumph when I reached the sea. Then he would hoist me on his shoulder and climb the steep hillside again, laughing and shouting to Mother that there was nothing to fear. "Na Luve ni Cava has the sure feet of a bird and runs like the wind" he told her.

It was from N'gardo that she learnt of the old gods of the islands, who even now are still believed by some to live in the mountains, and of the Tuka cult which promised its followers "everlasting youth and health, with an abundance of everything desirable and desired".

Perhaps the story of N'gardo's death, self-willed in the inconsolable grief of separation from his spirit child, implanted in the impressionable mind of the little girl the sense of personal loyalty and dedication that remained part of her character throughout her life. Character is made by the sum of a life's experiences, and it is too easy to find in such episodes an influence far exceeding their real significance; but Katharine at the end of her life did remember her father's stories of N'gardo and wondered whether "that dark, protective presence" of her childhood was responsible for the sympathy she instinctively felt for native people.

Her "first literary effort", as a proud father called it, is less likely to have been a real beginning. Kattie had been locked in her father's study as a punishment for some forgotten misbehaviour:

> When he thought the culprit had been reduced to a proper state of penitence, he opened the door to find she was thoroughly enjoying herself. She had over-turned the inkpot, and, seated on his writing table, was busily scrawling ink over the papers all round her. "Go away, Tom", she said severely, mimicking a tone he had often used to her, "I'm writing".

Kattie was three when the family left Fiji with her two baby brothers and lived for a while at her grandparents' home, "Clareville", at North Road on the outskirts of Melbourne. She remembered her grandfather as an affectionate, old curmudgeon who was fond of playing fearsome games with the children, hooking their legs in the crook of his stick as he sat by the fire muttering, "Fee-fi-fo-fum, I smell the blood of an Englishman", to their terrified delight. But it was her grandmother, Susan Mary Fraser, who first captured Kattie's imagination with the inexhaustible treasury of her Victorian drawing-room and stories from a miniature booklet, "Elizabeth, or the Exiles of Siberia", in which the virtuous heroine was prone to noble declarations, very improving for the young:

> Since the dawn of reason enlightened my soul, my parents have been the sole objects of my thoughts; their love has been my greatest blessing, and to contribute to their happiness is my only wish. They are miserable. Heaven calls me to their relief, and has led you to this spot to aid me in fulfilling my destiny.

Soon after Tom Prichard became Editor of the *Sun*, a weekly newspaper, he moved the family to Brighton near the sea, secure in the respectability of a position in which he could employ his flair for satirical verse, solid conservative though he was.

To Kattie, Miss Cox's school at Brighton was a place where you learnt to play trains, hanging on to the small boy in front who puffed about importantly being the engine.

> Then one morning, two small boys started fighting as furiously as cockerels. Miss Cox rushed out to the schoolroom and put a stop to it. "What's the matter?" she asked. "Kattie's my truck", sobbed the umbrella boy, with a bloody nose. "And Artie says she's got to be his truck, 'cause she's his cousin". "You naughty little girl," said Miss Cox. "Why did you let the boys fight about it?"

Recalling the incident, Katharine concluded that being anyone's "truck" had never appealed to her since.

Kattie was eight when she first went to that school. And a "perfect terror" she looked at the time: eyes gleaming with villainy in a pointed, elfin face, beneath an impossible Cherry-Ripe hat, one ruched leg of her drawers hanging halfway down to her knees, leaning on one arm against the photographer's chair with momentary nonchalance, ready to take flight again at the click of the shutter.

A change in ownership of the *Sun* left Tom Prichard out of work and on the verge of the nervous depression which eventually destroyed him. "Father no longer went to work every morning", Katharine remembered. "He was not busy in his study in the evenings as usual. Mother did not say when the boys and I were chattering noisily: 'Ssh. Father's writing!' " Closing the scrapbook of his political skits for the *Sun,* he wrote wearily:

Sunscreeds and Madcap Rhymes
Written by me
T.H.P.
Who, with a sigh, adds
More fool I.

Her father's appointment to the editorship of the *Daily Telegraph* in Launceston, soon after the birth of Kattie's little sister, Beatrice, gave the family a fresh start. To Kattie herself, it was the beginning of the wild, free childhood in the hills and gullies of the Tasmanian bush which she described in *The Wild Oats of Han.* The book was "almost auto-biographical", Katharine said later, although she borrowed the Christian name of her Aunt Hannah, concealed her family behind the transparent disguise of other invented names and transposed some incidents from earlier adventures to the house on the top of the hill overlooking Launceston:

> After his day's work, when he had toiled uphill in the evening, Peter would stand at the gate, looking back at the long rough way by which he had come, and at the township with its squat, square buildings, muddily-white and huddled together flock-fashion, like sheep in the twilight. Wiping the sweat from his brow, he would take his hat off, so that last rays of the sun, still striking the hilltop, might bathe his head and shoulders. Chin raised, drawing in the tranquil beauty, the evening calm, his soul uplifted, his face a prayer of gratitude, eyes welling, he would stand quite still for a few moments, then turn to the garden, and go into the house.

Peter and Rosamund Mary Barry were the names Katharine chose for her mother and father. They were gentle, loving and rather remote figures to a child, to whom all being unfolded as a wonderful game:

> They were lovers, Han's father and mother. Children had come to them in the nature of accidents — not unwelcome accidents, to be sure — but just circumstances incidental to their love. They had the tenderest affection for the three; but that was outside themselves. They were absorbed in each other.
>
> It was a shock to them when they discovered before they had lived on The Hill for many years, that they had a family. They felt accesses of parental responsibility for some time after, and corrected, expostulated, and expounded the law and the prophets to Han and the boys for days at a time. Han, and the two small brothers who had come to enjoy life in the hills beside her, bore with them patiently; but were in no wise affected. They went their own ways, without let or hindrance, as gaily as if nothing had been said to the contrary.

Kattie herself was "the wildest of all the little wild animals that lived in the hills. Her grass-straw hat was invariably torn . . . a solemn elfish looking child . . . her eyes are full of lights and shadows . . . She had no conscience, any more than the birds or the possums . . ."

She did of course. In the very independence of her existence, the simple logic of the child's revolt against convention, her sensitivity to beauty, and her pain in the suffering of other creatures, there is the essence of the personal morality of Katharine Susannah Prichard. And in Han's fervent belief in the fancies of her own imagination are the beginnings of creativity. Her awakening to the realities of her father's failure to find work posed the first, unanswered question from which social conscience grew.

Han could steal apples without consciousness of wrong; wander off to explore the gullies and creeks when she should have been at school, without caring:

> Silver wattles beside the road were downy with blossom the morning Han took the law into her own hands. Whether it was the breath from them, as they dipped and swayed by the roadside, or the breeze which came from the hills, who knows? But, when she came to a turn in the road where it wound lazily downhill to school, she hesitated. She could hear bees in the golden masses of bloom, parakeets screech-

> ing among far-away trees. Wings red and blue and yellow flashed past her and dived into the greenery. A voice seemed to be crying to her, crying and singing softly, subtly, insistently:
>
> "Come Han!
> Han, Han!
> Come, Han!"
>
> Books in her hand weighed a ton. The track among the trees beckoned like a crooked, gnomish finger. Han dropped her books in a hollow stump and ran up the track through the trees.

Han could swim naked with her brothers in the heat of summer and firmly believe that she could escape the outraged modesty of the town's tell-tale spinster by disguising herself in ferns like "goodly greenish locks all loose untyde", and dancing around the shocked lady like "a Flocke of Nymphs". (But that is possibly the "Spenserian legend" referred to in the Foreword to *The Wild Oats of Han* as part of the make-believe story of Han, rather than the true-life Katharine Susannah.)

It was Kattie who fought to save a goanna from being stoned to death by the boy next door, clawing his face with her nails to protect that most improbable "enchanted prince". Kattie who wept for a sheaf of withered wildflowers, collected lovingly from the hillsides in the early morning for a flower show:

> "Look at it", she cried, grief and rage gripping her, as she held out the sheaf of withered wildflowers for him to see. "It was so pretty this morning. It would have been the prettiest of them all . . . but we had to wait for Miss Elizabeth at the foot of The Steps . . . And she was so long coming . . . and it was so hot, they died. Somebody laughed at them, so I brought them away."
>
> Throwing herself on the grass, Han sobbed tempestuously. Sam left her alone for awhile. Then he went and sat down beside her. "I know", he said. "I know Han. It hurts — life's like that . . . full of pains and things you don't expect. You haven't known before — but you've got to meet 'em and take 'em . . . crackin' hardy. Not let on they hurt, too much. That's the way, Han. You've just got to shake your fist at Life and say: 'You can't break me. You can't!' And Life 'll get tired of tryin'. You see."
>
> But Han lying on the grass, could only sob over the dying breaths of the wildflower people in her withered bouquet.

At eight or nine years old, Kattie discovered the wonderful world she could make in her own mind. Books intrigued her, before she could really read, for the stories she was able to invent about the people in the pictures. Through Han she told of visits to the forbidden secrets of her father's study:

> Usually Han's visits were as surreptitious as the bees'. She just turned over the books for a few minutes and went away again. But one day she found, lying open on the table, a huge leather-covered book like the family Bible, with "Plays of William Shakespeare" carved in heavy gilt letters across it. There were pictures in the book. Han tried to read the fine dim writing beside them.
>
> Over and over again she crept into the room and with a mighty effort lifted the tome from the shelf where it stood, put it on the floor, and lay down full length on the floor before it to gaze at the pictures. Absorbed in her wondering about what they might mean, as she could not read the printing beside them, and making her own stories for every picture, one day she did not hear the door open and close again.
>
> She only knew her sin had found her out when she saw her father, Rosamund Mary, and Granny in the open doorway gazing at her. Peter's eyes were radiant, Granny's brimming with smiles, Rosamund Mary's awed and surprised.
>
> Han's guilty confusion changed to amazement when her father called softly, joyously:
>
> "Come here, Han!"
>
> He took her in his arms and kissed her . . .
>
> "I believe, dear", he said to Rosamund Mary, "our harum-scarum will be a credit to us, after all".

Kattie quite shamelessly allowed her parents to believe that she really had been reading Shakespeare, but when her father firmly removed Lempriere's classical dictionary, with its accounts of the immoral goings-on of the gods and goddesses of ancient times, and put it on the top shelf out of her reach, Kattie hooked it down with the garden rake and searched fruitlessly from cover to cover to find out why it was not a "fit book" for her to read: "For a long time, however, she was so hurt at having the book taken away, and so offended at this unexpected censorship of her reading, that she would have nothing to do with *Plays of William Shakespeare* or any other book."

She learnt that others could be entranced in the subtle magic of her imagination. Being sent to bed was no punishment when Kattie could tell her brothers stories about the tiny people decorating the Chinese bowls from which they ate their bread and milk. Her efforts at playmaking were less successful. Dreams of becoming a bareback rider in the circus ended with a disastrous performance when, dressed in mauve stockings and her mother's corsets, she leapt from the top branches of a tree and crashed to the ground, winded and unconscious.

Katharine confessed that Sam, the shingle splitter of *The Wild Oats of Han,* who lived alone in the bush near Han's home, was a "rather idealised version of the old man who used to cart wood" for her family in Launceston. In his words, the young Katharine Susannah expressed her own half-formed thoughts at the time the story was written, in 1908, rather than the ideas that may have influenced her as a child:

> "You see, if your untrammelled spirits carry you along, Han", Sam went on. "you're bound to have some wild oats, sooner or later — but you waken sooner. It's the wakenin' that's worth while. Lots of men and women aren't awake . . . they're afraid to think . . . afraid to feel. They carry theirselves around like cracked mugs . . . never realizing life. They never realize it because they never get to grips with it — know the rush and violence of joy and sorrow."
>
> "Don't they, Sam?" Han was trying to get the meaning of this. There was something beyond her in it.
>
> "By and by you'll understand". Sam said. "You'll waken . . . that'll be the soul in you burstin' like a rose."

Sam did not have as much to do with her awakening to reality as he is credited with in *The Wild Oats of Han.* "I worked that out for myself," Katharine wrote later.

And awaking came not like "the burstin' of a rose", but in the bewilderment and pain of her mother's tears. Returning from a picnic in the bush with her brothers, Kattie had been outraged to see the best family furniture hauled off on top of the grocer's cart. She could not understand why all the most precious treasures had been sold, even the hand-embroidered, red velvet chair that only very special visitors were allowed to sit on. She challenged her mother passionately with her treachery in "giving away" their "beautiful chair". Haunted by anxiety and fear for her husband's health, Kattie's mother tried to explain her problems:

> "Don't you know father and mother are very worried just now? Presently we shall have to go away from here. Father has lost his work . . . not through any fault of his own . . . but just because he is too good and honourable a man to do a mean thing . . . We are going away . . ."
>
> She broke down and cried pitifully, childishly. Han looked at her, wondering. To see Rosamund Mary crying like

> that made her feel very old. For the first time her mother was dear — her shape, and face, and soft brown hair threaded with silver.
>
> Han put her arms round Rosamund Mary.
>
> "Don't cry!" she begged.
>
> She could not bear to see Rosamund Mary crying; it hurt like a bruise, with an aching soreness.
>
> Rosamund Mary's eyes were tragic.
>
> "Oh, you will be good, dear, won't you?" she pleaded. "You won't make it harder for us."

It seemed to Kattie like the end of the carefree irresponsibility of her childhood. She wanted to grow up; wanted desperately for the first time to help; and with the moment of mature understanding that even a young and imaginative child is capable of, faced with truth, she knew there was nothing that she could do. But a conviction of personal responsibility was imprinted upon her consciousness.

Return to Victoria and a borrowed house did nothing to improve the family's fortunes. Kattie's father was "ill and dejected". Her mother sat up late into the night smocking children's clothes, or painting illuminated addresses to eke out her godmother's charity. Sometimes there was not enough money to pay the tradesmen's bills. Knowing that he was living on his wife's meagre earnings and relatives' charity humiliated Tom Prichard: "They argued and argued, tenderly, desperately. She trying to cheer him, he becoming more demented by fear that he would never again get a job on a newspaper."

And Kattie listened, learning in her own heart the bitter lessons of the impoverished, professional unemployed.

> Ever since that moment of revelation in Tasmania, I had been aware of my parents' worries. Disturbed and bewildered, I groped for the reasons why there was no work for Father, and why Mother had not enough money to pay the baker, milkman and grocer. With a child's intensity, I brooded over the catastrophe which had befallen my parents, feeling helpless, and yet responsible for finding a way out of their troubles.

A private school favoured by the relatives was financially impossible, but Kattie "begged to be allowed to go to a State School", like her younger brothers. She was eager to make up for lost time, but although she was admitted to the secondary scholarship class, her school record seems to have been distinguished mainly by her first revolt against established authority:

With one exception I got on well with my teachers . . . The exception was a headmaster who had a vile temper and used his cane too freely. When he had thrashed a boy unmercifully one morning I stood up in a front row and called: "Stop, you brute!"

The man was so surprised that he did stop, and came over to me. "What did you say?" he asked.

"I said, stop, you brute!" I told him.

"Get out", he shouted, his face livid with rage, brandishing his cane round me, and put me out of the classroom.

"She called me a brute," he explained to the class when he returned. "So you are," cried the girl who sat beside me.

She too, was turned out of the classroom.

To her bitter disappointment, Kattie found that, at fourteen, she was just over-age for the scholarship to South Melbourne College upon which she had set her heart. The headmaster's offer of a half-scholarship opened to her "the happiest and most valuable years" of her school life.

J. B. O'Hara, poet and teacher, was a decisive influence in Kattie's development as a writer. His interest and encouragement filled her with "joyous enthusiasm" for her studies. A contribution to the College magazine describing a school dance so caught the imagination of a professor of English at a German University, the husband of one of her teachers, that he wrote to say "the girl who wrote that sketch would become a famous writer some day".

How excited I was! To have my writing thought so well of was surprising. I decided forthwith to become "a famous writer", and began consciously to study the work of great writers in order to learn something of how stories should be made, and why some were more powerful than others . . .

Immediately Carlyle's gorgeous words and flamboyant style captured my imagination. That was the way I wanted to write, I told myself — until J.B. teased me about what he called my "rodomontade".

If my essays were to please him, I thought they must have elegant language, and poetic imagery, so I tried that. They did please him, but once when the subject of our weekly essay was "Gardens", I indulged an impulse to write as I wanted to. I knew that others in the class would be writing mostly about green lawns, rose-beds, and colourful masses of flowers, so I wrote about a neglected vegetable garden with a plot of seeding onions and an old horse feeding among the tall silvery drumsticks. It was sheer defiance of my poet schoolmaster's predilections but to my surprise it delighted him . . .

Kattie's opportunity to make a real contribution to the family came unexpectedly when a story entered for a children's competition in *The Sun and Society Courier* earned her first literary guinea. "That Brown Boy" was a simple yarn of a lad living nearby who "got into as much mischief as any mortal, or rather any little Australian who ever breathed". The story ended with a touch of romantic imagination when Brownie is drowned, and a neighbour, the main target for the young villain's tricks, "threw a greasy apron over her head and sobbed for that poor little Brown boy!"[1]

It was not Kattie's first success. She had been delighted when a contribution to a Melbourne paper was published in the children's page, before the family left Tasmania. But "That Brown Boy" was considered good enough to deserve the editor's encouragement to keep on studying the things and people about her.

Kattie gave her prize to her mother and father.

Success; the discovery of a way in which even a girl of sixteen could help; perhaps the sheer pleasure of using words to tell stories which would make people laugh and weep; whatever the reasons, Kattie decided to tell her father of her ambition to become a writer. He seemed amused by the idea, Katharine remembered; did not take her efforts seriously. "You'll need plenty of patience and plenty of postage stamps", was all that he told her, anxious, perhaps, to save his daughter the heartbreaking frustration and despair that he had known. He did not warn her that a writer needs to be able to face mockery and ridicule to survive. That she had discovered herself overhearing her grandmother and a collection of aunts in gales of helpless laughter over an earlier story called "A Soldier's Love". Kattie remembered. To write from reality, from her own knowledge of people and places, became a rule rarely broken.

Tom Prichard found work again and the Prichard family fortunes recovered; but not enough to meet the cost of university fees as well as the boys' education. Kattie passed her matriculation examination in seven subjects, with honours in French, in December 1902, but her mother's illness ended hopes of studying for a bursary.

> It seemed disastrous at the time; but Father and Mother never knew how deeply I was disappointed. The fear of adding to their financial worries had haunted me since that auction sale in Tasmania. I made a rule with myself not to ask them for anything, and I never did. Not a new dress, or a penny, ever!

To keep pace with her friends, Nettie, Hilda and Christian*, now well advanced in their university courses, Kattie borrowed all the books they were reading from the Public Library; bought the penny classics and second-hand editions of the great works of literature and philosophy and went on to devour the masterpieces of the French and German languages.

The determination to become a writer was never forgotten. Kattie loved dancing; she found joy in picnics in the bush and parties with her brothers and friends; but she was firmly resolved not to fall in love or to marry. Nothing would be allowed, she promised herself, to "interfere with her work as a writer".

Kattie was twenty when she won a competition for a love story in the *New Idea*.[2] It was one occasion when she drew very largely on imagination, and disapproved of herself thoroughly for doing so:

> I wrote "Bush Fires" knowing nothing about either love or bushfires. The story was a poor thing, really, but won the prize. I wonder, now, how it could ever have impressed anybody. But joy at the time reinforced my desire to be a writer. I decided, though, that I must know more about bushfires, love and the country beyond our ranges.

* Nettie Higgins, later Nettie Palmer; Hilda Bull, later Hilda Esson; Christian Jollie-Smith.

CHAPTER 2

ALL EXPERIENCE IS AN ARCH . . .

I am a part of all that I have met;
Yet all experience is an arch wherethro'
Gleams that untravell'd world, whose margin fades
For ever and for ever when I move.

— Tennyson

Life opened before her. The new horizons of the twentieth century beckoned. Katharine Susannah, a young woman of twenty-one, eager for all that life promised, grasped her independence gladly. In 1904 she set out to earn her own living, full of confidence in her determination to become a writer. For the next fifteen years she learned the lesson of life's great joys and sorrows; learned to know her own country and its people; found the misery of poverty in the great cities of the world, struggled with failure and despair, the soul-destroying tedium of the daily office round; saw war in its horrifying reality; searched for answers to the tragedy of man; wrote unceasingly, finding in all that she saw and loved and suffered the rich treasures of experience; delighted at last in success, and a love that even her resolute dedication could not resist.

She is a slim, pale creature with long, brown hair piled in a wispy French loaf over her forehead in the delicate, high-key photographs of that time; firm jaw and fine, half-smiling lips, with those same bright, brown eyes that look out of her baby photographs, unshadowed by the tragedies which gave depths of compassion to Katharine's portraits in later life.

Her father disapproved of her intention to accept a position as governess in South Gippsland; but with her mother's gentle persuasion, he gave Katharine his blessing and a poem to guide her:

Do thou the right:
Scorn to conceive a lie;
Not merely as estopping words untrue,
But, with purpose steadfast, pure and high,
Thy Spirit-self in Truth's own robes endue;
Fix thou thy gaze upon her radiant star;
Bear thou her image mirrored in thy soul,
Nor let a thought, a word or action mar
The sovereign solace of her sweet control.

She had little need of high moral persuasion. Her father had succeeded in coaxing her to confirmation in the Anglican faith by an appeal to the beauty of poppies unfolding in the morning sun, where a succession of clergymen had failed to answer her doubts. For some little time she communed devoutly with God in nature. When her eternally questioning mind grew restive with conformity, she was protected from transgression by her own resolve to avoid any emotional ties which might interfere with her ambition to become a writer.

Katharine soaked in the rough, undiscovered beauty of mountains, forests and the richness of the coastal farms of Gippsland. She filled the notebooks that were her treasury with descriptions of the bush and town, the people who were to become the characters of novels and stories as yet unconceived: stories of convicts escaping up the Tarwin River from the penal settlement in Tasmania long ago, which would one day become *The Pioneers* and win for her the fame which still seemed a remote, impossible dream.

Long afterwards, Katharine said that she had turned deliberately to an expression of the beauty and colour in the Australian scene in reaction to Lawson's "grey and distressing country".[3] Perhaps she did make such a conscious choice later, but the young governess who wandered through the bush at Yarram and drifted in a flat-bottom boat over Corner Inlet, where "Wilson's Promontory flung its darkening masses against the sunset", was enraptured by the beauty of the Gippsland bush, as if with a girl's first love. The beauty she found there overflowed into the ecstatic fantasies of "Diana of the Inlet", published much later in London.[4]

As her eyes found wonders of form and colour in the drab olive-green of the gums and wildflower weeds, Katharine glimpsed for the first time the passions which can move ordinary men and women. An elderly European doctor had offered to give her German lessons. He played Chopin and Schumann for her, "talked brilliantly about famous places in Europe and distinguished writers and artists with whom he was acquainted". She was shocked to find this old man calling again and again to see her, talking distractedly of his love and begging her to go back to Europe with him: "I was cruel and uncompromising in my youthful ignorance . . . 'You're old, over sixty,' I said. 'How could I ever think of such a thing?' He rushed from the house saying 'You will never see me again.' " Conscience-stricken, she learnt that he had taken poison. She reproached herself "for being so callous and stupid: for not understanding the state of mind this man was in, so that I might have caused some of his suffering".

The rejected elderly lover lived; but the fear of causing such pain to a fellow human being remained with her. "It left a psychological impression which was never obliterated", she admitted in *Child of the Hurricane.* Like other experiences that burnt into her consciousness, the memory of that brief passion and attempted suicide was reflected in the lives of her characters: perhaps in Arthur Henty's hopeless love for Sophie in *Black Opal,* and his despairing suicide when she, too, refused to go away with him. It was a memory bearing its own burden of regret, re-echoing through the future.

There was more gentle instruction in the ways of the human heart for the young Miss Prichard on her next governessing appointment on a sheep station in the far west of New South Wales, three hundred miles beyond Broken Hill. There the distant adoration of the red-bearded son of the owner captured her imagination and stirred thoughts not entirely literary:

> He looked my ideal of an Australian stockman: tall, slender, reserved and sensible; walking with the graceful slouch of a man more accustomed to riding than walking . . . Nothing was further from my thoughts than falling in love. I had vowed to myself never to fall in love or to marry. I told myself that I was "dedicated to my art!" I was to be a writer. Nothing else mattered. But for a while, Red Beard and I looked at each other as if we were a little dazzled by something inexplicable between us.

Red Beard proved a faint-hearted lover, too easily deterred by his father's warning to the attractive young governess: "No use your making eyes at my son, Miss Thinga-me-bob. He's engaged to the daughter of an old friend."

However, to do him justice, Red Beard did put up his fists for his lady when one uncouth fellow boasted in the men's hut that "he had seen Miss Prichard's drawers" as she whirled in an impromptu tarantella at the station fancy-dress ball.

So Red Beard became the improbable hero of Katharine's first piece of professional, free-lance journalism, the "Letters from Back o' Beyond", serialized in the *New Idea* in 1906 under the title "A City Girl in Central Australia". The series, partly fictional and partly descriptive of life on an outback station, was in the form of monthly letters from "Kit", a young governess, to her mother.

The "Letters" drew an irate reply to the Editor from her employer, protesting at her fanciful descriptions of drunken revellers in back-country pubs. "Let us hope that Kit's contributions to the next *New Idea* will smack of a little common sense and be tainted with just a hint of truth, for I know how 'Kit' travelled, and now speak as one in authority," the anonymous correspondent chided.

Katharine's father, proud of her achievement, was at the same time concerned that she would offend her host, Mr Quin of Turella Station, even more with a thoroughly unflattering picture of his family, "all cradled to the corroboree", "as dark skinned as little niggers", "as rough and ignorant as young savages". He reprimanded her gently in verse:

Our Kattie having taken wing
Most dutifully writes
A weekly budget, in the which,
Her mother's heart delights;
Although in spelling through its lines
She learns with some surprise
Her super-sylphlike daughter is
"Expanding mushroom-wise".

"Ah me" La Madre softly sighed
"I never yet was swift
To fathom cryptic phrases, so
I hardly catch her drift."
"Tut tut" exclaimed Le bon papa
"It means but what is said;
A touch of Quin-sy ending in
A case of swollen head."

Katharine learnt more of the country than she did of its people during her year at Turella, but the White Cliffs opal fields nearby and the life of the station were the first faint outlines from which the story of *Black Opal* grew. Katharine's cautious admirer had his part, too, in the lonely, pathetic son of "old Henty of Warria Station", afraid to love until love passed by him.

Tutoring in Melbourne after her year's assignment in the "Back of Beyond" gave Katharine time for night lectures in English literature and philology at the university. She was inspired by Walter Murdoch's lectures:

> His lectures were a joy. He introduced me to George Meredith and *Love in the Valley,* for which I've always felt a debt of gratitude. Most of his students, studying for a degree, didn't absorb the literary value of his lectures as I did, I thought. To me they were manna, and I rushed to read articles in the Saturday *Argus* by Elzevir, which Hilda and Nettie told me were written by Walter Murdoch. They called him "the Murdoch buddy" with the superiority of day students. As I was only a night student, he was too exalted a personage for me to speak of so familiarly — though by astute dawdling after a lecture I did contrive sometimes to catch the same tram to the city; and in his easy quizzical way Mr Murdoch talked to me some more about literature and the intriguing derivations of words.
>
> It was rather a blow to hear him say, after I had given him a story to read: "Better burn this, and write it again".

She thrilled to the revolutionary poetry of Bernard O'Dowd, "the thorn crowned laureate of the New Democracy", whose conviction of the poet's role in the world of ideas was later defiantly proclaimed in an address on "Poetry Militant" at the Melbourne Literature Society, to the disdain of the academics, and the delight of one inconspicuous, unknown young woman.

She stirred to the enthusiasm of Dr Rudolf Broda, visiting Austrian socialist:

> When I told Dr Broda I was saving up to go to Europe some day, he exclaimed indignantly: "But why? You have the most wonderful country to live in. A young country, a new country. Australia is the most progressive country in the world. You are making history here. You will write a new page in the story of the world. Helping to do that is more important than anything you can do, or write, in the old world — a world in decay, rotten with superstition and prejudices, soaked with the blood of wars. Ah, you do not realize the poverty and misery you would find there, my young friend. An almost hopeless task confronts us. But not quite, not quite! It will come, the new order of socialism. Your task in Australia will not be so difficult. You will show us the way.

Life also had grimmer lessons to teach her. Alan, the older of her brothers became critically ill: Alan, her childhood playmate, who had followed loyally, unquestioning, in all their wild adventures in the hills of Launceston, the grave, gentle boy who had danced with her, teased her, called her "Jemima", "Jammy", given her his devotion and love. Katharine knew that Alan might not live:

> Father walked up and down the hall all night, frantic with anxiety . . . I crept out of bed and went to try to comfort Father, putting my hand in his and walking beside him. "My son! My son!" Father kept saying, looking queerly tragic in his night-shirt, with his hair usually so sleek, all ruffled. "I wish it was me," I told him, feeling I would willingly have taken Alan's place. "I wish it were," Father said distractedly.

Alan recovered and Katharine told herself that she understood her father's anguish. "It hardly mattered what we said if only our love and longing for him to live could be expressed," she explained. But those words scarred her heart. The memory of her own helplessness to comfort him, her worthlessness in the balance of her father's grief, filled her mind when twenty years later she told of Mary Ann Colburn's grief for her son smashed to pulp in the timber mills of *Working Bullocks*.

The death of her father left a wound that would not heal; pain that returned through the years again and again; a question to which there was no answer.

> In the end it seemed the struggle and frustration of many years had caught up with him. He could not sleep, and sat for hours with an empty sheet of copy-paper before him. During the last weeks of his life he refused to eat, afraid that: "There would not be enough food for the children". Mother tried to reassure him. "But, darling, the children are grown-up now. They can look after themselves — and us." "A burden on the children?" he cried. "No. No. I'll never be that." Every morning he would pray. We all knelt down round him in the little drawing room, and long and earnestly he pleaded with God to restore him to health, give him another chance to provide for his dear wife and children. So humble and eloquent those out-pourings were. There was a natural poetry in them welling from the depths of his being. His beautiful voice broke with grief and emotion. Open-eyed I watched him, as he crouched over a chair, believing he was communing with God. It was torture to see the agony of mind he was suffering, and Mother's anguish as she wept quietly beside him. "God, if there is a god, help Father," I prayed, promising myself that if Father recovered his health and strength I would believe in God.

> But I was full of passionate resentment that Father and Mother should be suffering so cruelly; that their belief should require such humiliation. I felt it was a farce, a tragic farce, to imagine there was a God who could hear their prayers and would avert the sorrow which threatened us.

On 28 June 1907, Tom Prichard took his own life.

Katharine could not face the fact that the burden of living had become intolerable to that gentle, loving man. The manner of his death was never spoken of. After sixty years, she could not bring herself to say how he died until, fearing my despair at some inconsequential failure in my own life, she warned me of the self-contempt that fixed itself upon her father, sapping his will to live, as if the sensitivity of his mind coiled in upon itself suffocating him in his own pity. In *Child of the Hurricane* she wrote:

> I loved and admired my father. Often during those last months, when he couldn't sleep, he would ask me to sing to him. I sang for hours to soothe and comfort him. After Father's death, for a long time I couldn't sing at all. There was no song in my heart, and my voice would not lift.

For a year after her father's death, Katharine stayed with her mother. She had given her first earnings as a governess to her mother for Bee's school fees; helped her brother, Nigel, through medical college. The dreams that "Han" had dreamed of growing up and helping had been realized. Now Alan was able to share the responsibility.

Katharine wrote her first novel in 1908, turning from present sorrow to the joy-filled reality of her childhood. *The Wild Oats of Han* was not published until twenty years later, but in Katharine's mind it was dedicated then to her brothers, Alan and Nigel, playmates of those happy years of youth, as she prepared to leave her home for the "untravell'd world" of life.

In July, with a personal letter from Alfred Deakin, the Prime Minister of Australia, introducing "Miss Prichard, a young Australian lady journalist of great promise", as a talisman for her mother's peace of mind, Katharine Susannah made her first visit to London to report the Franco-British Exhibition for the *Herald*.

> Gazing at the low-lying, green-filmed coast of England through a misty drizzle at dawn, and realizing all the tumultuous miles of sea between me and Australia, I felt homesick and afraid of what the future might hold. It seemed that I had left childhood and youth far behind; and must struggle

now as an independent and adult person for the fruition of those hopes which had haunted me for so long.

There in the heart of the Empire, the British relaxed their visions of imperial glory under Edward's benign dalliance and dared to try a liberal government. Shaw slashed at shocked complacency. H. G. Wells played prophet of a technological Utopia under his scientific master-race. The first socialists sat in Parliament. The unemployed rioted in Glasgow. Hunger marchers filled Trafalgar Square. And women talked of voting. To the "young Australian lady journalist" everything was new and exciting. Impressions raced before the moving camera of her mind:

> Endless streets with their surging crowds and congested traffic . . . the grimy ancient buildings, horse buses . . . Covent Garden and the coster barrows, Soho, Piccadilly . . . dreary slums . . . the beauty and grandeur of ancient buildings, churches, palaces, green parks and gardens ablaze with flowers . . . children dancing round the hurdy-gurdies in the street . . . the music halls . . . Bank Holiday on Hampstead Heath.

Religiously Katharine reminded herself of the vows she had made to her ambition. Her companion on the long voyage from Australia had a career as a singer to think of and agreed that they should be "good friends", "no flirting or falling in love". Only once did they forget. Swept away by the gay abandonment of the Covent Garden Ball, they kissed and promised each other contritely next morning that "there must be no more of that sort of thing". Upon that gayly platonic companionship among the slums and bright lights of London, Katharine wove in her imagination the fanciful romance of Gene and Peter, the immaculate lovers of *Windlestraws.*

Her reports for the *Herald* were full of the enthusiasm and outrage of youth. London was "like an illuminated volume of poetry — a living history book", where in some out-of-the-way, old-world courtyard she could find familiar figures of literature; or "just the biggest, dirtiest, wickedest place I ever had room in my imagination for. I wouldn't have the poor of London on my conscience".

The appalling misery of poverty in London was a horrifying revelation to Katharine. She was shocked by the queues of starving men outside the soup-kitchens, women with their feet wrapped in newspaper sleeping all night on the Embankment, sickeningly stinking shelters crammed with homeless people.

> The horror of such poverty in the great and wealthy city remained with me. The problem of how such poverty and suffering could be prevented, haunted my mind.
>
> One night, dining with English friends at the Savoy, I couldn't help thinking of those people on the Embankment. When I spoke of them my friends did not believe me. They thought I was exaggerating, or that what they called my "fertile imagination" was playing tricks with me.
>
> Our table was near a window. I got up and pulled the curtain aside.
>
> "There they are," I said. "You can see for yourselves. And they've been there every night, all through the winter."

It was more than ten years before Katharine found her own answers, but she was marked among the poor of London. It was her blooding in the stuff of revolution.

In Paris, she had her first introduction to the ideas of the Russian revolutionaries which were to have such a significant influence upon her later life. At the time, she pitied their impossible ideals and jotted them down in her notebooks to be used one day as incidental background in *Windlestraws*.

Katharine had arranged to meet the man she called her Preux Chevalier in Paris. A middle-aged friend of her father's with three daughters of her own age, he had taken an interest in her when she first returned from governessing in the back-country of New South Wales. Now, amid the romance of autumn in Paris, the promises exchanged in London went unmentioned. Katharine remembered him fondly, her charming escort of those days in Paris:

> The Preux Chevalier used to say: "Some day, I will show you Paris". I never dreamt it would happen. But there he was, at my hotel, one morning soon after I arrived . . . They were wonderful days, spent at the Louvre and the Luxembourg, driving in the Bois and to Versailles in the glory of its autumn gold, walking along the rive gauche, browsing over the bookstalls, and wandering through side-streets to discover historic places, L'église St Geneviève and La Sainte Chapelle. There were déjeuners and dinners in all manner of out-of-the-way restaurants, nights at the Comédie Française, the Odéon, the Moulin Rouge, a gala night at the Opéra, and suppers at Maxims and the Taverne Olympia.

Her own family never knew of their alliance and Katharine refused to mention his name, even when, as an old woman, she wrote of their affaire. But she warned my daughter, Karen, of the price she paid in years of possessive jealousy; of his demented threats to shoot himself when she attempted to leave him; of her regret for independence bartered to a man capable of the cowardice and deceit of playing upon her fear of suicide, knowing that she could not face the thought of becoming the cause of his self-destruction.

Through the great, grey kaleidoscope of London, Katharine saw the infinite diversity of mankind. She talked to flower girls, cabbies, charladies, artists and writers, the eager partisans of a new golden age, heralds of the twentieth century. She interviewed the great and distinguished women of the day, Sarah Bernhardt, Melba's teacher, Madame Marchesi, and the Countess of Dudley, whose husband had been appointed Governor-General of Australia; grieved with George Meredith for the passing of his youth:

> As he held my hand to say goodbye, the grief which had oppressed me all the time I was with him, surged. A tear or two dripped on his hand. He patted mine.
>
> "There, there," he said, as if he understood what was distressing me. Then he kissed my hand with a gentle, gracious gesture — and I fled . . .
>
> Somewhere along the path, downhill out of sight of the house, there was a hawthorn bush. I sat down under it and wept and wept. Why I don't know — except that I had the overwhelming sense of tragedy, and my youth was reproach to me.
>
> I felt that I should not be young and Meredith old: that I should not have gone from the sunshine into that darkened room and stood in the doorway in my light summer dress. Perhaps I had stirred some tender memory; or merely my youth and being on the threshold of my life's work had intensified the realization that his was nearly done. He was waiting for death, and I somehow had broken in on him, like his Daughter of Hades.

Finding a footing in the English press proved to be a tougher task than the interviews and articles commissioned at home. Katharine was glad enough to retreat temporarily and accept an appointment on the Melbourne *Herald*. After a year of tormented apprenticeship learning "to avoid literary airs and graces" under threat of the Editor's blue pencil, Katharine accepted the General Manager's offer to renew her appointment: "Allow me to take the present opportunity to express our high appreciation of your always fine work — marked, as it has been, by a high ability, strict care and punctuality and a splendid enthusiasm," he wrote.

Even such a finely ornamented commendation could not compensate for the stultifying routine of the women's column, society gossip, fashion notes and housekeeping hints. When the second year of her contract expired, Katharine decided to leave:

> After nearly two years of staff journalism, I began to realize it was sapping my energy for creative writing. The experience had been invaluable as discipline and training for exact and condensed expression, but I became restless and dissatisfied because there was no time for the sort of writing I longed to do.

Free-lance journalism was impossible in Australia, she found, and decided to try her luck in America. The visit was disastrous: "Your stories are too Australian," an American editor told her. "No use to us. We want stuff about the United States . . . plenty of love . . . murder . . ."

Cold, friendless and rejected, with her savings exhausted, she retreated to the nearest haven: England, Huntingdonshire and spring.

More than once the kindly, conservative Fraser cousins rescued Katharine from defeat in her long struggle on the "inky way" of Fleet Street from 1912 to 1915. They welcomed her to "The Elms", their Huntingdonshire mansion, set in a "wilderness garden" where "daffodils, bluebells, primroses and forget-me-nots rioted in a tangle of grass and ivy under the trees, old oaks, larches and limes"; fed her hot-house fruit, cherry brandy and good English food, after she had collapsed trying to exist on a diet of porridge, because Carlyle had been able to do it when he was a young and struggling writer. "I could have had a dolce far niente existence in this stately old mansion, and in the garden and woods surrounding, if only I had been content not to worry about my conflict with London," she recalled.

When her cousin turned away a deputation of hunger marchers empty-handed from the gates of "The Elms", Katharine returned to London to face again the disappointment of the editor's regrets:

> Manuscripts kept on returning with "editors regrets" slips, day after day, week after week . . .
>
> I decided to apply for a staff job. Walking home along the Embankment after a discouraging series of enquiries at newspaper offices, despair got hold of me. It was late afternoon of a cold, grey day, misty rain falling, unconsciously my tears were falling too. An oldfashioned closed-in cab drove along the edge of the road. The cabby hailed me. I shook my head at him. "Sorry," I said, "I've got no money." "Ee don't need no money", he said. "I be joost drivin' home. Joomp up and I'll give 'ee a lift" . . .

> That gesture of kindness, though, coming it seemed from the great heart of the people, broke through my despondency. I was ready to fight on.

The occasional paragraphs on women's suffrage in Australia, fruit-bottling or co-operative housekeeping were hardly more encouraging to a young woman hoping to become a serious writer.

London was to be her proving ground. She explored the new ideas of the Freewoman Discussion Circle, the Guild Socialists, Syndicalists and Fabians, throwing aside the mysticism of Christian Science and theosophy which attracted some of her friends. Ardently Australian and feminist, she told the conservative ladies of St Ives Primrose League:

> Every day, the women of Australia are making history, proving to the world that women's power in public affairs is for good; that when women vote a great power for the purification and betterment of public life is brought into play.

It was her first public speech, and the present-day supporters of Women's Liberation may have found her hopes a little over-optimistic. The ladies of the Primrose League were no doubt relieved that such experiments were conducted in the colonies.

She worked with Mrs Pankhurst's Women's Social and Political Union, but withdrew when she saw that it was interested only in votes for women and opposed the wider goal of universal adult suffrage.

Strangely, a story written in the quiet of Huntingdonshire won her entry to the harsh world of the London press, thundering the threats of war in Europe. Katharine wrote lingeringly of the willow harvest on the Ouse, the ancient crafts of the basket weavers, the herb gatherers and flower sellers. Soon her work began to appear in six or seven newspapers.

Resting at Clovelly, a fishing village on the English coast, Katharine wrote the verses that became the first published volume of her work. "Clovelly Verses" was a tiny, twenty-page booklet in grey cardboard, printed in April 1913, and dedicated to her mother. She placed no importance upon her poetry. It was accidental, she said, "the altogether naive murmurings of me to myself":

> Zephyrous airs
> That the earth and sky have taught me,
> That the wind and sea have brought me,
> You are not worth the pence
> Of a wise man's money,

Or one sweet drop of wild bee's honey,
Clearly, clearly!
You are love songs merely
For those that dream.

When war came, Katharine was swept up in the patriotic fever. She tried unsuccessfully to secure an assignment as a war correspondent and to join a women's auxiliary unit. She was to recall that, "Neither I, nor anybody I knew, had much sympathy for pacifists and conscientious objectors in that period of patriotic illusions about the war . . ."

She wrote pathetic stories about the children of men who would not return, and in March 1915, obtained permission to visit an Australian Voluntary Hospital at Wimereux, north of Boulogne, within sound of the artillery bombardments at the front. Katharine made light of the casualties in her war-time reports. She chattered flippantly of the problems of satisfying the French police that "she and her passport agreed in gender, number and case"; made the standard, stiff-upper-lip jokes about the wounded Tommies' pronunciation of Ypres, and, in her heart, grieved for the tragic lines of gaunt, weary men swathed in bandages. "The misery and waste of war struck me more forcibly than it had ever done . . ." Katharine remembered. "I was consumed with desire to find some way of preventing the diabolical slaughter caused by war."

Her own brother's death in the third year of the war hardened her resolution: the aching need of a young and sensitive woman to relieve the suffering she had seen became the unyielding determination that drove Katharine to devote her life to the cause of peace.

Success in her own campaign against the battalions of Fleet Street won time for Katharine to write her entry for the Hodder and Stoughton All-Empire £1000 Novel Competition. Protected by a notice on the door of her top-storey flat in Chelsea Gardens saying she had "Gone to the Country", Katharine hunted out the notes made in Gippsland eleven years before and began to work. She wrote "all day and far into the night". *The Pioneers* was finished in six months and sent off to stand its chance in the competition "with acute consciousness of its many defects".

One of her closest friends, Sumner Locke, wrote an appreciation of Katharine during those London days for *Every Lady's Journal*:

> In a swathing of brownness, demure-eyed and tender she seeks out the little, unwashed city children, and finds in them an excuse for her shrinking bank balance . . . A slender, restful brown-bonneted, brown-eyed figure, guiding the un-

lucky ones among the mazes of mediocrity into the open, breezy channels of a beautiful and great simplicity. It is of the real things in life that Katharine Susannah Prichard teaches in her writing . . .[5]

But there was a great wealth of love in Katharine's reality and her dreams were a part of it. She was known as the "Lavender Girl", Sumner Locke said, for the little lavender-filled sachets she sent with a poem to her friends:

I'll send you lavender
To lay among your thoughts of me,
That I, forever in your dreams,
May dwell with fragrance —
Breaths undying,
Subtle, mysterious and sweet —
Of these herb flowers I love so well.
Lo, I am a witch
And weave the spell![6]

Almost a year after her manuscript was submitted, Katharine's expectations were raised to the skies by a journalist's tip that she had won the Hodder and Stoughton competition; and dashed again by a routine rejection slip:

It was a crushing disappointment after months of waiting, and those last weeks of anticipation. I went out and wandered about London, walked for hours. Didn't know where: or why I was wandering. Late at night I got a bus and climbed to the top. It was raining, and I sat in the rain without a coat or umbrella. Presently a man came and sat beside me. "May I hold my umbrella over you?" he said. I said "Thank you", and we sat without another word until I was getting off the bus. Then he said, "Please take the umbrella". I said: "No thank you," and we lost sight of each other in the crowded street.

Next morning there were apologies and congratulations. Katharine Susannah Prichard had indeed won the £250 prize for the Australian novel; not £1000, but still "a fortune!":

It had been a dull, misty morning; but as I emerged from Paternoster Row, and came out on to Ludgate Hill, the mists cleared. A shaft of sunshine fell across the smoke-grimed buildings and wet pavements. It was as if all London lay before me. I wanted to sing and dance as I went down into Fleet Street. "Buy a rose! Buy a rose, lidy dear!" flower-girls on the kerb were saying. I told them my good news, bought all the roses I could carry, and went on to find friends in the newspaper offices, the happiest girl in London that day.

The Pioneers' success was a decisive factor in the development of Katharine's career as a novelist, despite her own doubts, then and later, as to its literary merits. It secured her reputation abroad and made it possible for her to return to Australia, the source and inspiration of all her future work. It gave her confidence in the possibility of attaining her ambition; gained time for creative writing, free from journalistic chores; earned wide critical acclaim in England, almost universal praise in the Australian press, and astonishingly enthusiastic reviews throughout the United States of America where the Los Angeles *Times* alone found the story of *The Pioneers* melodramatic and the development of the plot lacking in skill.

"We think it would have taken an uncommonly good story to beat it", pronounced the London *Times* . . . "Shows merit of such a high standard as to border on genius", said the Melbourne *Herald*, discreetly reminding readers that Miss Prichard was once a member of the *Herald* staff. Only the good old Sydney *Bulletin*, deliberately mistaking the judge's name, couldn't resist slinging off: "*The Pioneers* couldn't be worse than any novel written by her judge", the "Bully" said — and promptly apologized to Charles Garvice and *The Pioneers*, admitting that it was after all "a splendid Australian novel" and that "it did not even remotely resemble garbage". The *New York Times* announced that *The Pioneers* was "unquestionably a worth while book, interesting, with plenty of spirit and a good deal of significance".

It was enough. Katharine at once arranged to return to Australia.

Before she left England, Katharine was to meet a young Australian soldier, Lieutenant Hugo Throssell of the 10th Light Horse. There was a confident, carefree charm about Hugo Throssell. She could not help being impressed by his "gay, irresistible manner", although he was awaiting an operation to remove a bomb fragment from his shoulder. Afterwards, he swore that he had fallen in love with her as she walked towards him along the terrace of the Royal Automobile Club for tea with the Colonel of his Regiment; but that was a story Hugo Throssell told to many young women.

> There was an indefinable attraction to each other . . . Colonel Todd, who came with us, was perturbed by what he thought were symptoms of love at first sight. Bluff and forthright, he declared: "You can get engaged to him, if you want to, but you can't marry him till the end of the war".

With the promise of the career she had yearned for at last a reality, Katharine had not the slightest intention of abandoning her newly won independence. If the thought had occurred to Hugo Throssell there and then, Katharine's career might have been as easily swept into the compass of his arms as it was three years later. Now, a soldier at war, he had his own triumphs.

Shortly after their first meeting, Lieutenant H. V. H. Throssell was awarded the Victoria Cross by King George V at Buckingham Palace, for conspicuous bravery at Hill 60, Gallipoli on 15 August 1915. Katharine visited him several times in hospital where he was recovering from meningitis, intending to write about the action in which he had won distinction, but she abandoned her own article when Sergeant MacMillan who had been with him at Gallipoli told the story of "The Man I want to Follow" in the London *Daily Mail*.[7]

In Perth, the Western Australian Parliament placed its appreciation of Lieutenant Throssell's bravery on record. A trooper of the 10th Light Horse in a letter published in the *Daily News* told of his men's tribute:

> The day I got my little lot, poor old "Jim" Throssell got his hit. If ever a man won distinction on the battle field it was our officer that day. He took all kinds of risks, and he is such a tender-hearted chap! Every time one of his men fell "Jim" would insist on returning and doing his best for the poor beggars. He simply took no care of himself at all. And when he got potted and the doctor who was fixing him up told him where to go, he said, "Oh, I'm going back. I'll gallop better with the colours up." And gallop he did. He was fine to watch — never faltered. "Come on boys, we'll get 'em; good old 10th," he called until he was knocked about so much he was ordered out of action. His biggest grief was for his men, and he always made light of his own wounds. I could tell you more about him, but it will do for the present. I only hope his conduct reaches the proper quarter, because he is a good 'un, and above all, he is such a bonzer chap with his men.

Hugo had almost recovered from his illness when Katharine was due to sail:

> We said goodbye in the midst of my luggage, packed cases of books and belongings. I couldn't believe there was more in his feeling for me than a sort of bushfire flare that would pass. So we parted, shaking hands, sadly . . .

CHAPTER 3

AS THE SEA LOVES

Oh, I pray the elements
that they may blow through my soul
and make me whole.

That I may be
as a tree,
tall, green-leafed, casting deep shadow,
for wanderers to rest in;
having great arms
for wild things to nest in.

That I may lie,
as the sky,
over all in my thought,
spacious, serene, recking nought
of castes, horizons, or creeds.

That I may love,
as the sea loves:
as the sea loves the shore,
evermore, evermore!

—Katharine Susannah Prichard

After five years abroad, Katharine returned to Australia in February 1916. All the banners of joy were flying for her: to be home again; to have won the improbable duel with London; to find friends eager to acknowledge her triumph. "Miss Katharine Prichard is the woman of the moment in Melbourne this week," *Punch* declared, "and we are just tumbling over one another to say 'we are proud of you, and welcome home'."

It was a more wonderful homecoming than she could ever have imagined:

> There were many welcome home parties and receptions by literary organizations. Greetings and warm-hearted congratulations poured in from hundreds of unknown readers. I could never have imagined people would be so responsive to the success overseas of a young writer belonging to them.

The Premier of Victoria, Sir Alexander Peacock, gave a luncheon in her honour at Parliament House and presented her with a free pass on the Victorian Railways for six months. (The New South Wales Government followed suit.) There was tea at the Overseas Club, and a dinner at the Café Français for "a handful of women journalists and a small army of brothers-in-ink".

The Sydney *Truth* reported the occasion in its own fashion:

> Having won the prize, the inky are proud of Katharine, and one she-scribe has informed the listening world that the author is beautiful as well as brainy. It is not often ink-slingers admit anything like that, but you see Kathie is on the topmost wave of prosperity for an Australian scribe.

Katharine, "wearing her laurels very modestly and with all her old sweetness of nature and charm", sat at the head of a table decorated with boomerangs and huge masses of gum-leaves. With her first two editors, J. E. Davidson of the *Herald* and W. Somerset Strum of the *New Idea* on either side, she listened to toast after toast of greetings and congratulations. There was a poem sent by Nettie Palmer:

> Tell me not friends, I am unkind
> That from the witchery
> Of Katharine's pen and Katharine's mind
> To Katherine's self I flee . . .

And Mary Fullerton's glad welcome:

> Bring your laurels and tell your tale
> Gladden our ears and eyes,
> Where you have been and what you have done
> Under the old North skies.
>
> Welcome enough your precious self
> Had you never a tale at all
> Of life and days in the old grey land
> Where the rough winds call.
>
> But there's no place like the old place
> To home returning eyes,
> *Isn't it good* to be home again
> Under the old blue skies?

To Katharine that night of gaiety and rejoicing was a symbol not so much of achievement but of dedication. She wore the Honiton lace collar her mother had made for the time when her wayward daughter would at last find her man and marry him.

> "But I don't want to marry anybody", I assured her. "I'm married to my work."
>
> Then, on the night of that wonderful dinner party, she gave me the bertha to wear on my dress, as if it were a wedding gown.
>
> "If you don't want to be a wife and mother, dear," she said sorrowfully, "you might as well have the lace now."

Windlestraws was published in 1916. A gay, unlikely romance of two adventurers adrift in London, with which Katharine had first attempted to please the English publishers, it did little to enhance her reputation as a writer. "*Windlestraws* may be a little impossible but otherwise it is wholly delightful", said the *Daily Express*. Others, too, saw the book as a fairy story without a moral. She herself thought the book immature and unimportant, and chose to withhold *The Wild Oats of Han* already in manuscript, until there was something more substantial upon which to risk her newly won laurels.

Longing to rediscover her own country, for a month Katharine lived alone in a cottage on the shore of Port Phillip Bay. She filled a penny exercise-book simply titled, "Notebook: Australia I: Titree Studies, 1916", with her brief, unfinished word songs: fragments of language, lingering pages of her day-dreaming, phrases chipped from the clear crystal of imagination. Day by day she wrote of the trees, the wind, sky and sea, tuning her own heart to the moods of Australia: "Oh it was good to go down to the sea this morning . . . Each wave broke against me with the shock of a kiss, fierce, hungry . . ."

It was as if she rejoiced in freedom from the journalistic inhibitions of the years in London and again loosened her imagination in revelry with the elements:

> A wild night. The sea a lace of foam for seven lengths of breakers from the shore.
>
> I have no soul tonight. I have given it to the wind and the sea and the ti-trees . . . Dark. Dark it was under the trees — and good to be mad for a while. To stretch my arms over the sea and swear that I belong to the world — and to no man . . .

And when her solitary communion with nature came to an end, there was something of a lover's fulfilment in her gratitude: "The last day. You couldn't believe how I have loved it all. Something of the blue of sea and the sky have gone into my soul . . ."

She learned again her love of the inland, travelling by horse-drawn coach from Orbost along the coast to Sydney:

> Driving from dawn until sunset through the southern forests, seeing again the thronging columns of mountain ash and messmate, the tangled fern gullies, breathing the fragrance of sassafras and dogwood, with a whiff from early pale blossom on the prickly scrub, hearing bellbirds tinkling in the deep shadow, made me feel as if I were being newly baptized into Australia.

Her journey took her on, over the barren desolation of the inland plains, to the opal fields of Lightning Ridge where the ideas first conceived at White Cliffs ten years before stirred to life. Opal, black opal, "the dazzling beauty of its red fires", was to be her symbol for Australia in the new novel forming in her mind.

Katharine retired to the solitude of a cottage at Emerald set in acres of untouched bushland in the foothills of the Dandenong Ranges beyond Melbourne. It was a place where she could work and dream; a place where she could listen to the yearning of her own heart and confide her fears and her joy in the words of poems. Emerald was home to Katharine. There she knew friendship: of Vance and Nettie Palmer, Louis and Hilda Esson, Frank Wilmot and Henry Tate. Emerald could not claim her from the world, but it was for a time her sanctuary, to which she returned in spirit fifty years later when her last novel, *Subtle Flame,* was written.

At Emerald, Katharine began work on *Black Opal,* waking early in the morning when the first bird songs stirred the silence of the bush; working until she was too tired to go on. From Emerald, she wrote to Frank Wilmot: "So tired tonight — can scarcely think one thought after the other. My hand and head goes dog on writing after 6 or 8 hours of doing it."

It was not all work though. Sometimes the music of the bush called to her, as it had called to Han, and she deserted her pen and paper to listen. Once Henry Tate, whose music was derived from the "lucid harmonies" of the bush, came with her and found inspiration for his "Dawn Symphony" in the morning song of the birds:

> With overcoats over our pyjamas, like unquiet spirits, we went out of the house and sat on a stump at the edge of the clearing. It was very cold, owls still muttering among the dark trees. But with the first light came *Eopsaltria Australis,*

> the psalmist of the dawn, as this yellow robin is called. He sat on the branch of a wattle-tree near us and tuned his little harp.
>
> It was incredible luck to see and hear him like that. I had met him often before, and heard his shy, lovely song along the tracks. He does sing during the daytime in thick quiet scrub, although he is supposed to sing only at dawn. That morning he sang for Tate as if he were doing his best, to oblige me. Then the native thrushes awoke. A cuckoo's quavers flew with their wild sadness: whipbirds, golden-breasted whistlers, all the warblers, wrens and tree-creepers, tossed their ripples and runs into the air, while magpies and butcher-birds fluted and yodelled, kookaburras laughed and hooted away in the back hills.
>
> We might have been wood-bugs, Tate and I, we sat so still as the bird-music drifted this way and that, drew to a mighty paean, and subsided.

They were her dearest friends, Henry Tate and Frank Wilmot, while Hilda Esson, the confidante of Katharine's girlhood, was abroad with Louis. They discussed their work together, shared their dreams and gave each other gentle sympathy in disappointment and sorrow. When Vance and Nettie Palmer decided to move to Queensland, Katharine arranged a farewell party and insisted that Frank Wilmot and Tate must be there: "You and Tatey — the nicest people I could think of. What is the masculine gender for 'bonzer tart'?" she asked.

With Frank Wilmot, whose poetry written under the nom-de-plume of Furnley Maurice, stirred her with its beauty and zest, she maintained a gaily reverent raillery. "Honoured Sir", she would write. "I'm that flattered at the thought of being mistook for a really truly poetess . . . me that never had a rhyme or metre to me name."

And he might as gaily reply in verse, dedicated to Katharine Susannah Prichard, shouting aloud that "Life's a Brawl":

> Here's to the habit of swift forgetting!
> Here's to the habit of no regretting!
> The triumph you giddily threw away
> Returns tomorrow or some other day.
> Smile deep and true with tranquil heart
> And you'll carry the world in your donkey cart![8]

A mood of rare abandonment for Katharine, and Frank Wilmot too. Both of them were passionately committed to the campaign against conscription as the war ground agonizingly on through its last terrible years. Wilmot wrote his despairing cry, "To God from the Weary Nations" and Katharine appealed to him: "Your God is the Power of Good, or just Good, isn't he? In particularly desperate states of mind one says 'Oh God!' without meaning Javeh any more than any other divine peanut, it seems to me."

She sought her own solution to the world's insanity in a more earthly salvation. With a small group of friends she talked of war, socialism, syndicalism — and found her questions still unanswered. Theory meant little to her, unless there were some proof that it could be made effective. The revolution in Russia was her signal-fire to action. She seized upon the works of Marx and Engels and was convinced that in their theories lay the promise of the future.

> My mind was illuminated by the discovery. It was the answer to what I had been seeking: a satisfactory explanation of the wealth and power which control our lives — their origin, development, and how, in the processes of social evolution, they could be directed towards the well-being of a majority of the people, so that poverty, disease, prostitution, superstition and war would be eliminated; people of the world live in peace, and grow towards a perfecting of their existence on this earth.

Katharine's discovery of communism did not at once transform her life, as if by a mystic revelation of truth. Generally, life flowed on as it had before; but now Katharine knew where she was going.

She returned whenever she could to Emerald and *Black Opal.* It was hers now, a gift from her mother: a legacy from Alan. She felt herself drifting in "the whole ineffable silence — deep as the sea, in which everything lives and moves and has its being". She heard the "shifting and singing of the leaves"; heard the throbbing of a bird's song, "as if a single note were being struck on an eastern prayer bell". And it was the sound of her tears for her brother. Among her notes from Emerald she wrote her poem of grief for him:

> No fruits are sweet now,
> The flowers are done;
> I have no light
> Of the moon or the stars,
> No joy of the sun.
> My way is like this way
> Which goes through the hills —
> A rough path — it seems to ascend, ascend:
> But I know it will come to the sea,
> And the long day end.[9]

In her sorrow, Katharine clung to her resolution to live alone, but yearning for more than the love of wildflowers and bush places filled her with regret when she wrote to Nettie Palmer one of those "inconspicuous murmurings", in which she sometimes spoke to herself with deeper truth than a word spoken allowed:

You — little mother
You have your home
Among the trees:
You have your mate
And your baby.
I have only
The ache of my heart;
The windy way —
The breeze:
And a will of thorns
For lover.[10]

In 1918, Hugo Throssell came home. Katharine's "will of thorns" was no proof against his overwhelming assault. Once before he had returned on leave, swept aside her promises to the elderly lover, who still held the threat of suicide over her, leaving Katharine shaken by a love that she had not previously known. After that first tumultuous homecoming she had written:

As a vase of earthen ware,
  I am filled to the brim
With the golden wine
  Of my joy in him.[11]

Now, he would hear no excuses, accept no opposition: "He stood at the foot of the stairs, a tall, masterful figure in uniform — returned from the maelstrom of war — my irresolution vanished. He held out his arms and I walked down the stairs into them." The end of the war removed the only remaining obstacle to their marriage.

> We had been spending the day at Emerald, and were walking to the train at twilight when flares lit up the distant hills.
>
> Hugo gazed at them, a strange expression on his face. So moved and silent, he was, as flare after flare cast a yellow light across the sky.
>
> I asked anxiously: "What's the matter?" thinking the flares might be reminding him of bomb explosions and the havoc they cause.
>
> His arms folded round me. "The war's over", he said. "Those are armistice rockets. We can be married now. I won't have to go away again."

They were married on 28 January 1919. "The ceremony was exceedingly quiet," the press reported when it caught up with the news a week later, "only the immediate relatives being present . . . Captain and Mrs Throssell are spending their honeymoon at Emerald. Bushfires have been raging around their bungalow, near which burnt trees have been falling . . ." Katharine's promise to herself had endured for twenty years. Her life for the next fourteen years was to be dedicated to my father, in love and happiness; and in the pain he brought her.

CHAPTER 4

NOT FRANKINCENSE OR MYRRH

> To you, all these wild weeds
> and wind flowers of my life,
> I bring, my lord,
> and lay them at your feet;
> they are not frankincense
> or myrrh,
> but you are Krishna, Christ and Dionysos
> in your beauty, tenderness and strength.
>
> "To Jim" — Katharine Susannah Prichard

"My husband is truly, I believe, the best thing that ever happened to me", Katharine wrote to Frank Wilmot from "Wandu", the sprawling ten-roomed house on the upper slopes of Greenmount where Hugo Throssell first brought her for their West Australian honeymoon.

> We lived in only two or three rooms, and on hot summer evenings disported ourselves like Adam and Eve in the garden.
>
> During those honeymoon months I gave Jim Engel's *Socialism Utopian and Scientific* to read. As he sprawled over it on the verandah, often there would be a yell of: "Hell, girl, what the blazes does this mean?" I would go out to explain, his arms stretch out, and usually our political discussions end in love-making.

Hugo Vivien Hope Throssell was thirty-four years old when they were married: Katharine, by the calendar was thirty-six, but he flatly refused to be the junior partner of the firm, and with fine contempt for the Registrar's records declared her to be his own age too. He had been known as Jim since his boyhood in Northam, a country town on the Avon River in the farming lands fifty miles from Perth. Jim was the son of George Throssell, shopkeeper, landowner, conservative politician, at one time Minister for Crown Lands and briefly Premier of Western Australia. The old man had fought successfully for the extension of the railway from Northam to the goldfields of Coolgardie and Kalgoorlie and was known in the local press as "the Lion of the Avon", "Father of Northam".

Young Jim Throssell, the youngest of thirteen children, grew up in an atmosphere resembling as closely as possible the life of the landed gentry of County Cork, once the family seat in Ireland.

At Prince Alfred's College, in Adelaide, he became a champion gymnast, athlete and captain of the school football team, learnt a little Latin and returned to the leisurely life of Northam. He was given his own horse and trainer; picked up prizes in the picnic races and sports events; boxed and wrestled the visiting champions; hunted kangaroos with his brothers in the scrub country beyond Northam and played the romantic lead in *Niobe* with The Idlers, the town's amateur dramatic company. Jim Throssell loved horses and cattle, and with no other qualifications with which to earn a living, found himself a job on a cattle station in the north-west once owned by his father. Shortly before the outbreak of World War I, George Throssell made Jim and his brother Ric, a gift of a thousand acres of rough, uncleared land at Cowcowing on the outer fringes of the Western Australian wheat belt. The two brothers worked like bullocks from daylight till dark, clearing the scrub and cultivating the land for their first crops; but the poor soil was a hopeless proposition in the long, dry spell of 1914. Jim and Ric tossed in their hand and enlisted.

The war brought glory to Jim Throssell, and tragic disillusionment. Ric was killed at the second battle of Gaza. Jim crawled over the battle-field searching for him, calling, whistling the notes that had been their rallying-cry; and found only the nameless dead and dying. There was no glory in the war for him after his brother's death. The strange joy of battle that inspired him and the men he led at Hill 60 withered in the horrible reality of war.

To the people of Western Australia, he remained Hugo Throssell VC, a dashing, romantic figure, though many were shocked by his announcement at the victory celebrations in 1919 that the war had made him a socialist. Katharine wrote to Nettie Palmer:

> Peace day at Northam was an event! Jim led the procession in that little country town — looking very splendid on a great bay charger. The crowds cheered and cheered him. And then at night, my dear, he said his say. The Premier on the platform. Northam's [the] chief town of his constituency and he's an old friend of Jim's. You could have heard a pin drop. Jim himself was ghastly, his face all torn with emotion. It was terrible — but magnificent. Now Mitchell is wondering

> about his seat. It's the opinion of most people that Jim could have it as easily as he liked, if he liked. But he doesn't want to go into Parliament — at any rate not yet — if ever.

Katharine had seen to his political education; but his conviction was completely genuine. There were no ideological differences between them. With Katharine, he attended the Labor Study Circles which she organized, and spoke in support of the strikers at the Esplanade Hotel when five thousand unionists confronted a contingent of armed police and barbed wire barricades on 20 June 1921.[12]

Hilda Esson, unaware of the extent of Katharine's active involvement in the creation of communist organization in Western Australia, was amused by her enthusiasm and assured Nettie Palmer:

> I find Kattie talking "high politics" in her last letter. It doesn't seem to be necessary for her somehow. I was delighted with the naivete with which she solemnly assured me that she didn't have much faith in political action, as if it were a new discovery . . . Of course all these ideas are more emotionally than intellectually stimulating to her, and I don't want her to worry her heart out over things for which she has no particular faculty and which may weaken her in other ways. She is such a purely artistic personality.[13]

Jim bought two acres of bare land on the slopes of Greenmount, and a square, two-bedroomed, weather-board house with a narrow apron of veranda perched on naked jarrah posts. It had none of the charm, then, of their honeymoon home at "Wandu", but there was a sweeping panorama for thirteen miles over the coastal plain to Perth. Verandas were added later, dressing the place with a show of spaciousness. Climbing roses, wistaria, jasmine, honeysuckle and grape-vines grew, softening its bare symmetry. Across the Old York Road, Jim took up 140 acres of good grazing land surrounding the gravelled prominence of Sugar Loaf Hill. He ploughed, planted fruit trees and stocked the paddocks. And Katharine wrestled with her conscience about employing a maid. "I have wanted to do everything myself, but if it's a case of my work going to the wall, I think Jim will put his foot down," she told Nettie.

> My idea has been of course that I don't want us to be employers of labour. But there are ever so many people wanting work for their living just now . . . Isn't it just sweating yourself and keeping the other bloke out of a job? To a certain extent it is. And yet I'd rather do everything if I could.

A lady novelist was a rather doubtful quantity among Katharine's new sisters-in-law. Sweet natured, loving creatures, they all adored their youngest brother and gathered protectively to make sure that Jim was being properly looked after. Katharine was determined to show her paces as a housewife and win their confidence. She prided herself in being able to do anything she set her mind to. It was not so difficult, she found. They were only too glad to embrace anyone who loved their Jimmy, although Katharine did shock the dear things a little by actually using the family Royal Doulton and by filling Jim's silver trophies with flowers. Katharine's literary friends in the eastern States were more surprised to find that she really enjoyed the simple domesticity of Greenmount. "I truly am a peasant at heart and cannot deny the demand of the land," she confessed later to Nettie Palmer.

But it was a refined peasantry — and enjoyed in smallish doses. She was as proud of her cupboards of jams and preserves as any good farmer's wife, and found that for years the interviewers faithfully reported that the well-known authoress, Katharine Susannah Prichard, also made pickles and jam. She fed poddy calves with her fingers before they learnt to drink from a bucket; rode with Jim over the hills to look at the cattle fattening for the Midland sales; milked sometimes, when he was away on the business of the Land Settlement Board, and fell embarrassingly in love with a pet piglet christened "Goldilocks", until it grew up and to her grief was surreptitiously sold to the butcher.

Katharine and Jim found complete fulfilment in their love and confidence in each other in those first years of their marriage. "I never thought life could be as good as it is", Katharine wrote to Nettie Palmer:

> Jim is so unbelievably thoughtful, devout and adorable in all the little every day ways. I'm surer every day of the rightness of having married him . . . I really think I've been happy lately for the first time in my life.
>
> I remember, you asked me in the letter — before the last two — whether expecting happiness wasn't asking the gods for too much. I've always thought so, and that we've got to be immeasurably grateful for a very little! I didn't think happiness could ever happen to me, the Furies had chased me so far and so hard. And now this tranquil backwater where I just live and am afraid something may happen! The only way with happiness it seems to me is not to seek to hold it, not to peer at it too closely — to be very humble about it and try to be worthy of it — by being willing to sacrifice even it to the great objective values.

From those rich years of contentment, Katharine's work grew to full maturity and confidence. She stored away in her mind the small, unnoticed dramas of Greenmount, material for stories like "The Curse", "The Cow" and "The Grey Horse", which were regarded by some as her best short stories.

The unremarkable people who were her neighbours, tradesfolk and friends lived again at the touch of her pen: the blacksmith of "White Kid Gloves"; the old Scottish orchardist of "Sour Sap"; the English immigrant of "A Devout Lover", and the Italian quarryman in "The White Turkey" — they were all there, a little more faded, perhaps, a little more easily overlooked among their fellow men than they appeared in the sharply drawn detail of Katharine's portraits.

Everything she saw was inspiration to Katharine. Jim took her with him on trips to pastoral areas of the south-west, on to the timber country and outback to the wheat lands. "I'm simply gorged with stuff to write", she rejoiced. A trip to the farm at Cowcowing, three hundred miles by motor bike and car, was a triumphal procession:

> The former guaranteed to reduce a respectable married woman to the mental condition of a scrambled egg in the shortest time on record. But the journey was gorgeous! Every stockman and drover on the road knew Jim — and of course it was a case of pull up and yarn with everyone!
>
> "Hullo Jim" from the men on the road and "come and see my missus" from Jimmy after the first few minutes.

Black Opal had been completed and submitted to Hodder and Stoughton in London before Katharine and Jim came to Greenmount. "H & S wanted me to cut the book by 50,000 words and alter two chief characters. I told them to 'go to Hell' — or words to that effect," she told Nettie Palmer in August 1919; but later discovered that the cut could be made:

> The book from a literary point of view loses, but its propaganda will go further in present form — although now to me it has no longer any interest, I'm not going to submit the m.s. to H & S again, or any more m.s. It's a waste of time to send to a firm who suggest altering characters, for all the world like requiring the grandfather in *The Curiosity Shop* to fall in love with, and marry Little Nell, in the last chapter.

In 1921, *Black Opal* was published by Heinemann, with a royalty of ten per cent on British and American sales, and "threepence per copy sold in the colonies". To most Australian critics it was a marked advance upon her previous books. "The best Australian novel we have read for a long time", said the *Triad* and gave its congratulations to Captain Throssell VC! Professor William T. Goode commended the book's truth to type, to setting and conditions; found it had "a singular delicacy of perception"; but warned that "as in all novels with a purpose, the purpose militates against the artistry of the book".[14] The *Bulletin* revelled in the fact that "an Australian, using an Australian setting can confidently challenge the interest of readers both at home and abroad". But in England comment was decidedly less encouraging than it had been for either of the two previous novels. Katharine learned the bitter taste of public ridicule from the anonymous reviewer of the *Yorkshire Observer* who accused her of "slovenly English" — a criticism which cut deeply into Katharine's pride in her craftsmanship.

Seeing the book in the cold perspective of print, Katharine was dissatisfied with *Black Opal*. She worked over the novel again, simplifying the language, seeking greater clarity of expression.[15]

H. M. Green reassessed *Black Opal* in 1931, with Katharine's later work as his bench-mark:

> One would not have imagined that a young woman who had published only two novels, one a sentimental potboiler and the other of no great importance except by merely local standards, could do work like this. It represents at once the world of life and the world of thought, as reflected in or glimpsed behind a mirror of the daily doings, the joys and sorrows, tragedy and triumph of one little Australian mining community.[16]

After the publication of *Black Opal*, Katharine retired temporarily from all major creative writing and gave herself wholly to the quite complete happiness she found in being a mother. I was born on 10 May 1922. On my birthday Katharine always remembered how it seemed to her then:

> I am thinking of that first day — so wild and stormy it was, with torrents of rain . . . My Jim, poor darling, hadn't been to sleep all night, because you didn't arrive until the dawn. Then Mrs. Parker found him hanging on to the clothesline in an agony of mind. "Mr. Throssell," she said, "the baby has come, and I *think* it's a son." (Knowing well it was.) . . . My heart sang all the magnificats you can imagine. Then I saw you so fat and red and lovely, and they bathed you beside the fire and I said: "Put on his Bolshevik gown,

> please". That was the little gown I had embroidered with wheat ears and a hammer and sickle. So many years ago it all was — and yet like a cinema in my mind, every incident of that glorious day . . .

Katharine had hoped to meet D. H. Lawrence who was staying in the hills a few miles away with Molly Skinner, his collaborator in *The Boy in the Bush.* She had been captivated by *Sons and Lovers* and wrote telling him of her admiration. He replied from Thirroul in New South Wales: "Your letter, I suppose, means you are up and about and wearing your little V.C. like a medal at your breast. May he be a rosy cross."

And shortly before he left for New Mexico, Lawrence wrote again explaining how he felt about Australia:

> My, how hopelessly miserable one can feel in Australia: au fond. It's a dark country, underneath — like an abyss. Then, when the sky turns frail and blue again and the trees against the far off sky stand out, the glamour, the un-get-at-able glamour! A great fascination, but also a dismal grey terror underneath . . .

Australia held no "dismal grey terror" for Katharine. The country itself breathed beauty, as if it were blossoming in harmony with her own happiness. Lawrence's terrors were an alien thing, shadowing the land she loved and clouding her admiration for the man himself. When *Kangaroo* was published she was deeply disappointed in the lack of integrity in his treatment of Australia. "Our philosophies were too far apart for my mind to have been influenced by his style and outlook as has sometimes been suggested," she explained.

Critics found echoes of Lawrence in the luxuriance of *Working Bullocks,* the first book to appear after she began work again, although later literary analysts recognized the superficiality of the comparison, and Katharine herself was not aware of any direct influence. She acknowledged the freedom which the "evanescent brilliance" of Lawrence's style had revealed for writers of her day, but her literary development, she believed, grew out of her own experience. The joy of life which she had discovered in Greenmount had more to do with the release of new creative vision in her work than the vicarious enlightenment of *Sons and Lovers.* Perhaps Captain Throssell could have more justifiably accepted the *Triad's* congratulations for *Working Bullocks.* He and Katharine were like young lovers. After a week away in Sydney, she wrote to him to say:

> Never felt so thoroughly un-kissed — and it don't agree with my peculiar temperament . . . Oh dear we must have a honeymoon in Sydney some day. Coming home across the harbour the other night I felt it was dreadful for you not to be having it with me — and no other man among the surfers a patch on my man. Nor any other man-thing in the city of the least use to me.

The origins of a work of imagination are difficult to trace; often forgotten by their creator in the elaboration of the idea, like the long process of growth that transforms the seed into the fruit. Who knows where *Working Bullocks* began? But it is tempting to see the first spark from which the new novel smouldered into flame, in the words of Michael Brady defending the independence of the opal miners of Fallen Star Ridge. "What good would they be . . . if the men sold themselves like a team of bullocks to work the mines?" . . . "They'd have their wages — like bullocks have their hay." Working bullocks — the very words were surely the essence of it.

Notes for *Working Bullocks* were written before *Black Opal* was published. On Boxing Day 1919, Jim took Katharine to the Greenbushes races and log-chop on the outskirts of the great karri forests of the south-west. She was enthralled by the casual drama of the contest, the easy confidence and quick flashing power of the axemen. The pages of her notebooks spilled over with impressions: the competitors, the crowd, raw chips of language, facts — the size of logs, times, axes. As if captivated by those first glimpses, Katharine went on to the mills at Big Brook, in the heart of the timber country. She heard the "scream and moan" of timber under the saws; watched the felling and hauling; saw a bullock-driver at work, "a young Irishman — with a long narrow sun-red face . . . muscles on his arms, sunburnt, sweating as though they were oiled in the hot sunlight. His flannel shirt cut open at the arms . . ."

As the bullocks manoeuvred the huge logs across the slopes of the hillside, the muscle-tearing strain of the great, placid beasts driven again and again to impossible effort by the cut of the whip and the bullocky's command, was branded upon Katharine's imagination. "The most tragic thing in the bush — the working bullocks", she scrawled in her notebook.

The novel germinated in Katharine's mind for five years, competing with the claims of her political conscience and the demands of motherhood, until it, too, irresistibly demanded birth. In September 1924 she confided to Nettie Palmer:

> I've been just sick to write lately, but so damned tired always. It's difficult to have leisure, or energy. Ric is adorable, but exacting, and the weather is perfect for out of door playings . . . I haven't been able to do much lately — though ran away from home last week and addressed a meeting of timber workers on strike.

The strike was a gift from the gods to Katharine. It gave historical authenticity to the inner logic of the novel, the basis in fact that her literary credo demanded.

Two years later, *Working Bullocks* was published; and the scene recorded in her notebooks became the first chapter of a book that was to pour a flood of new life into Australian writing.

> The bullocks jostled and hustled each other as they backed, chains slackened, heads tossing, horns clashing, terror of the whip in their eyes. When they were huddled against the log, Red stepped out before them, swinging his whip. He shouted to the leaders:
>
> "Come up, Lively!
> Lively! Snowy!
> Boxer! Rogue!"
>
> The long slim cord of plaited cowhide was spinning circles, semicircles, dancing serpents, in the air about his head, as the fine lash cracked, no more than a flick reaching the hides of the bullocks.
>
> The leaders lurched forward. The team strained and struggled . . . The whim wheels moved. They rolled on to the skids. The bullocks pulled, shoulders and heads down, coughing, spewing froth. Beasts, whim, log and men drew to firmer ground in the centre of the track. Red Burke rounded the team, heading it for the siding, and halted up.

Fellow writers were caught in the lyrical sweep of the new novel. "We are reading Kattie's novel in manuscript, *Working Bullocks* and it is astonishingly good," Louis Esson wrote to Vance Palmer on 31 December 1925. "It is most unconventional, and it is less like an ordinary story than actual life. You feel you are living in the Kauri (sic) forests. Men and women are put against nature and everything is simple and elemental . . ."[17] Nettie Palmer confided her impressions in the journal originally intended as "a record for herself and perhaps some day one or two friends":

> *Working Bullocks* seems to me different not only in quality but in kind. No one else has written with quite that rhythm, or seen the world in quite that way. The creative lyricism of the style impresses me more than either the theme or the characters. From slang, from place-names, from colloquial

> turns of speech, from descriptions of landscape and people at work, she has woven a texture that covers the whole surface of the book with a shimmer of poetry. As you read you are filled with excitement by the sheer beauty of the sounds and images . . . It is a break through that will be as important for other writers as for KSP herself.[18]

Vance Palmer wrote to her questioning the change in viewpoint from Red Burke's in the early part of the book, to the girl Deb's in the closing chapters. Katharine replied:

> You're right about the change of "venue" in "Bullocks". I held myself up to consider it at the time of writing. Did realize it, and weigh[ed] the consequences; but could not be satisfied with a Red vision of the Karri. I had to have the Deb outlook as well — indeed don't ever want to get behind a definitely male consciousness, or subconsciousness; but to see the thing from my own, or objectively. I mean that I can't endure to stalk a man, as it were, behind a female signature.

Working Bullocks was hailed enthusiastically in the press. According to John Sleeman, it represented "the high water mark of Australian literary achievement in the novel so far, and marks a very great advance in Katharine Prichard's mastery of her art".[19] The title seemed to be the only part of the book disliked by the critics. "It does seem as if a more attractive name would have been more expressive", complained the *Times Literary Supplement,* on behalf of the women readers, making it quite clear that the TLS itself understood its meaning.

But financially *Working Bullocks* was disappointing. "My first royalties account was for £23 — dears what do you think of that?" Katharine asked Vance and Nettie. "My typing bill for 'W.B.' was £25 incidentally . . . My royalty is 7d. or 9d. — I forget which. (Think I told Hilda it was 3d.) But looking up the contract the other day to discover how I was going to fare on the American edition, saw it was 9d. — I think, or 7d."[20]

Thirty years later, Vance Palmer recalled the impressions of those days:

> Young people of today may not be fully aware of the flood of new life Katharine Prichard poured into our writing. Such vital freshets from the underground springs of creation flow into the main stream and are absorbed, perhaps their force and volume forgotten. But to the writers and readers of thirty years ago what a revelation *Working Bullocks* and *Coonardoo* were . . . they brought indisputable evidence that a new writer had arisen, one of lyric freshness, of original vision, of dramatic power.[21]

CHAPTER 5

THE WELL IN THE SHADOW

> Coonardoo, they called it, the dark
> well, or the well in the shadows . . .
> — Katharine Susannah Prichard

All through the years of my childhood, I remember Katharine sitting in the mornings with her notebooks and paper at the end of the wide veranda that surrounded the old house. When the gully winds roared, hot and dry through the gum-trees, she retreated to the polished, jarrah table in the dining-room: far away; writing, writing. There were rules about interrupting when Katharine was working; but it was hard for a little chap to understand why she didn't seem to hear when she was asked the inevitable question, "What are you doing, Mum?"

Later a workroom was built fifty yards from the house and the distractions of household chores: a one-roomed, oiled weatherboard cottage with ceiling-high cupboards for her manuscripts, lined with bookshelves and warmed in winter by a huge stone fireplace. There was a jarrah writing table, a bit uneven and rickety on its pins, strewn with her papers in the ordered disarray that only Katharine herself understood; a couch covered by a possum skin rug and a couple of saffron cushions. The loquat bloomed in a mass of sweet-scented flowers by the door in spring. Jonquils grew wild in the new grass. The double casement window looked over the rose garden and a summerhouse, thatched with the fronds of zamia palm, and overgrown with morning glory and ferns.

Katharine woke early in the morning, with the first bird song she used to say, and wrote propped up in the high double bed, scrawling her notes in longhand in black school exercise-books or cheap scribbling blocks. There was breakfast on the back veranda before my father made his morning dash for the bus to town, braces over his shoulders, his coat with its Cecil Brunner buttonhole in one hand, a piece of toast in the other. I raced after him to hand him his bag at the gate. A quick kiss: "Goodbye, old chap. Look after Mum!" And he'd be away down the hill as the bus rounded the corner. "Never missed a bus in my life", he boasted.

When the family was despatched, Katharine retired to the workroom and usually worked through until lunchtime; took a spell in the early afternoon and would be at work again when I came home from school, peeping in through the french windows to see if a visit would be acceptable. I knew that I'd have to wait for her company until evening when she smiled and asked from miles away, it seemed, "Hullo darling. Had a good day at school?"

In the cooler weather when the grass was long and green in the orchard, Katharine wore the calf-length, soft-soled boots of possum skin that my father made to keep her feet warm as she sat writing.

The workroom became unbearably hot in mid-summer. When the temperature hung around 110^0 for a week on end, the whole family stripped to the minimum clothing until it could face a ride of two or three miles for a swim in the rock-pools of the Jane Brook, or make the long trip to the sea at Cottesloe, driving home after sundown when the "Fremantle doctor's" breath of cool air reached the Hills.

Before the first copies of *Working Bullocks* had arrived in Greenmount, Katharine was already seeing new dreams in the mirror of her mind: dreams of a stark, bare country; quiet, dark people, still shadows in her imagination.

From a friend, she had heard the story of an aboriginal woman, mustering cattle with her child slung against her body, who had flung the baby from her in desperate rage and abandoned it among the rocks of a dry creek-bed. Before she could write the story of that simple, primitive tragedy, Katharine believed that she must see and know the country; try to understand how a woman could be brought to such terrible madness. With a four-year-old son in tow, she travelled to the end of the railway line at Meekatharra, and four hundred miles further on by truck to Turee Station in the far north-west beyond the Ashburton River.

In the harsh, drought-racked country of the north-west, the drama of man's conflict with nature seeped into her. From the yarns of the men round the fire in the long kitchen on cold nights, or stretched out on the veranda after the heat and glare of the day, she learnt the folklore of the north-west, the tragedy and comedy of everyday life. She saw the sad domestic scene, and sensed a deeper torment which whipped man and woman like the eddies of the willy-willy sweeping dust and dry leaves from the red earth. For hours, day after day, it seemed to an aggrieved small son, she sat at the edge of the station veranda talking to the shy aboriginal girl who helped in the homestead kitchen; rode with her sometimes to the dry creek-bed near the aborigines' camp. In her soft monosyllables, the grave depths of her eyes, the smiles that flashed at some shared understanding, Katharine discovered an affinity with the girl, an almost instinctive sympathy and insight into the mind and emotions of a fellow creature caught between the primitive culture of her own people and ways of the white man. Katharine wrote:

> It's terrifically hot — and the dust storms — suffocating. But I've been riding nearly every day, and am the colour of red mulga and henna-ed with dust (make what you can of the verb, Nettie dear). Sometimes one of the gins rides with me, sometimes mine host, who is really a bit of the country, and sometimes Mick, a stockman who has lived here all his life . . . And of course I'm enciente with stories, delighted and quite mad with the beauty and tragedy of them. The only fly in the ointment that my hostess has aspirations to literary efforts . . . and I'm afraid won't ever be able to do anything but the small and sentimental. I mean has no quality of language, capacity for imagery, or ability to see natural values. You know what I mean, weaving our psychology and sentimental morality over native legends. I've been trying to show her how to do them on their own merits — to see things as the blacks see them.
>
> And the blacks are most interesting — fair haired — and I find them poetic and naive. Quite unlike all I've ever been told, or asked to believe about them. I'm doing some character studies. But feel "to honour bound" not to touch the legends.

I learnt to play with the station children, turning awkward somersaults in the dust, tracking imaginary bungarras,[22] running in convincing terror when one of my aboriginal playmates shouted, "Narloo comin'! Narloo'll get yer!"[23]

Katharine watched; and our games became the childhood of Coonardoo and Hughie, out of which the tragedy of an aboriginal girl's love for a white man grew.

Towards the end of her stay at Turee, on 1 November 1926, Katharine wrote a long letter to Hilda Esson sharing with her the excitement of the new life she had discovered:

> Letters two days ago the first since I've been here. For nearly two months that is. We seem to be cut off from the rest of the world by long shimmering plains, blue hills and pink, mottled with purple, dove-grey millions of miles of mulga, the mirages, and frame of red dust, infinite, exquisite skies, of the most miraculous, changing, asphyxiating (can't even spell it, because of that) blue. I have loved being here — it has been a wonderful experience — though difficult. My hostess being a city girl, nervy and at loggerheads with everything. She has had a very trying time, physically, and needs to get away. The story of the place and its people — as it is — simply writes itself. I'd give anything to set it down as I see it — but the laws of hospitality . . . My host — even his name is just right for him. And how can I get away from it? The most likeable type of Irishman — I like him immensely — I'll send you a snap of us riding. I have a large sympathy for him, though of course he has the limitations of his type . . . The homestead is of corrugated iron — unlined. The flies and heat and dust — almost unlivable — to us other folk. Flies crawl all over your food, and you just take them off — the dust storm powders your meat while you eat. And at present — we're on salt meat, the flour is flavoured with petrol: butter ran out a few weeks ago, and the new butter has betrayed our confidence. It stinks. No fruit, almost no vegetables — very few green turnip tops and so on. But the interest of everything makes up to me, and Ric though pale and thinner — is quite well — really he has been a fiend as to behaviour though and worn me to frazzles often enough. I'll be very pleased to hand him over to Jim. And we go down before the worst of the summer — by the coastal boat from Onslow on Nov. 23 . . . Jim is really wonderful to me. To let me come on this journey for instance. And next week I'm going on a ten days muster with men of the place, no other female, except perhaps a gin, with the complete assurance of Jim's understanding and eagerness for me to have all of the life up here, I can.

Katharine did not immediately turn to the story of the north-west which had seemed ready to flow at white heat from her pen. She was both afraid of offending her hosts and instinctively reluctant to disguise the truth of their lives in discreet anonymity. Firmly she put the idea aside; but neither courtesy nor discretion could entirely restrain the creative fever which gripped her imagination. She poured her impressions into a play, already roughed out at Turee Station, and two short stories, each in its own way a preliminary study of the tragedy of *Coonardoo,* chancing her luck that the real "Brumby Innes" would be unlikely to meet himself on the stage. Within six months the play was finished and sent off to the *Triad* competition, without much hope for its success. "I suppose [it] will be considered unproducible," Katharine admitted to Vance Palmer.

> But the thing wrote itself. I couldn't help it. As I saw the corroboree, it was the most thrilling and dramatic performance I've ever seen. It could be produced; but Jimmy doesn't like the play at all. It's too brutal he thinks. But it's true in every word and detail really.

Her earlier plays[24] were slight pieces written to amuse herself mainly, and to support the "Pioneer Players", the amateur theatre company founded by Louis Esson in Melbourne. Louis was the playwright, Katharine believed. Vance, too, had far more experience in the theatre. Her own theatrical ambition was to write an "honest to God" comedy. A second play was entered for the *Triad* competition, a domestic comedy, but Katharine doubted whether her touch was light enough. She expected, and hoped, that Vance or Louis would pull off the prize: " 'Strike me breath,' Vance dear, I'd give anything for you or Louis to win this stunt. Not that it counts much in itself, but that it opens the door," she explained.

But, celebrating the arrival of her first American royalty cheque for *Working Bullocks* with Jim in Melbourne, Katharine heard that her play, *Brumby Innes,* had won the *Triad* three-act play competition. "A very remarkable work, comparable to some of the best of Eugene O'Neill's," Gregan McMahon, one of the judges, announced.

Generously, Louis concealed his disappointment that Katharine should have beaten him at his own game. His startled reaction to the play was indicative of the outcry which greeted *Coonardoo,* when the novel that Katharine was trying futilely to put out of her mind would be restrained no longer. There was no profanity in the play; no love scenes. The mere notion of sex-hunger as a natural appetite, the very idea of intercourse between a white man and an aboriginal woman, was outrageous. Louis told Vance:

> Apart altogether from its literary and dramatic quality, I didn't think *Brumby Innes* had a possible chance. It is a powerful and picturesque work, beginning with a wonderful corroboree, but the episodes are startling enough to make most people shudder. A Repertory or any other audience will get the shock of their lives when it is played. A few cuts may be made, of course, but nothing can prevent it being a terribly daring play.[25]

The short stories, "The Cooboo" and "Happiness" had been published by the time Katharine and Jim returned to the west. They were both highly successful in capturing the character of the north-west and its people. "The Cooboo" was greeted as a masterpiece in miniature: "What a world of tragedy and strange beauty she has compressed into a couple of thousand words! It is a marvel of economy as well as feeling — so little stated directly, so much implied," Nettie Palmer wrote in her journal. Louis saw "Happiness" "as a perfect picture, and a simple human drama that becomes extraordinarily poignant as seen through the eyes of an abo woman".

As if the play and the stories served to key her mind to the outback, Katharine found that she could no longer concentrate on the circus novel, already half-finished, which she intended entering for the *Bulletin* £500 prize novel competition. "Today I'm not writing," she told Nettie in February 1928.

> Have turned a bored and haughty stare at my stray leaves and notes for the new book. Can't be reconciled to 'em, interested in 'em. Damn 'em! I'm tired . . . head tired . . . have been ever since we got home from our dash East. It was a glorious spree, but everything went wrong at home in the meanwhile. Fires have destroyed all the feed in our paddocks, burnt the hillsides black — rabbits ate 60 per cent of the crop — and the summer's been the most trying I've encountered. I'd rather do no more work at all this year — and will not unless my head lets up. It has been aching incessantly — with blackouts like the one I had with you at Emerald once. And yet there's so much I want to do . . . things I'm aching to do . . .

Katharine did not believe in inspiration. Writing to her was a skill learned in a lifetime of conscious effort, an awareness of the tools of her craft, practised sensitivity in observing reality — "an infinite capacity for taking pains" — and work. All of that was in the writing of *Coonardoo;* and something else. The story had entered her mind as the aborigines believe the spirit of a child enters its mother.. Fathered by reality, it grew in her imagination and demanded creation.

With the closing date for the *Bulletin* novel competition only three months off, Katharine began to work with a concentrated intensity and a speed quite beyond anything she had ever attempted before. By the time entries closed, the book was completed. In July 1928 she wrote:

> I've just finished a long novel, 100,000 words, for the *Bulletin* competition, but too tragic and sombre to pull through I think. Also not in serial form. The story of the Nor' West I've been trying not to write, and it sort of arrived and sat down upon me when another quite respectable yarn was three-quarters done. "Damn!" I says and never thought it would be finished by the end of June — what with all the upsets of the early part of this year. Financial crises and Jimmy down to it. Also my sister and her kiddies staying with me. Four rooms our shack has, old dear, and nowhere for a woman to write, but a corner of the verandah or the hill-tops.

There were 542 novels entered for the competition, most from Australia, but 75 Australian-born writers submitted entries from New Zealand, Papua, Burma, Rhodesia, Italy, America and England. It seemed too much to hope that Katharine's string of successes could continue; but on 18 August 1928, the judges of the *Bulletin* story competition announced that *Coonardoo* by "Ashburton Jim" had won first prize, sharing the honours with *A House is Built* by Marjorie Barnard and Flora Eldershaw.

Katharine was overjoyed. She had bowled a "hat trick", Jim told her, with prizes in succession for a short story, a play and a novel. It seemed as if the world of Australian arts and letters rejoiced with her. Hilda Esson wrote to Katharine:

> I've been re-reading *Coonardoo* aloud to Louis . . . I am still more amazed and delighted at the quality of it. Every phrase, every picture, character, incident, becomes more vivid, and the beauty and strangeness of it have fascinated us both. It is probably your best work — the best ever done here . . .

Such spontaneous praise from her closest friends, and her most revered personal critics, was manna to Katharine, more important to her inner satisfaction than public recognition. "I feel I owe so much to your sympathy, criticism and always generous support," Katharine told Louis. "I mightn't have had the courage to gang my ain gait but for you and Hilda sooling me on."

"*Coonardoo*: like a woman lying against the heart of her lover", Hugh McCrae told her in one of his exquisitely composed letters. And a group of Melbourne poets wrote to say: "We the citizens of Melbourne having dined and being somewhat the better for drink, rejoice exceedingly in your successes . . . We understand that congratulations of this kind always bring the congratulators a free signed copy".

Katharine replied through Frank Wilmot promising copies of *Coonardoo* for "those cobbers of yours who invoked Bacchus to my well-being": "Darlings all of you. My *Bulletin* news itself did not give me so much delight as your letter: Evoe Evoe! Life is almost too good to me just now. I'm grateful and almost afraid."

The serialized version of *Coonardoo* in the *Bulletin* was a serious disappointment to Katharine. She objected strenuously to their editorial liberties and blamed herself for not insisting on seeing proofs of the story. She wrote to Vance Palmer, whose *Men Are Human* had won third prize:

> I worked fearfully hard, and went through the m.s. at least six times, before it left me. Wish to Gord I could have seen proofs all the same. The "Bully" is dropping in "thes" and "thats" and "withs" and so on . . . Some sentences I could never have written as they are with their little alterations. I've protested — but this is to warn you to get proofs. One of my big disadvantages is that I can never see my proofs, and all my work suffers through sub-editors and printery ministrations. Damn them! I'd rather stand and fall by my own imperfections!

Among the public, *Coonardoo* aroused a minor storm of controversy, although literary critics in Australia, England and America recognized it as a major achievement. "A novel of which Australia may well be proud", wrote Leonard Gould in the London *Observer*. Correspondents questioned the validity of the novel's characterization, the reality of the station life depicted and complained in shocked protest at the casual sexual relationships between white men and black women which the book revealed. It was an attitude by no means confined to the suburbs: "What an appalling thing *Coonardoo* is", Mary Gilmore wrote to Nettie Palmer. "It is not merely a journalistic description of station life, it is vulgar and dirty."[26]

Others swore to its authenticity and applauded the frank handling of relations between black and white, until that time a forbidden subject. Cecil Mann, one of the competition judges, believed that in refusing to keep off the subject of "black velvet", Katharine Prichard had tried the almost impossible task of making "the Australian aboriginal a romantic figure". So ingrained were the old racial attitudes that he could say: "With any other native, from fragrant Zulu girl to fly-kissed Arab maid, she could have done it. But the aboriginal, in Australia, anyway cannot excite any higher feeling than nauseated pity or comical contempt." Of the book he concluded that "with the white flame of the author's creative power burning through it, (it) is itself vital — a harsh but living piece of literature".[27]

The *Bulletin* itself declined to print *Men Are Human* because "our disastrous experience with *Coonardoo* shows us that the Australian public will not stand stories based on a white man's relations with an Australian aborigine". The Editor added jocularly to Vance Palmer, "There is no chance I suppose of you white washing the girl?"[28]

Katharine commiserated with Nettie and urged Vance not to give up:

> It's damnable of "the Bully" to behave like that to Vance and of course he's right not to concede anything. They only cut a few oaths and bowdlerised some of my remarks — the which I didn't see or know about until they were done in *Coonardoo*. But Prior kept sending me ridiculous letters from anonymous correspondents.

She took wicked delight in arranging a stream of letters to the *Bulletin* from each port of call on her way to Broome: from Perth, Carnarvon, Onslow and Cossack.

> As I go around Australia, Prior will be pot-shotted with demands for *Men Are Human*. And the variety of his correspondents! You and Vance would love the mixture — a young prostitute cum bar-maid, and a ship's doctor, the Hill Station folk and two young men surveying aerodromes (can't spell it) on the overland route.

Katharine found other ways of hitting back at the wowsers. When Norman Lindsay's *Redheap* was banned shortly afterwards, she wrote in protest to *Smith's Weekly*, "the only Australian author who has had the courage to denounce the outrage openly, and the insight to realise exactly what it means to future Australian authorship", Kenneth Slessor told her. The letter was not published, but Norman Lindsay wrote personally to thank her:

> I am quite reconciled to having *Redheap* censored to get in return such a magnificent tribute as yours. It quite startled me to think that anyone in Australia could think like that about me. Many thanks for giving me the pleasure; a genuine pleasure, for the power of your prose is its own sincerity.

Katharine affected unconcern about the controversy aroused by *Coonardoo*. To a friend in New York, she wrote:

> I feel it doesn't really matter what anybody says. I have my own row to hoe — and hoe it I will, in my own wilful way — though the reviewers treat my work well enough these days, and occasionally it is exhilarating to find that somebody has recognized something underlying. For instance, the *Spectator* that *Coonardoo* among other things is a study of two opposed moralities![29]

She had been at pains to explain in the introduction to the first edition that the people of Turee Station were not the characters depicted in the book. Long afterwards, when *Coonardoo* had been accepted in the canon of Australian literature and reached its tenth edition, Katharine replied to the suggestion that Hugh was an idealized character, and Coonardoo, herself, more a symbol of the land than a real person:

> I had models for Hugh and Coonardoo. When the book was published I was always afraid that Geary would come some day and take to me. Hugh did: appalled that a man's inner conflict should have been so revealed . . . Coonardoo? She is an aboriginal woman I was close to (in all but the end which happened to another woman) . . . I'd rather *Coonardoo* was thrown on the scrap heap and forgotten than be regarded merely as background and poetic symbolism . . .[30]

CHAPTER 6

THE LIGHTEST, BRIGHTEST SHOW ON EARTH

Much of the symbolism discovered in *Coonardoo* had been largely unconscious, Katharine insisted. In *Haxby's Circus,* the fourth novel of the first fruitful years of her life in Greenmount, she set out deliberately to suggest a parallel between the world of the circus, and the circus of life. In *Child of the Hurricane* she recalled:

> A novel about circus life had been haunting me ever since the circus rider with the broken back had been brought into Nigel's surgery in Victoria. When a circus came to Perth, Jim arranged for me to travel with it through the country districts in order to obtain details for this story.

As a condition of his agreement to her travelling with the circus, Katharine had to promise Mr Wirth, prototype of Dan Haxby, the genial, ruthless head of the family circus of her story, that she would not smoke so that the Wirth girls would not learn the habit.

"She took all her characters from the circus — the dwarf and everybody", Doris Wirth believed.[31] But Gina, the crippled bareback rider, was in fact largely a fictional character, and the story that Katharine told was not Wirth's own story; the atmosphere of the sawdust ring, the dedication of the circus people, their brave insistence in the face of disaster that theirs was "The Brightest, Lightest Little Show on Earth", were part of Wirth's world. "Our assistant lion tamer", they called her; and to thank the circus people, Katharine arranged a fabulous party. Louis Esson, a little dazed by it all, described the celebrations in a letter to Vance Palmer:

> Kattie and Jimmie arrived this week and will leave for a week in Sydney after Cup Day. They are both in excellent form. Jimmie, who is enjoying every moment of life, insisted on us jazzing; so I had my first lesson on the night when Squizzy Taylor and Snowy Cutman had their duel to the

> death at the other side of the Gardens. I had the honour of being Kattie's dancing partner. I had never seen her looking so well or in such gay spirits. She gave an extraordinary party last night at the Green Mill, a party, as Bill Dyson said, that nobody except Katharine could possibly have conceived. It was for the members of Wirth's Circus, with whom she travelled in the West. They were interesting people of different nationalities, American, German, Danish, Norsemen, trapeze artists, bear-tamers, head balancers, mixed in with Dyson and Bancks, Tom Roberts and other highbrows. The ladies were delightful; and there was dancing, and an elegant supper, with sparkling hock and whisky under the tables in the boxes. Dyson announced himself as a wombat-tamer and Jimmie never missed a dance. Kattie is working on a circus novel which will be very different from the sawdust and spangles kind of thing.[32]

Katharine turned back to the half-finished circus story, undisturbed by the demands of a second brain-child. The success of *Coonardoo* gave her new confidence and some immediate relief from financial anxiety. The book was finished before the end of 1929 and entered under its original title, "Fay's Circus", in Jonathan Cape's £1000 novel competition.

Exhausted by the intensity of her creative effort over the past two years, Katharine set off by sea for Broome and Singapore. It was meant to be a holiday, but Katharine promised herself that she could check her facts on the circus's purchase of wild animals in Malaya. Like drugs to an addict, the scent of new places, new stories stimulated her unresting imagination: "I've been awfully used-up really," she admitted to Nettie, "and this place has gone to my head — so that I've been scribbling like mad, when I didn't want to at all."

Slowly, the tensions relaxed and Katharine was able to drink in the strange sights and sounds of British Singapore, Johore and the jungles of Kuantan. After two months, she was glad to be home:

> Life has simply been too lovely since I came home. Sunshiny days, and my two dear men so riotously glad for me to be at home again — with a stolen hour or two on my beloved old Wyburn among the deep hills — where not the sight or the sound of a soul but ourselves and the birds.

There was good news of "Fay's Circus" too. Not long after she reached home, Jonathan Cape wrote to say:

> We are very pleased indeed at the thought of our being the publishers of "Fay's Circus". We like it here very much

> indeed and we have considerable hopes of our achieving a good sale with it. The book was a very close runner-up in our Prize Novel Competition. It was within an ace of getting the prize. We had over 600 manuscripts submitted and "Fay's Circus" got into the last six.

Katharine could hardly complain that the new novel had been so narrowly beaten, although the prize-money would have made a great difference to the financial affairs of the family. She did argue determinedly with Cape's about their proposal to change the title. Jonathan Cape was apologetically adamant:

> We were afraid that until one had read the book, that Fay would be thought of as a girl's name, and the word "circus" has been misused and used sometimes in a derogatory sense.
>
> Furthermore, here in England it denotes a locality, witness Piccadilly Circus. Haxby is a good old-fashioned English surname, probably from Yorkshire, and *Haxby's Circus* is a straightforward title. At any rate one can scarcely be misled by it.
>
> Well, here's the best of wishes to *Haxby's Circus*.

It was a minor triumph when the American publishers, W. W. Norton and Co., decided to revert to the original title, and even more gratifying when they invited her to reconsider some chapters dropped from the English edition, although when it came to the point she found it extraordinarily difficult to remake her people once given independent lives in print. On 13 August 1930 she wrote to Norton:

> I have been working on the "dropped" chapters for the last month, and after a reading to my husband who does not like them, decided to cable Mr. Higham that they were unsatisfactory. Then your letter came, and I thought I should send them anyhow, so I cabled Mr. Higham again to say that I would.
>
> The trouble is that having my mind set to the mould of the book, it is difficult to disintegrate and live those phases again. I do not know whether you will like them. I am dissatisfied with them at present myself because they take action away from the circus and are a development of Gina rather than of the circus as a whole — and yet intended to give the cruelty of life (in the circus maximus) as compared with cruelty in the little circus about which there is such a sentimental fuss. Within the time you mention, though I hope to get this effect more clearly. It was part of my original plan and I was very foolish to depart from it in the first instance. Have been vowing that never again will I do such a thing.

Katharine would have been less amiably disposed to W. W. Norton if she had known that he had also written to Nettie Palmer suggesting that she might pass on some criticisms of "Mrs. Prichard's" style. Evidently Nettie Palmer declined, and Norton summoned up his courage and passed on personally Hartley Grattan's criticism:

> I have read *Fay's Circus* by Katharine Prichard with immense interest. Miss Prichard continues to amaze me with her ability to live into diverse situations and I am more sure than ever that I was right in calling her the hope of the Australian novel. If she accomplishes nothing else she will have justified herself from the sociological angle by the very range of life she has encompassed in her novels. But of course she is getting beyond the merely sociological and has a marked and unusual ability to tell a story. If there is any present-day writer who merits the word dynamic it is Miss Prichard.
>
> But *Fay's Circus* raises an interesting issue. I have noted before that she has a bad habit of writing too rapidly and too carelessly. If she could be persuaded, in some delicate fashion, that her work would be more enduring if she spent a few weeks on it with a blue pencil, I am sure it would be extremely profitable.

The main reason for Grattan's criticism was "the inadequate way", as he saw it, in which the novel explained the circus' sudden change of fortune, through a bequest of £100,000 from Rocca, the Italian dwarf, to Gina, the cripple who had befriended him. Nevertheless, Grattan had the highest admiration for the sharp irony of the book's conclusion:

> I think Miss Prichard has admirably indicated the crucial importance of the Italian dwarf in the development of Gina's (unquestionably, incidentally, a powerful character) life and thinking. Though he figures in but a few pages he overshadows the whole book. And I am sure that it was a major stroke to have the book close with Gina accepting the dwarf's point of view with regard to the crowd's reaction to his deformity and going into the ring as a clown. I wonder if it occurred to you that here we have "Laugh, Clown, Laugh" raised to the thousandth degree and made, not sloppy sentimentality, but a genuinely moving tragedy.

It was not Rocca's gift itself that dissatisfied Grattan, but merely the extent of the dwarf's generosity to the one person who had treated him as a fellow human being. As an alternative,

Grattan suggested that the bequest might have been in stocks, so that Rocca might die without realizing the amount he was leaving. Katharine ignored the suggestion; but the accusation of carelessness, now made for the second time, struck home, though she regretted in the later years of her life that she had been too much influenced by others' advice, and felt that she had lost some of the freshness and spontaneity of earlier work because of it.

Important though Hartley Grattan's advice was to her at that time, it was an exaggeration to suggest, as he did when visiting Australia in 1965, that he had "edited" the book for its New York release.[33] In the end, the American edition of the novel contained one additional section, a description of a boxing match, which had little of the bearing upon the "circus maximus" that Katharine intended.

To some, *Haxby's Circus* was Katharine's most successful work: Henrietta Drake-Brockman, writing as "Henry Drake", said "undoubtedly it is the best and most moving story she has yet written".[34] It was highly commended by authoritative critics in England and America. But now Katharine needed cash more than critical acclaim, as the strangling fog of the Depression seeped across Australia. When the novel was attacked by one American reviewer Katharine wrote lightly to the United States publisher:

> Has somebody sprinkled salt on that nasty *New York Times* critic for me? It's the only thoroughly mean review of my work I've ever seen. Didn't think anybody could find the circus folk dull. He must have had a liver, poor dear. Should I send him a prescription for it, "with the compliments of the author of Fay's Circus"? Or a bottle of honest-to-God Australian sparkling hock? I know of nothing better for blue devils of that sort. "Pig, I ses, and swep' out!"

But there was depression beneath her own clown's make-up, and it was difficult to "crack hardy". She told Norton:

> The first cheque for *Fay's Circus* was a little ray of sunshine; but this reverse, the only American review I've had so far, will overcast your plans, I'm afraid. I'm more distressed on your account than my own really — though it matters so much for the book to go well.

I had no sense of my parents' anxieties as the slow decay of the Depression engulfed them. I did not see the moods of exhaustion that swept my father's spirit; I did not know how the idyll of their life together soured. The camp for the unemployed at Black Boy just below our home had no meaning to me. The men and women in black-dyed Army greatcoats who tramped up the York Road looking for an hour's work or a meal were strangers. My world seemed full of the good things of living: the shadows passed me by. Life was still a circus, and ours "the lightest, brightest little show on Earth".

We lived well, even when financial worries racked my father, and debts mounted in the bank ledgers. There was a mob of fowls and white muscovy ducks in a separate paddock below the house. Turkeys roamed half-wild through the bush paddock, until they were picked off by hungry men looking for a cheap feed. The cattle and horses, all except Katharine's own gelding, Wyburn, were sold off, one by one.

Katharine's visit to Broome and Singapore ate into the *Coonardoo* prize-money. There was little left by the time the new workroom in the orchard was finished, and the stone wall of the open veranda facing the hills had been laid. Katharine always gave her royalty cheques to Jim: "You're the financial brains of the firm", she told him. He was not an entirely satisfactory financial adviser. "Jimmy's supposed to be my business manager," Katharine had explained to Vance Palmer, apologizing for her own helplessness with figures and percentages, "but he wants to deal with a book as you would with a lb. of tea — or something of that sort."

She was afraid of his careless extravagance; but believed that it was necessary to show that she had confidence in him. A man had to be master in his own home, she said; quite content to have her own way in most things by gentle persuasion. It was a shock to her to find that his romantic, adventurous spirit was less able to cope with the mundane struggles for existence in a world which had no need for heroes.

There were innumerable schemes to recover the family fortunes: a wheat-bag loader, which someone else succeeded in patenting; shares in an oilfield in the north-west, which produced only worthless wax; an equally useless steeplechaser, surely the clumsiest horse that ever lived; a mining lease at the Larkinville rush, which yielded enough gold to replace Jim's wedding ring, worn to a sliver by hard work with the pick and shovel. Katharine wrote to Nettie Palmer:

> Have been so full of things to do lately. Jim has been away at the rush for nearly two months and I have had to do all the odd jobs, looking after the horses and farm yard generally.

> Milking in the evening, feeding chooks and chasing turkeys, to say nothing of wrestling with bush fires, and such like.
>
> Last Saturday night, having gone to bed with a migraine epouvantable, up comes a fire. When I went out at about 12.30 to see how it was behaving, our hill and the next one was ablaze. Had to waken Ric and Bill, his small cousin, aged 10, also Rose, my maid-of-all-work, 16 or thereabouts, to turn out and help me bring in the horses, cows and turkeys. There seemed no chance of beating the fire, but when we found it had just jumped the creek we tried, and some lads from further down the road, coming along, we did manage to stop it for a distance of half a mile or so . . . We lost all the feed in about 140 acres, but otherwise not much damage was done, a few posts down that was all. And several turkeys cooked.
>
> Was glad to see Jim home this week end, with a pocketful of "slugs", and messages and yarns from all our mates on the rush. My "mates", too, because I was camp slushie while I was there and loved it. We took a day off, at the sea to celebrate, but haven't had much sea this year. The car being a thing of the past, and our daily surfings memories now. The worry and all, has prevented me from writing much and nothing I do is any good. But perhaps, after all I'm more of a peasant than anything else. Reading this article on H.H.R., I realised that, strenuous and distraught as my life is, I wouldn't swop one moment of it, for her life in London.

There were still the long holidays at the beach to look forward to. We sang at the tops of our voices on the long, slow trip to Fremantle and out through the sandy scrub and limestone towards the sea. Katharine led us in the bush songs she loved: "The Old Jig Jog" and the "other" version of "Waltzing Matilda". Her clear, gentle voice was drowned as the kids picked up the chorus and yelled their joy in it all. Jim would throw back his head and lead off with "Pack up your Troubles", "Daisy", "Yip-Ay-Addie", or his pet, mock-melancholy melody from *The Arcadians,* ". . . a short life, but a ga-a-y one".

Katharine loved the sea. She would run hand-in-hand with Jim to the water's edge and do a little skipping dance through the surf to join him, as he raced away to dive into a breaking wave. The sea to her was "the eternal mother of us all" in whose arms she refreshed her soul. She didn't swim well and could not manage heavy surf; preferred to play in the white water or lie lazily in the still, crystal-clear shallows of the bays and inlets where we camped. In the early morning, or in the afternoons when the sting had gone out of the sun, she sat for hours under a green-striped, rust-flecked, beach umbrella, with a wide straw hat fringed with faded apricot-coloured tassels to keep the flies away: writing; dreaming; trying to capture the gaiety and sparkling beauty of the beach.

Katharine herself forgot the anguish of the Depression years; put aside the pain of her own disillusionment in Jim's defeat by financial disaster, and made an ideal of his "beauty, tenderness and strength". Katharine's poem of dedication, "To Jim", was forgotten when Sunnybrook Press published a limited edition of her verse, *The Earth Lover,* in 1932. To her he was and remained "Krishna, Christ and Dionysos". To others he seemed lost in Katharine's world, out of depth in his own. "There's something in his attitude to her writing that isn't quite happy," Vance Palmer confided to Nettie after visiting Greenmount on his way to London in 1930.

> He's proud of it, but he's afraid of her letting it "worry" her as though it should just flow out of her at odd hours . . . Jimmy's got "land" on the brain. He puts all the money they have into land, consequently they're always short. He's bought an estate near "Wandu" and has got it plastered all over with ridiculous go-getting placards. Of course he takes it half humorously but it's the sort of humour that must be a bit wearing.[35]

Katharine remembered only the "halcyon days" in Greenmount before anxiety and stifling domestic triviality settled about her. She forgot that in the end even those carefree weeks by the sea became a mockery to her. "This holiday is a sham," she wrote in desperation to Nettie Palmer from the holiday camp at Rockingham. And among the old photographs of skylarking children in striped, woollen bathers, Katharine's face looks back to me through forty years, lined with weariness, desolate.

The Depression darkened. My father lost his appointment on the Land Settlement Board when the Returned Soldiers' League withdrew its support. His real estate business collapsed. He lost heavily speculating in wheat futures. Block after block of land in Greenmount and Northam was mortgaged to meet arrears of rates or his debts to more pressing creditors.

With no money coming in, the girl who helped in the house, more one of the family and playmate than a maid, had to go. Katharine turned to the domestic chores that had once been pleasure, and somehow tried to write: "Overdrafts and the debacle of wheat have me so frazzled for the moment that I dare not think of a new book—though several are brewing . . ." she wrote to W. W. Norton. "But for the time being I'm doing short stories to raise the wind, and having been born in a hurricane, pray that my old gods of the storm do not desert me."

Katharine threw herself into the organization of the unemployed[36] and stretched her own energy to breaking point to find the family's living expenses. There were times when there seemed no way out of the morass. Her letters screamed her weariness and protest:

> I wish to goodness I could shake the dust of this humpy from off my feet . . . I've been working, so hard, and badly, because Jimmy is dashed hard up and fretted to frazzles over it. Has little debts amounting to something like £4000 and for the first time since I've known him has gone down to it, dropped his bundle and funked; really I can't stand that—weakness, and I don't expect it of Jimmy. I'll carry my own and his bundle, but a lot will be lost in the doing. It always is—Damn! Damn! Damn! and again Damn!
>
> And I milk the blasted cow and feed the chooks—make the jam and kill and pluck the blasted brutes—and it seems a very good idea to sit on the verandah and drink beer. Only there isn't any beer!

Katharine found that she could not work under the whip of urgency. "I seem to have done nothing worth while this year. A sort of blight of the spirit, or something," she told Hilda Esson. "And I begin to feel pot-bound in this damned bourgeois environment. There isn't anything worth working for except communism, I'm sure."

At the cost of her own strength, little by little the financial position improved, although Katharine could barely recognize the lightening of the load in her own weariness and anxiety. In August 1931 she confided to Nettie Palmer:

> I'm worn to frazzles myself, not sleeping and trying to work—au desespoir about everything. Jim with no job and colossal debts, having to be sheered-off and cheered-off nervous breakdown all the time. Working myself to keep things going—though have got that fixed for a year at least now. And the short stories—if the damn things would only sell—are to appear in the autumn shoal, I believe.

Katharine dedicated her first collection of short stories, *Kiss on the Lips*, to Louis Esson, and when he wrote to thank her,

Katharine's spirits lifted. She was even able to forgive Jim for using Louis' letter of appreciation as a testimonial:

> Your letter was better than any champagne ever vinted . . . But I must tell you, Jimmy was due for an interview with his banker the other day. A heart to heart talk about a little over-draft of several thousand pounds, you understand, and your letter was produced to indicate that the financial prospects of the firm are — incalculable!
>
> I was furious with my James for stealing your letter for such a purpose, of course. But he looked so naive and hurt — it had to be condoned. Me, on threepenny royalties and a lousy £50 in advance, look you, old dear. Wasn't it priceless?

I remember my father's show of triumphant achievement when he announced that he had been given a job in the Department of Agriculture; how he marched onto the back veranda, with his coat slung over his arm, flourishing the gladstone bag he carried on his business trips to Perth, and threw out his arms: "Hullo, old chap! How do you like the new Inspector of Fertilizers?" he shouted.

But there was a puzzling kind of sympathy in the way Katharine greeted him: "Oh, Jim . . . Isn't that wonderful, darling!"

Inspector of Fertilizers sounded pretty grand. What was there to be so sad about? It was not until I went with him on one of his rounds through the wheat belt, stopping at each of the small country towns, taking samples of superphosphate, potash and blood-and-bone for analysis, that I began to realize his frustration; saw how his songs on the long drive through the bush petered out into brooding silence, and sensed his despair in the futility of a job fit only "to earn a crust". It offered no hope of relief from the debts that weighed upon him; not an earthly chance of freeing Katharine from the household cares that consumed her vitality. He yearned to be able to give her again the joyous inspiration of their first years together. "Nothing's too good for my little woman", he had boasted. He wanted to give her the Earth; and all of his dreams had become a mirage, beyond his reach, beyond his strength, almost beyond hope. It was no good pretending any more. The show was over.

Katharine tried to reassure him that she was content with the simple life of Greenmount; did not need to lead a ladylike existence. She made him promise not to give up the relative security of a regular job for some wild scheme in the hope of making a fortune. But it was clear that her own health could not stand the strain much longer without some relief. The dazzling confusion of migraine split her vision into a hundred jazzing fragments. For days she lay in a darkened room barely able to lift her head until the attack passed, leaving her exhausted and depressed. Katharine recalled in *Child of the Hurricane:*

> My sister, who was making a trip abroad begged me to join her and be her guide to Paris. She sent the fare and Jim insisted that I should take advantage of it to meet my English and American publishers in London, and, perhaps go on to the Soviet Union.
>
> "I'll never forgive you," he said, "if you don't try to see what's happening there. We must know whether what we've been told is true."

Katharine and my father were talking in the garden when I first heard that she was going away. She leaned against him with her head resting on his chest, his arm around her. There was a gravity in their voices, and a sense of parting, something strained in his reassurance . . . "of course you must, darling".

Those words, half remembered: "Mum's going away for a holiday. We'll be all right, won't we, son?"

CHAPTER 7

FOR VALOUR

"I feel destiny driven and wonder why," Katharine wrote to Nettie Palmer from the ship on her way to England in June, 1933.

> Meant to do tons of work — and brought it. But my beastly head played up and I had to resign myself to making the most of such a marvellous opportunity to loaf — in order to arrive in London in good order and condition. The whole jaunt was decided on at a moment's notice. My head the chief reason — and I still find it almost impossible to believe I'm here . . .
>
> I didn't bring anything to read except a Russian grammar and the Aborigines Act — and the A.A. remains unopened. And although I started with four hours a day on the grammar have had to drop it — and humour my damned — beastly — stupid — rotten head . . .
>
> My book still in the rough and feel as if it will never be done now. I hate not being able to work — like hell. Tons of stuff to do — and only a damned ache to do it with.

There were letters from London, Paris and Moscow. Photographs of curious, shaven-headed youngsters at a Russian school; pictures of Katharine in ankle boots and a long, cloth coat posing with the group of foreign writers with whom she travelled through Siberia: Walt Carmen the American, Helios Gomez the Spaniard and Sigmund Lund the Dane; Katharine in earnest discussion with the director of the cinema train which took her through the Urals; talking with the peasants on a collective farm; wearing proudly her Udanik medal for outstanding workers. It seemed a different world. Letters were our only link with her distant reality. She told me of a broadcast she was to make from Moscow shortly before leaving for home.

> I'm going to see about my boat for going back to London today, and will be in England again before you get this. Kiss Dad, for me — and look after you both, won't you — because I simply couldn't bear it if you weren't both quite well.

My Dad and I climbed out of bed early in the morning to hear Katharine's broadcast on a neighbour's short-wave set. We managed to catch a few phrases among the crackles of static before her voice faded again into the senseless, jungle whistles and chatter of the sound-waves. We walked down the hill, silent and disappointed. My father put his hand on my shoulder. "Never mind, old chap. She'll be home again soon", he said.

He had told me of his scheme to get the sales of land in Greenmount moving: a grand rodeo, buckjumping, exhibitions of stockwhip cracking, boomerang throwing, pony rides through the bush. It would bring the crowds and let them see the place to build a weekender or a home in the hills. The scheme was first suggested by some casual visitor who had seen the dude ranches in America. My father believed that he "stood to make a packet" if he could unload the Greenmount land. He could not resist the temptation to show Katharine he could make a go of it.

As the scheme developed, the rodeo took more and more of his attention, until it became an end in itself. His original purpose was lost in everything that went into making a show. Stockyards were built in a natural amphitheatre above the creek, ringed by rough seats. Horse-lines were put up in the triangle of land where the Old York Road joined the new Great Eastern Highway. There was a kiosk thatched with reeds for the sale of sweets and soft drinks. Some ten ponies and riding hacks, a white donkey and a couple of mules were lined up, each one named after one of Katharine's novels or stories.

Two thousand people streamed up to the hills for the Sunday opening of the "Lazy H Ranch". My father was everywhere; an impressive figure in his crisp, white shirt with casually rolled sleeves, faded riding-breeches and boots stained with the patina of the saddle. The Perth dailies reported the event enthusiastically; but father's face was strained with anxiety when he came home that night, exhausted and depressed. The story was told in the final paragraph of the *Daily News* account of the opening:

> Captain Hugo Throssell, V.C. and his band of returned soldier helpers have struck upon a unique manner of entertaining Sunday pleasure-seekers, and as a result of yesterday's efforts charity will benefit considerably.

As a Sunday entertainment, no admission charge was permitted. The proceeds of a collection went to charity.

My father lost heavily. The Returned Soldiers' League declined its support. Crowds dwindled as the heat of summer hit the hills.

Those who came climbed through the open fences to avoid paying a two shillings admission charge on Saturdays, or threw a threepenny bit into the hat at the Sunday shows. The Roads Board complained about interference with the traffic. Anonymous neighbours wrote wanting the rodeo closed down. My father was forced to walk with a stick when one of the horses trod on his foot, crushing a bone in the instep and injuring a nerve. "By cripes it hurts, old man," he told me. "Worse than anything in the war."

He hated the physical limits the injured foot forced upon him; hated hobbling about or being helped onto his horse. He carried on; but he was again heavily in debt. Within a few weeks the show collapsed. The stock was sold off and the rodeo gear disposed of for what little it would bring.

I was sent to stay with friends who had boys of my own age, a mile or two away. I saw little of my father. I would walk through the orchard after school on the hot summer afternoons and find the house empty. I fossicked for Minties among what was left of the kiosk's stock of sweets in one of the big veranda cupboards; played with the remaining bow and arrows, or wandered aimlessly through the house just looking at the things I knew. There was strangely little comfort in a handful of free sweets. The house was a lonely place. I was grateful for the warmth and friendliness I found with my friends, but there was an emptiness that I couldn't tell them about.

My father took me to the pictures in Perth one Saturday. He paid for us both, not using the gold pass that Hoyts had presented to him. In the depths of his depression he had tried to pawn his Victoria Cross and had been offered ten shillings for it. We sat in the darkness of the cinema watching the film. He took my hand.

"Do you love your old Dad, son?" he said.

Not long after a car called for me before I left for school. There was a murmured conversation.

"Oh, no!"

"We'll get his things later".

"You must be a brave boy, Ric."

"Daddy's had an accident."

In Perth, my aunt, so gentle, so loving, wrapped me in her arms, sobbing, sobbing.

"You poor, poor boy."

"We mustn't cry, must we."

Tears streamed down her cheeks.

"He doesn't understand."

"Too young to realize."

"Mother will be home soon."

Katharine was in London when my father died. A telegram breaking the news had been delayed. She first learnt from a newspaper headline that he had killed himself.

There are few words of her pain and bewilderment at that impossible, undeniable fact in the closing chapter of *Child of the Hurricane;* but even thirty-five years later she could not bring herself to speak of it without reawakening the terrible memory of her grief. "I had absolute faith in him and don't know how I survived the days when I realized I would never see him again. The end of our lives together is still inexplicable to me," she wrote.

Like the bush creatures she loved, Katharine kept her wounds to herself, hidden away in some secret place until the hurt was healed. She felt too deeply for it to be seen by others. It was impossible for her grief to become a public display. Only to the closest friends would she sometimes speak of the tragedies in her life: and, later, to me.

Several years before her death, Katharine told me of the terrible doubt that she had borne in secret through the years. She had left the unfinished manuscript of *Intimate Strangers* in her workroom at Greenmount: perhaps my father had found it there; perhaps in his despair he had seen himself as the unwanted husband of the story and taken his own life, as Greg had done in the original conclusion of the novel. We talked late into the night before the tail-end of a log fire in the sitting-room at Greenmount. Katharine's eyes were filled with tears. Her face, scarred with age, worked with the fear she had suffered alone for so long. Her hands, frail and gentle, clasped and unclasped in mine.

I think, at last, she accepted my explanation that his despair was caused by much more tangible things: the inescapable burden of debt, the stark reality of failure, the physical fact of anxiety and sleeplessness. He had longed for an end to it all, and the only end seemed death. She searched my eyes as if to find the truth; sighed with the loneliness of those long years without him; leant her head against me, as she had leant against him.

"He was such a wonderful man. There was never anyone quite like him," she murmured.

The weeks until Katharine returned by the long sea route from London were endless. There was a broken scrap of a letter from

London. She would be home soon. I must be a brave boy till then. I longed to have her back; to tell me why. I returned to school and endured the cruel curiosity of my classmates. After a month of eternity the ship arrived at Fremantle. I yearned to be able to cry in her arms. Katharine was helped down the gang-plank. I hardly knew her. Her eyes were sunken; her face drawn and splotched with grief. She could barely walk without assistance; so hunched and thin. There was no welcoming smile, no arms to hold me: a murmured, "Nicky darling", between her tears. I knew that it was I who must comfort her; and knew, too, that there was nothing I could do.

CHAPTER 8

MOURN NOT THE DEAD

Mourn not the dead that in the cool earth lie—
  Dust unto dust—
The calm sweet earth that mothers all who die
  As all men must . . .

But rather mourn the apathetic throng—
  The cowed and the meek—
Who see the world's great anguish and its wrong
  Yet dare not speak!

—Ralph Chaplin

That summer in Greenmount went on for ever. I could not understand how Katharine could bear to go back to the locked, empty house: rooms closed and still; blinds drawn that were always open. Dead gum-leaves were piled by the gully wind against the door, making mounds in the corners of the veranda. The stink of rotten apricots drifted from the orchard where the fruit lay fly-blown and putrid on the earth. Over the verandas grapes hung in withered wreaths. The wild oats, parched dry and silvered by the sun, were hip-high in the dying garden. Everything about the house reminded me of him. I wanted to be able to forget. Katharine found some comfort in remembering. "But darling, we were so happy here," she said long after when I told her how hard it had been to go back to Greenmount.

Someone had kept an eye on the remaining stock. There was one milker, dry and hollow-gutted, in the big paddock; a few fowls sheltered from the heat under the water tank, wings half extended against the earth, beaks gaping, mad-eyed. Day after day climbed over the century, airless and still. The galvanized iron creaked on the roof against the heat of the sun. In the night simmering with cricket noises, the seed-pods of the wattles snapped, scattering a dry hail over the house. Then as if the air boiled, the gully winds roared, hurling gum-nuts on the veranda roof, howling and howling, thrashing the trees . . . No tears . . . "Crack hardy, old man."

Katharine went about the household jobs, remote, withdrawn; doing what had to be done; somehow making it home again. We didn't talk about him; couldn't, either of us, but the place at the end of the table became less empty. His things became just things again: the old, Army greatcoat in the hall; the pliers that hung on the back veranda . . . "A place for everything and everything in its place". There were no ghosts for Katharine; just the reality of living without him.

She was shocked to find how far my father had sunk into debt. All his land-holdings were under mortgage. There was a heavy overdraft to meet and debts in thousands of pounds outstanding from the fiasco of the "Lazy H". Even his modest life insurance policy was in jeopardy. Liabilities were assessed for probate as £9659 15s 11d. Her own account was exhausted from the expense of the return from Moscow. Katharine fought desperately to find some way out of the financial quagmire which had destroyed my father. She had always played the helpless female in money matters. Now she blamed herself. By persuading the executors that she was herself a major creditor of the estate, she was able to save the house at Greenmount and the double block of land around it.

Katharine forced herself to debate with the authorities the cause of my father's death. She was horrified when it was suggested by some official fool with notions of protecting my father's honour that he had committed suicide while of unsound mind. She wrote movingly to the Repatriation Department and succeeded in persuading them to accept her view.

> The facts, I think, are well-known. Nervously and physically, my husband's magnificent constitution was impaired as a result of war service. The Medical Board has the record of his wounds and periods in hospital for meningitis and malaria: but I resent the idea that his mind was ever in any way deranged. He feared that it might become so . . . I am convinced that he believed he would be insuring a pension to me and my son by his last act—although he had promised me that this would never happen.
>
> I consider that his "grateful country" made it impossible for my husband to live. He thought he had to die to provide for his wife and child. As far as I am concerned, I could not accept anything that cost him his life: but I feel that I have no right to interfere with what he sought to do for his son.
>
> My own health is uncertain and I may not be able to provide for our boy who is eleven years old.

It was a dreadful struggle for Katharine to make ends meet. She could not face the final revisions of *Intimate Strangers*, but forced herself to get back to the notes of her journeys through the USSR. Each afternoon when I came home from the little, two-teacher school down the hill, I would find her at her table in the sitting-room strewn with paper, typing away in frowning concentration, or gazing through a mist of cigarette smoke back to the excitement of those days: perhaps to the conference of the Literary Circle at a Siberian steel works . . .

> Rain or shine, it was always an adventure, going down through the factory yards, past the spray ponds and the blast furnaces, glimpsing the ant-like swarms of workers on the subway; to see the new crane of red iron stretching a gigantic claw across the silver threads of rails which penetrated into cavernous depths of the coke plant and the rolling mills. At night, the great buildings leapt to the eyes, high glass galleries brilliantly lit as for a ball, flames spouting up to the stars, the open hearths and torrents of slag casting a ruddy glow into the darkness.
>
> From the rain and splintering lights, we went into a big white hall packed with people. Between three and four hundred day workers from every department of the steel plant were attending the conference.

Katharine intended her book on the USSR to be more than a mere traveller's tale, more than a political pamphlet about the "Russian experiment". She had travelled, she said, about 30,000 miles through Russia, Siberia, the Ukraine, the North Caucasus and the Tartar Republics:

> I want to write about them in splashes of colour, gouts of phrases as Walt Whitman would have, or Mayakovski: paint them after the manner of the French symbolists, images seething and swarming over each other, as they lie in my mind. "The shapes arise."
>
> Ancient buildings of dead beauty, slums of the middle ages, sullen rivers, dark pine forests, pink and white churches with gilded domes, ragged mountain ranges under perpetual snow, fretted scaffoldings stretching above: new cities of glass and steel, dove-grey concrete, crowding in on them: a black mouldering village beside its stripped fields: harvest fields flooded with sunshine.

The Real Russia was serialized in the Melbourne *Herald* in April 1934. Introducing the series, the *Herald* announced:

> She has sought to find out and to convey something of the life of the ordinary people in Russia today — their habits, how they live and work, and whether they are happy or oppressed.
>
> In these articles she has succeeded to a remarkable degree in presenting her impressions graphically and picturesquely. In many directions her views differ entirely from those expressed by other writers who have dealt with modern Russia; and by many her conclusions will be found provocative.

Katharine told of the people she had met: "old Bolsheviks who had never dreamed of watching their dreams come true . . . gypsies, Cossacks, kulaks, aristocrats of the old regime, Esquimaux students, leaders of the Communist Party, udarniks (best workers) of the steel plant and coal mines, workers on the roads and railways, collective farmers, mechanics, women engineers, doctors, dentists, poets, artists, actors, musicians, street sweepers and officers of the G.P.U." She told of the places she had seen: cities and towns; the remote village at Ulitena, where "The Little Lamp of Lenin", as the electric light was called, burned in every home. E. J. Brady, poet and publisher of the roaring twenties, long silent, acknowledged the stirring enthusiasm of Katharine's account:

> That "Little Lamp of Lenin" good Comrade Katharine,
> Has fired with inspiration this weary Muse of mine . . .
> A lamp for human guidance, a torch of human worth,
> Long may its light englamour the workers of the earth!

The Real Russia was published in book form later in 1934. It was a shoddy publication, littered with printer's errors: her name mis-spelled on the fly-leaf. Katharine was disappointed with the book; felt she had not done justice to it. It was hard for her to recreate the zest and confidence of those Russian workers she wrote about, when her heart was tight with grief and the anxiety of living from day to day pressed upon her. But, despite her own desolation, *The Real Russia* is alive with remembered laughter. The vital statistics of the young Soviet state are seen through the eyes of a hopeful generation. There is no echo of Katharine's own sorrow, alone in Greenmount. Years later, she wrote: "Only my belief in the need to work for the great ideas of Communism and world peace helped me to survive a grief so shattering".

Others thought her devotion to the Communist Party damaged her work. Even her friends Hilda and Nettie regretted her political commitment. Hilda tried to persuade her to leave political chores to others. "I've always said to Kattie others will do that better than you can — but they can't write as you do . . ." Hilda told Frank Dalby Davison.[37]

Nettie took a more practical approach, appealing for Alan Marshall's help in securing some recognition of her importance as a writer among her political friends, and some relief from organizational chores:

> We have in Australia a few real writers and Katharine Prichard is one of them. Hartley Grattan, as an American observer and critic puts her first of all. Without question she's very important to all of us, and her international reputation in England, America, Russia — makes it more possible for Australian literature to gain consideration . . .
>
> That is one side of the picture. The other is that I doubt whether even the members of the Writers League know of her value . . . It's time they were told: or can't they be told, are they only willing to think of Katharine as a party hack who is willing to lick envelopes and sometimes drops into literature in her spare time? Katharine's work for the Party and its affiliated bodies is beyond all praise or thanks but some of the very Party members seem to think less of her because of it . . .[38]

As one of the founders of the Movement against War and Fascism,[39] Katharine was expected to attend the national Anti-War Congress arranged in Melbourne to coincide with the city's centenary celebrations in November 1934. A Czech journalist, Egon Kisch, was to be the guest speaker.

We travelled steerage from Fremantle, sharing a miniature, two-berth cabin six feet from the water-line in the bows of the old *Westralia,* where every wave was a nauseating, roller-coaster ride and every roll, by some ingenuity of marine engineering, became a loop-the-loop. Katharine loved the sea and was quite immune to seasickness. Half an hour out of Fremantle, she found me on my face by the winches on the foredeck within staggering distance of the rail. I spent the first few days of that journey stretched out on the top bunk, with my nose eighteen inches from the ceiling, like a very crook herring in a can. She bathed my face, tried all her most infallible remedies, gave me barley sugar to suck, anointed my wrists and temples with eau-de-cologne, sang to me:

> Rikki-tiky-tavi was a little mongoose,
> Brave and strong.
> He fought a big snake in the garden
> Of the world,
> All day long, all day long . . .

Even the lullaby that had always been proof against all the fears of my childhood was no consolation.

Kisch was refused permission to land in Fremantle. In Melbourne, the Congress went on without him. There were two empty chairs on the platform: for Kisch and the banned New Zealand delegate, Gerald Griffen. Katharine at once joined in the work of "The Kisch Defence Committee" and, with other writers, protested against his exclusion as an undesirable alien. Years later she remembered:

> When the others left to attend the proceedings in Court, I remained with Kisch. We had been warned that he might be shanghaied on to a German gun-boat, which was lying in the harbour, quite near the *Strathaird*. I had been requested not to let Kisch out of my sight, and to send word immediately if such an attempt were made.[40]

Fortunately Katharine's services as a bodyguard were not needed. "He did not know I had been his shadow that day," she wrote, "but he recognized me when we met later in Sydney."

Kisch refused to be excluded. He jumped from the rail of the *Strathaird* as the ship pulled out from the wharf, broke his leg in two places and was bundled back on board for the trip to Sydney.

Katharine and I went on to Sydney by train and found a one-roomed flat with gas-ring and balcony, closed-off at one end by ill-fitting sheets of mildewed plywood.

Kisch's case was taken to the High Court. We met him while he was on bail awaiting the appeal. He was still on crutches, his foot in plaster. Such a little bloke to have so much guts, I thought. Dark hair pushed back from a sloping forehead. Keen, laughing eyes and a greying, toothbrush moustache, like Hitler's. I wondered why he didn't shave it off. After coffee in the restaurant below our flat, he entertained me by dropping a coin into my cup.

> "I shake it. You can hear it, is it not? Now look. It is empty! Look, I will do it again. Watch carefully. It is a trick I learned — when I had a little time, you know," he explained.

Katharine understood him. "In Germany?"

"The concentration camp," he said.

Katharine sat beside Kisch on the platform at the stadium when Gerald Griffen, still a fugitive from the police as a prohibited immigrant, was to speak. It was believed that the police would try to arrest him at the meeting. Katharine wrote:

> Looking out over the sea of faces in the semi-darkness of the vast sporting arena, I realized that there would be a riot if they attempted to do so . . . It was a sensational moment when a spotlight was turned on the young man who stood up in the crowded amphitheatre and spoke clearly and steadily for several minutes. There was a move at the back of the hall to approach him; but it was obvious that a number of husky young workers were surrounding Griffen. Then the light went out, and in the darkness we heard the noisy rattle of a motor car. There was a rush from the building and some shouting. Kisch clasped my hand. "Don't worry," he said. "It will be alright." It was. The meeting went on. Not until next morning did we learn that detectives had chased that motor car and taken the men in it to the police station. None of them was Gerald Griffen. He had remained seated in the audience and walked quietly away with the crowd leaving the building at the end of the meeting.

Kisch was eventually permitted to leave Australia without the deportation order being enforced. All costs of the proceedings against him were met by the Commonwealth. He visited Katharine again in Greenmount on his way home, and told of his visit in his book *Australian Landfall,* although his picture of the place, with dingoes howling in the garden, possums peering from the branches and koalas playing in the gum-trees, seems to have been constructed with full journalistic licence.

Katharine stayed by herself in Greenmount when my father's old school friends from Prince Alfred's College offered to meet my fees at boarding school. I accepted my two bob a week pocket money; grew out of my clothes and asked as a matter of course for a pair of football boots. Katharine rationed herself during the week so that there would be "proper food" for me to eat during my weekends at home. She made do with calf's liver and soup; invented a dozen different ways to prepare the stuff; ate a meal with me at the weekends and somehow saved enough from her war pension to be sure that I was provided for. Her sacrifices were carefully kept from me in those years, although with the almost subconscious awareness of a child, I learned that there were reasons why you didn't ask for some things.

In public Katharine could conceal her grief in work for the "great objective values", for which she once believed even the fragile happiness she had discovered with Jim should be sacrificed. Alone in Greenmount she mourned for him:

The grass is green again,
and you're not here,
my love.
What can I say to all the spring
without you?

The loquat blooms:
its perfume wafts my senses
to their old wild spate —
and you're not here, my dear,
to make its warmth and mystery
our own,
for one lost hour.

The foam of wild flowers breaks upon the hills:
the hills you loved and worked among,
ploughing the orchard,
driving cattle through the rain —
your great glad voice,
singing Appassionata,[41]
when the west wind hurled itself among the trees.

Oh, yes, the spring fulfils its magic everywhere:
a native cuckoo calls.
But neither sun nor bird songs
wake you now,
and I must live alone.
How could you leave me so,
to take the beauty of the world with pain,
because you are not here, my love?

Katharine published little in the first years after my father's death. Grief dried up the joy of life which had been so much a part of her and her work. An intolerable loss to some has meant artistic death. Katharine, however, was incapable of retiring into sterile melancholy. Sheer necessity compelled her to keep working; but short stories were her only source of income from writing in those days. Residual royalties from the earlier novels fell to as little as £1 10s for six months sales. Reprints were unheard of.

Each year the *Bulletin* accepted one of her stories. As if to outface fortune, they were often stories full of warmth and laughter: "Buccaneers", the story of a carefree, holiday romance between a trio of middle-aged businessmen and three young women caught bathing nude on a remote beach; "Jimble", the fable of an aboriginal boy's first Christmas at an outback pub; "The Mayor of Bardie Creek", a yarn of the hotel cook's attempt to rig the four-forty at a country sports meeting.

The demands of her political work absorbed her time and energy relentlessly. Pressed almost to the limit, she wrote to Vance Palmer in October 1935 in desperate protest:

> Gord . . . he knows whether I'll ever get another book done. One day a month is all I get sometimes and working 18 hours a day sometimes on Party affairs. It's devastating . . . quite impossible to get any concentration. And I'll be stony, motherless broke if I don't earn something soon. Summer coming too, and you know how one's brain boils in the heat.

In 1936 the Spanish Civil War flamed into ill-disguised international violence. All over the world the people of the Left were stirred to the defence of the Republican Government. Katharine poured herself into the organization of the Spanish Relief Committee in Western Australia. Often during the weekends, friends called, sometimes with the grave-faced, quiet men wearing the black beret of the International Brigade. Letters poured in, plastered back and front with postage stamps of the Republic; pamphlets and magazines proclaiming the defiant slogan *Non passeran,* told of Spain's savage struggle against German and Italian intervention; the destruction of Guernica in the German Air Force's rehearsal for total war. Katharine wrote articles in support of the Spanish Republic; addressed meetings against the non-intervention policy of the British Government; marched in demonstrations through Perth and spoke to a rally on the Esplanade appealing for support for the Spanish Relief Committee.

The stands of the regular Esplanade spruikers for salvation and inner cleanliness were down to a handful when Katharine spoke. She detested public speaking; had none of the tricks of the professional, party speakers. Every appearance was an ordeal. She had been warned that some of the Catholic Action supporters were expected. No VC now to see she got a fair go. But when she spoke, they listened. Her voice, thin and clear as a cry in the night, rose and died with such sadness that it seemed to contain all the grief and tragedy of Spain. She looked frail and alone there on the platform, her hands clasped tightly behind her, her head thrown back and tilted a little to one side, with the defenceless defiance of a bird with a broken wing. That gentle voice so full of conviction, passionate in its plea for the dying Spanish democracy, had great power to move those who heard her. It was after a meeting like this, that a long, thin fellow with sunken cheeks and staring, blood-shot eyes staggered out of the audience and, swaying before her, declared solemnly: "I wouldn't go on my knees to Jesus Christ, but I'd go on my knees to you". And to Katharine's immense embarrassment tried unsuccessfully to do so.

Moved by the tragic death-struggle of Spain and accounts of the heroism of ordinary people defending a democracy they had barely glimpsed, Katharine wrote *Women of Spain,* a fiercely partisan one-act play which adopted the direct political appeal of agitation-propaganda. She had first used the method in a dramatic sketch written for the Actresses' Franchise League in London in 1914.[42] *Women of Spain* was performed for the Spanish Relief Fund by the Workers' Art Guild[43] in the Perth Town Hall in 1937.

Her plays in the thirties[44] were largely a matter of conscience, part of her political duty to the things she believed in and the people she cared about. She did not regard them as significant work. Certainly they made no contribution to her livelihood as a writer, even though she was a good deal worse-off than the shop-girls and the miners she wrote for.

Katharine was never able to order her life so that it fell in nicely defined order. The three strands of her existence were interwoven: her work, her political commitment and her love for those close to her. Aidan de Brune was mistaken when he wrote: "We may be sure that she is inspired by artistic and not political reasons when she walks with the unemployed in street demonstrations. . ."[45] Katharine marked that passage from Book News with a significant exclamation mark. Her artistic and political purposes were not so easily separated. She could not deny the people with whom she identified herself; could never achieve for long the solitude that her work demanded; could not abandon the art through which she sought "to understand the world and make others understand it". She needed the love of those she loved.

The demands of a major work might become her main preoccupation for as long as the rest of the world would allow her. A political crisis could fully absorb her immediate attention. The personal tragedies of life might for a time sap her consciousness of all other concerns; but these were the knots and ties in the total fabric of her life that made of an end a new beginning.

CHAPTER 9

INTIMATE STRANGERS

In the stillness of Greenmount, Katharine took up again the manuscript of *Intimate Strangers*. The early morning bird songs were the only sounds about the house to wake her now, as the pale jade light of dawn lightened the sky behind the hills and the morning star shone in dying brilliance against the last fringe of darkness. Sometimes still the native thrush sang her heartbreaking, beautiful song alone in the vast, silent stage of the morning. Katharine knew all the bird songs in the garden at Greenmount: the chestnut-breasted warbler, the superb warbler, the yellow-rump tit-warbler, the melancholy heart-cry of the pallid cuckoo in spring. She delighted in the brief, flirting visits of the blue wrens, and the redbreast's tiny, crimson flag flaunted from a fence post in defiance of the winter rain; the daredevil willy wagtail chasing a marauding magpie from his nest with a machine-gun volley of scolding profanity. She tolerated even the mock-innocent twittering of the hordes of silver-eyes raiding the grape-vines, despite her most ingenious defences: bits of brightly coloured rag, brown paper bags and tins filled with pebbles designed to rattle terrifyingly in the wind. Katharine was satisfied to make a gesture of defence against those miniature invaders by clapping her hands and calling, "Shoo! Shoo! Oh you naughty birds!" The silver-eyes took it for applause. Katharine, as if to excuse their liberties, set fruit bearing the mark of their thieving on the breakfast table: "The bird-pecked ones are always sweetest," she would explain.

Years before, Katharine had written down word for word a story that my father told her. As a schoolboy he had seen the English actress, Henrietta Watson, play the leading lady in *The Three Musketeers* and reckoned she was wonderful. He came across a photo of her in an old magazine when he was working in the North-west and wrote to her—in indelible pencil, squatting in a corner of the shearing shed with a kerosene box as a desk. He told her of his memories of her, promised that "he would find a gold mine or a bird's nest"; come to England and live happily ever after. Signed himself "Northam Jim", and addressed the letter: "Miss Henrietta Watson, Actress, London". Three months later she replied. "Perhaps it is destined we shall meet some day," she told him.

When he was in hospital in London, after being wounded at Gallipoli, he wrote again, "just saying I had not found the gold mine nor the bird's nest, but as soon as I was well enough she could expect a bearded bushman to be knocking at her door and announcing himself as 'Northam Jim' . . ." They met often during his convalescence and visited theatres together. He went to her home and she showed him the dilapidated envelope addressed in indelible pencil: "Henrietta Watson, Actress, London."

"Of course," he said, "in a proper story, we should have got married and lived happily ever after, but this is a true story so we remained the best of friends, or, as she aptly put it — 'intimate strangers'."

Katharine's novel owed its title to Jim's story, no more; but by the strange irony of life, it was at Wandsworth Hospital, where he had first met his intimate stranger, that he also met a young Australian journalist, Katharine Susannah Prichard.

The ideas for the novel were first explored in a light-hearted domestic comedy, *Bid Me to Love,* probably the second play submitted with *Brumby Innes* to the *Triad* competition. The characters were the characters of the novel; the setting was unmistakably the veranda at Greenmount; the plot was marriage, discussed in terms familiar to the permissive society of the seventies, startlingly unorthodox in the Australia of the nineteen-twenties. The play has remained unknown. Its central situation was fully developed in more serious vein in the novel that had tragic parallels with Katharine's own life. In November 1928 she had written to Louis Esson:

> There are two things I want to get on to and finish. Both pull and I'd like to dispose of the circus yarn and get on to *Intimate Strangers* which is to be a study of the married relation, urban, and as close in as possible. Probably I'll make notes for the latter when I feel like it and work steadily on the other. Things litter the floor of your mind so, until they're chucked out . . . don't you think?

Her notes for the novel were begun in 1928. Among the scribbled descriptions of the sea, a crabbing party at sunset, Greenmount after rain, there is the story of a wedding. The bride dreams of the fisherman she had loved and the man she is to marry: "Nice young haberdasher . . . dear sweet young haberdasher . . . she mocked herself . . . You'll smell of clothes with him . . . unbleached calico and moth balls . . ." It was Dirk's wedding in the novel still unwritten.

Not all of the pieces fitted so easily into place. There are notes from Remy de Gourmont's *Natural Philosophy of Love*; musings on the nature of love in men and women:

> Watering the garden — an ache for it all — an ache of passion and fear. It is the late summer of life which is the season passional of women . . . In women who have known the disillusion of life and love the flame is stronger.

Opinions, compared, weighed; a man's eyes; a New Year's Eve party and "a tall golden-haired girl in flounced tulle, yellow and ghastly", sick in the hand basin; the fish markets at Fremantle; names: Greg; Dirk — Dirk swimming out alone beyond the breakers:

> "I don't mean to . . . and then I can't help it . . . I wish people would leave me alone." What subtle peace came to her out there in the deep dangerous water . . . Always she came in with a gay, satisfied, almost shy look on her face, a girl coming from the embrace of her lover, exalted, satisfied, remote.

Tentative, disjointed passages of a woman's unspoken thoughts to her lover:

> You're very charming and lovable — quite fascinating when you smile . . . But you're not capable of typhoons — passions which overwhelm and carry all before them . . . Your eyes have no depth. There is something mean and shrewd in them . . . Oh yes, I like you best when you laugh, mon cher . . . But I don't like you at all when you say my name. You slop over it, as if it were a caramel, some large soft lump of toffee which sticks to your teeth . . . The bushfires and typhoons of emotion — passion, lust, jealousy, grief, I go down like a butterfly on the wind for. That's what my man has. No other man I know has just the same force of feeling. Only marriage, familiarity, the commonplace has sated his capacity to feel like that for me. That's why I explore you . . . He thinks I'm captured, because I've married him. You know it isn't so. I'm not captured — only captive . . .

Little by little, the impressions resolved. Incidents fell into place. Images of the sea and cities coalesced. The story of distant, middle-class lovers torn by family duty, the memory of old ecstasy, the fantasy of new love and the grinding reality of unemployment, grew in Katharine's mind.

Intimate Strangers was begun in 1929. Under the growing financial pressures of the Depression, sometimes she despaired of it ever being completed: "As for me, the book of this coast I hope may be done during the year. It was begun when we were here three years ago, and I haven't been able to get back", Katharine wrote to Nettie Palmer from Rockingham in 1932.

A year later it seemed no closer to completion and Katharine told Vance that she was "in despair of its ever being published". Even when she wrote to Nettie from the ship on her way to London in 1933, her despondency continued: "My book still in the rough and feel as if it will never be done now," she said.

Henrietta Drake-Brockman suggests in the "Australian Writers and Their Work" series that *Intimate Strangers* was not more than half-written in 1933, when Katharine visited Russia. She goes on to say, however, that the ending of the novel was changed before it was finally published:

> Her husband's death altered the structure of this novel: it had been her original intention that Greg Blackwood should shoot himself. When this conclusion seemed no longer possible lest people came to regard the work as auto-biographical (which was certainly not the case) she had to seek another solution.[46]

Katharine's own fear that my father's suicide had been influenced by the original conclusion suggests that the book had been completed in draft before her visit to Russia; her letter to Nettie from the ship implies that the rough draft had been finished, although a great deal of revision remained to be done.

No one can know now what torture Katharine suffered remaking, god-like, the lives she had created. Even to read that final chapter of *Intimate Strangers* must have been anguish, raw acid in the wounds of her mind. Reliving the terrible doubt: had Jim read the manuscript, searching for some reassurance of her presence in his loneliness; yearning perhaps to be able to give her a word of encouragement in the desolation of his failure? He was always the first to read a new story: the finished typescript laid on his pillow, an offering to her household gods:

> To you, all these wild weeds and wind flowers of my life, I bring, my lord . . .

And if he had read those last lines . . .

> *Her eyes strayed to the letter. She saw the revolver lying beside it. Her heart contracted with fear. "Elodie darling — " the letter began, "it's no good. I'm not fit to live. I've made such a mess of things. And there's no other way out that I can see. Try to forgive me, and remember that I loved you. I've been a fool and a blackguard . . ."*
>
> *His arm had fallen across the page. "Sold the house . . . the money's all gone . . ." Elodie read.*
>
> *She stared at the straggling script. It leapt and crawled away under her gaze as though it were alive . . .*

Could he have seen himself in Greg: shared his failure and despair? *"Sold the house . . . the money's all gone . . ."* Could he have believed that Elodie's thoughts were her own?

> *As Elodie went over the details of her arrangements, everything seemed quite simple and practicable. There should be no need for any ill-feeling, she assured herself. Greg and she had become business partners, more or less. The spirit had gone out of their relationship as husband and wife. They were no longer lovers. Their life together was bankrupt of happiness for either. All the real values for both of them were outside the framework of their marriage and domestic entanglement. No doubt Greg would be as willing as she to make an end of the farce between them.*

He could not have imagined that this withered relic of domesticity was their life together, their love! . . . And yet there were those familiar details that he might have recognized and given greater significance than the carefully observed background to another's story: the faded blue shirts that Greg, too, liked to wear; the tricks of speech echoing his own words: "Cripes, I was gone on you when I wrote this"; the inconsequential incidents of daily life, children's illnesses and quaint sayings; Elodie walking the curving foreshore of a deserted beach with the crimson parasol that Katharine used to carry; Elodie swimming side-stroke in the shelter of the reefs, as Katharine did. Places so near, painted with all the vividness and light of reality: *"Bougainvillaea growing near the verandah cast a purplish glare over her. Magenta, aniline and virulent, it thrust a tower of bloom against pale blue of the sky. Light showed through its thin silken leaves as if they were stained glass . . ."* Had he seen this as the same bougainvillaea that grew by the veranda at Greenmount where he died?

"I can't sleep," he had written, "and I feel my old war head. It's going 'phut' and that's no good for anyone concerned."

Katharine rewrote Greg Blackwood's story:

> *She pulled open the door of the workroom. Greg was sitting beside his carpenter's bench: he had fallen asleep writing. A shabby old dressing-gown over his pyjamas, he sat stooped across the table, his head on his arms. The light on the bench flared over him.*

She could not rewrite her own tragedy; could not know what it was that led the man she loved to destroy himself. Those powers of an author to do what she alone willed with the creatures of her imagination were confined to make-believe lives, into which reality had broken devastatingly.

The revisions of *Intimate Strangers* were completed by the middle of 1936. The finished novel was at last sent off to Jonathan Cape in London, some six years after it had been begun. Edward Garnett, Cape's reader, reported:

> Very good, very good indeed, this novel of an Australian woman's married life. Mrs. Prichard already knows what she wants to do, and here has track of her subject with her usual cleverness and intimacy . . . The story is interesting all through, bright and picturesque in the setting, and the scenes, out of doors mostly, are worked into a clever, intriguing pattern. The novel gives, we should say, a true and intimate picture of the Australian woman's life in the rather free and easy society of a seaside town.

Jonathan Cape added his personal impression that the story at the outset moved too slowly and was over detailed: "I don't think this can be avoided as it is by the accumulation of detail that you build up your effect," he acknowledged. He asked all the same that Katharine should do "some slight pruning"; suggested she should refer to "swimming suits" instead of "bathers"; chided her gently for inconsistency in the use of colons and semi-colons: "Possibly punctuation is something which you do by 'feel' and not by principle or method. Very few authors are strong on punctuation."

The novel that had cost her so much had become a picture of married life in the "free and easy society of a seaside town". The catastrophic pressures of the Depression, against which the lives of the people were set, passed without comment. There was no mention of Greg's intended suicide and the tragic irony which allowed a shadow to live, while a man died. In the publisher's cool, professional eye it was a matter of pace and pruning, of colons and semi-colons, of words understandable to English and

American readers. It was some consolation to Katharine that, with her publisher at least, she was safe from the personal identification of the author with her characters which the public often assumes.

Cape understood the faculties which allow a writer to absorb the experience, emotions, attitudes of mind of other men and women and re-create them with such clarity and conviction that they seem to spring from the most intense personal experience — and yet are fiction.

Katharine's "rage for privacy", the reluctance to reveal the intimate details of her life as a young woman in *Child of the Hurricane*, her wish that personal papers should be destroyed after her death: these things make it clear that Elodie and Greg were fiction, even to those who did not know the depth of understanding and companionship between Katharine and her own returned-soldier husband. It would have been entirely contrary to Katharine's character and to her whole method of work up to then, and after, to make herself the central figure of her novel and to expose the naked yearnings of her own heart.

In *Intimate Strangers* Katharine had dealt for the first time with a situation close to her own way of living; her own time. She wrote of an artistic, middle-class family; Perth and the coastal beaches she knew. As always she drew on observed reality. It was inevitable that much of the detail of character, incident and setting was recognizably associated with Katharine herself and the people she knew. She denied that *Intimate Strangers* was autobiographical. "The novel was a simple story of two friends who recognized themselves immediately when they read the book", she wrote.[47]

She explained in a letter to Ian Reid, of the University of Adelaide, that *Intimate Strangers* had been written during the Depression years: "They were the natural background of my characters, like Elodie and Greg. The distress of those years impinged on the middle class of course. I deny the focus of the story changed. It was only the end which was affected by tragedy in my own life . . ."

The book was received enthusiastically by the local reviewers. The Perth *Daily News* devoted half a page to the novel:

> It lives up to — in fact, it surpasses — the high standard which Mrs. Throssell set in *Coonardoo* and *Haxby's Circus*. It is perhaps the finest modern novel written by an Australian . . . It can be said at once that Katharine Susannah Prichard

> has accomplished brilliantly the task she set herself. She has played with sure touch . . . Her work is interpretive as well as reportorial: it is creative, not read meticulously from a score. When this is adequately done, a novel is a work of art, its author an artist. It has been done triumphantly in *Intimate Strangers.*

Once the work had been completed, Katharine put the book aside and tried to forget the painful memories associated with it. She paid little attention to the reviewers' reactions, rarely referred to it in accounts of her work and accepted without comment the fact that it was often ignored in the assessments by later critics. "When I'd finished 'I.S.', I didn't know whether it was good, bad or indifferent," she told Nettie. "Nothing ever seems to measure up to what it was during the process of conception. But I had to do this thing: try to do it at any rate."[48]

Katharine continued to believe herself that the book had failed, and made her own self-appraisal. "Why was *Intimate Strangers* a failure?" She wrote to Jack Lindsay in 1961:

> I think because it did not remain true to its conception. The m.s. was drafted, and in the rough, when I went to the U.S.S.R. In it the husband shot himself and Elodie, disillusioned in her affaire with Jerome, seeks to identify herself with the universal flow of life towards that better earth — whose "margin fades forever and forever as we move". When I returned home my husband had died like hers. It was too painful then to write of what had happened to me. I changed the end. My literary conscience failed the test, I suppose. So the book was a failure.

It was not until 1967, when Henrietta Drake-Brockman wrote her careful appraisal in the "Australian Writers and Their Work" series that *Intimate Strangers* was fully recognized as one of Katharine Prichard's most interesting works:

> For the first and only time, Katharine Susannah Prichard is chiefly occupied with middle-class attitudes and people given to self-analysis, critical of life, with civilized responses and informed interest in the arts. In many ways *Intimate Strangers* is the most thoughtful of the novels; at the same time it is designed to show the emptiness of middle-class existence . . . Katharine Susannah Prichard is now, like Lawrence, occupied with the nuances of a woman's sexual experience: she sets out to dissect the sensations of love-making, not clinically, but for effect at the moment and later. With considerable frankness for a woman writer of the thirties

> (delicately, by present-day comparison), she explores, within the limits of Elodie's knowledge, the erotic life of an intelligent woman, imaginative, sensitive and tender, whose romantic, or poetic, vision of life is frequently sharpened by the irony of actual living.[49]

Katharine was grateful for Henrietta's recognition of *Intimate Strangers*. When in the last two years of her life she told me of the fear that had haunted her for so long, she asked whether I believed she should release the final chapter of *Intimate Strangers* as she had first written it. I knew what it would mean to her to relive her grief, to awaken the memories of those terrible days when my father died. I could not ask her to do that, although I knew, as she did, that the logic of the novel required Greg's death.

The first version of the ending of *Intimate Strangers* was not among the papers Katharine left for me at Greenmount. She had burnt it, I suppose, with those other "wild weeds and wind flowers" of her life which she had once given to Jim.

CHAPTER 10

THE FIRE AND THE FURY COMES

Wake, my fellow Australians,
The fire and the fury comes;
Now comes your hour of nationhood,
With the rolling of the drums.

— Ian Mudie

Katharine sat, chin in her hand, elbow propped on the polished, jarrah table where she worked, gazing out across the garden and the hills of Greenmount beyond: "the dark, quiescent earth heavy with trees and shadows, indigo, purple, young green a film spreading over it . . ." She had written lovingly of those quiet hills in her notebooks, seeking the words and images which would reveal the beauty of familiar things, recording impressions coloured by the moods of evening, rain and summer sun, testing out the rhythm of words upon her pen: "Trees after the rain, under a swift flash of sunshine glittering as though cut in silver."

It was hard to believe that we were at war. So often the newspaper headlines had screamed of invasion, ultimatum, threats and counter-threats. But there was no mistaking the gravity of Neville Chamberlain's voice, pulsing with the ebb and flux of the radio waves; nor the careful solemnity of the Prime Minister's announcement of Australia's declaration of war. I imagined Katharine hadn't heard the announcement from the other room.

"Mum! Did you hear that? We've declared war on Germany", I called.

Katharine sighed for all the fear, the pain and suffering she knew must come, and turned from the peace and simple beauty outside her window.

"Yes, darling," she said, her eyes filled with tears.

The war came as no surprise to Katharine. She had worked, organized, spoken and written against the twin evils of war and fascism, convinced that if facism could be overcome war could be avoided.

> Those who work for peace are forced into the difficult position of either supporting the League — the weakness of which has been apparent in the past — or of aiding and abetting Fascist arrogance, and with it a perpetuation of a system which depends on war for its existence. To be apathetic and cowardly when our energy will help to remove the menace of war and fascism from our lives and the lives of our children is unforgivable, surely? Are we all mad to sit quietly and listen to explanations of how populations will be wiped out by aerial warfare — and do nothing to prevent it? Why not work to prohibit the manufacture and sale of poison gas, rather than be duped by talk of futile preparations against it?[50]

Now she knew that only war could stop a Nazi triumph. She saw in Nazism the antithesis of all the things she believed true and good. Knew, too, the horror of war. Remembered the death of her brother, Alan, in France in 1918. Saw her son, unaware, unknowing, seventeen . . .

Katharine was convinced that the new barbarism of Nazism under Hitler had to be wiped out in the interest of civilization. She had passed through Hamburg on her way to Russia; saw the strutting arrogance of the Nazi officers; had read accounts of the Brown Shirts' terror in the Communist press; heard from Egon Kisch the terrible reality of the concentration camps and Gestapo gaols; saw the insidious spread of German military strength through the Saar, Austria and Czechoslovakia. She, who loved life and beauty, loathed Nazism with the same intensity that the world learned when the lessons of five years of war, the evidence of Belsen, Dachau, Auschwitz and the judgments of the Nuremberg war crimes trials had provided their incredible, tragic proof. Katharine shared wholeheartedly the initial decision of the Australian Communist Party that "the first aim must be to defeat Hitler",[51] until the stalemate of the "phoney war" led the Left to suspect that the governments of Britain and France aimed to turn the Nazis' ambitions against the Soviet Union.

Early in 1940, a series of police raids on the homes of known Communists heralded a tougher attitude by the Australian Government to the Communist Party's opposition to what they persisted in regarding as an imperialist war, despite the fall of France and the Battle of Britain. Katharine had learnt from previous experience.[52] Piles of forbidden books, pamphlets and magazines were bundled into an old tin trunk and hidden in the middle of a thicket of plumbago, protected from the law by a flimsy barricade of sticky, blue blossoms. At 6 a.m. the next morning the police arrived and sifted through the bookshelves and cupboards, taking possession of anything that struck them as subversive, including my schoolboy history notes on the Peasants' Revolt and a volume of the poems of Percy Bysshe Shelley.

On 15 June 1940, The Communist Party was declared illegal. Joan Williams records the events leading to the declaration of illegality in her manuscript, illegality in "The First Furrow".

> Before the actual declaration of illegality, raids had been conducted simultaneously on leading Party members, with a number of others thrown in for good measure. Mrs. Throssell's Greenmount home was ransacked and much of her library removed, but her literary prestige apparently made it too difficult for the police to proceed.[53]

Katharine had once written to Vance Palmer during an earlier period of anti-Communist activity, speculating about the implementation of the Crimes Act:

> Goodness knows what will happen if it's ever put into operation. I'm beginning to think gaol's the only place I'll ever get any peace to write in. So long as you all demand political rights for me so that I can write. Don't forget, if it does happen, to stir up the craft for me on this issue.

Now, when the prospect of gaol seemed more real, Katharine was not deterred by the possibility of prosecution or imprisonment from the pursuit of her beliefs and the cause to which she had dedicated herself. She drove herself relentlessly in the defence of those arrested for possession of the Communist Party's illegal newspaper and similar political offences: "I feel thoroughly exhausted after the causes and legal battles about which I was concerned," she wrote to Hilda Esson. "Bail, remands appeal, and interviewing legal counsel for the defence."

Katharine was not immune from intimidation herself. She told Hilda of a meeting with the Crown Prosecutor in a Kalgoorlie pub:

> Was staying with friends, and went into the "Palace" for my letters, when who should walk into the office but the Crown Prosecutor. I've never met the man, or spoken to him — only seen him in the police court, so you can imagine how amazed I was when he said:
>
> "Oh you're in Kalgoorlie, too, Mrs. Throssell!" I didn't reply.
>
> "You're not here for the same purpose as I am, I suppose."

"I hardly think so," I said.

Then with a jerk of his thumb, he sent the clerk out of the office, and leaning across the visitors book, said:

"Holding the intolerant opinions that you do, why do you allow the Prince Alfred College boys to pay for your son's education?"

He spoke so thickly, I realized he had been drinking and said:

"I beg your pardon."

He repeated what he had said. I replied:

"What makes you think you are entitled to speak to me in such an insulting way? My husband and I were in perfect agreement as to my point of view. I don't wish to discuss the matter with you." As I turned to go away he said:

"You've been shown a great deal of toleration."

I said: "I don't desire to discuss that either", and walked away.

"Oh well, you know where you get off", he said.

Did you ever hear of such impudence? Or such discreditable behaviour on the part of a man who is supposed to be representing the Crown in the interests of justice, law and order etc.

Katharine was quite sure her letters were intercepted by the censors and anything of interest passed on to the police. She took the opportunity to make it clear that she did not intend to be silenced by a spell in gaol:

> I'm only telling you this in case coming events may have cast their shadow before. It was such damned cheek to accost and try to intimidate me in that way. So ridiculously undignified and malicious! I don't in the least mind going to gaol, when and if it is necessary. "All experience is an arch where through gleams that untrodden world", you know, and, of course, any experience de la sorte would provide me with material to write about.
>
> For the present I'm not engaged in any political activity, but am trying to write this book and make a good job of it. If anything occurs to interfere with my work, the Civil Liberties might be interested to hear of the episode aforementioned. No doubt, the "gentleman" in question would like to take action, but it remains to be seen whether he will find a suitable pretext. My point of view is well known, of course, and I have no intention of denying it.

On another occasion, official displeasure took a more concrete form. A series of lectures on Australian literature at the University of Western Australia was cancelled. Katharine wrote angrily to the Professorial Board protesting against the decision:

> By cancelling the addresses which I was invited to give in the course on Australian Literature at the University, you are well aware, no doubt, of the implications of your action.
>
> That those, who should defend intellectual integrity, have thrown the first stone at me, is a matter for surprise and shame. But what I feel more deeply is, that by repudiating the value of my knowledge of Australian literature, for political reasons, you are destroying the principle for which the University is supposed to stand, and which is supposed to be the basis of your own work.

The University's action was not without opposition. "I still remember feeling stunned by the fervour of the Chairman's objections to having a notorious Red on the staff if only in a temporary capacity," Professor Allan Edwards recalled.[54]

The Fellowship of Australian Writers[55] forgot political differences and for once stood solidly with Katharine on the issue. To Gavin Casey the show of unity was an achievement in itself:

> People who loathed and feared just about every political idea and ideal in Katherine's head were as solid as those who habitually stood and cheered whenever she spoke. This was injustice of the worst sort and in no circumstances to be countenanced.[56]

The Fellowship's protests at least secured the payment of a fee for the cancelled lectures, which Katharine could ill afford to forgo. She continued to eke out a living from the occasional short story; but, on the advice of Hew Roberts, later Director of Adult Education in Western Australia, she was anxious for me to enrol in a drama course at the University of Iowa, and later at the Meyerholdt Academy in Moscow. It seemed an impossible dream. Katharine staked her luck on the chances of film production.

The theatrical possibilities of film had long interested her, despite the disastrous treatment of *The Pioneers*.[57] She had been impressed by the possibilities of a film centred on Broome and the pearling industry and set out to write a romance filled with the colour and intrigue of an exotic setting, which she hoped would provide for my future and buy time for the major work she wanted to do.

Katharine turned back to her notes of the visit to Broome and Singapore ten years before; the harbour, the streets, descriptions of the crowd at a Chinese circus; the sea, "clear, silver, glittering, opalescent"; junks carefully anatomized, "three sails ribbed like a duck's foot. The largest centre—stained muddy brown and faded, the others tan and sepia, or brown paper — each segment folding separately to a bone of bamboo." There was a Malay proverb she had recorded for the time that it might be used: "Look not at the setting sun for fear you may be led to untrodden paths." Snippets and scraps of stories: "The doctor David — boon companion — no good threw it away — threw it away — diamond ring . . . threw it away". Here, perhaps, in this disjointed fragment, was the conclusion to the romance of the pearl of ill-fortune, the "moon of desire", whose malevolent influence would only cease when it was returned to the sea:

> He threw the pearl into the sea. It shone like a little moon falling through the dark water. A moment later the moon disappeared from the horizon leaving only a frail radiance on sky and sea.

Katharine was intrigued by the exotic atmosphere of Singapore and the Malayan jungle, but she saw it as foreign territory: "I want all new words . . . another vocabulary to paint Malaya . . . to do it in batik . . ." she wrote in her notebook at Kuantan.

The lure of a handsome Hollywood cheque for film rights was enough to make Katharine forget her disillusionment with the cinema, but it was not so easy for her to be satisfied with work which she could not completely believe in. There was a basis of fact in the story of *Moon of Desire*. The central character was drawn from life. The settings in Broome and Singapore were described as she had seen them, with the heightened colours appropriate to a romance. The operations of the pearling industry were factually accurate. But there was little of the "illumination of the consciousness" which Katharine came to regard as the criterion of a work of art. She was impatient with the contrivances of plot which she thought necessary for film.

By the time it was finished, Katharine was fed up with *Moon of Desire*. "Wish I hadn't done the thing now," she wrote to Hilda.

> It's just a yarn, though has got a few decent bits. All the same, I feel I've let myself down on a concocted story. Just felt I had to do something to save the financial situation for next year . . . Have been so utterly weary — of this damned book, chiefly. Will be relieved to get it off my mind altogether. It seems so flat — and stiff and futile — although I have got in some bits of the real K.S.

Even when publication in the United States appeared assured, Katharine continued to be dissatisfied with *Moon of Desire*. She told Hilda:

> The American publisher wants to change the title. Why I don't know — and don't care. It's a rotten book. Just a yarn for film production. If it sells, that ought to mean relief from financial cares for the rest of my life — and a chance for Ric to study film production. Seems too good to really happen. But so far the prospects seem fair. T'any rate all I'm concerned about in connection with it, is the sale of film rights.

Her agents advised against a direct association with a film company: publication of an American edition of *Moon of Desire* had been arranged and their own representatives would look after things in Hollywood. Katharine received an advance against US royalties — less 10 per cent commission, less 7½ per cent alien tax, less interim copyright fees, leaving £37 5s 9d.

In August 1942 came the blow that, not only had no contact been made with the film industry, but the American publisher had decided to abandon publication of fiction and relinquished his contract. Copies of the typescript were sent belatedly to Fox, Selznick and Paramount — without result. Reluctant to abandon the hope of film production, Katharine wrote again pointing out that "although this book is not representative of my best work, the setting is surely of particular interest just now, when Broome and Singapore, as a result of war, have become places to which the attention of Americans is directed".

Although friends in the United States made further inquiries, the war disposed of any immediate prospect of *Moon of Desire* being filmed. It was a dream, like many others, which did not come true:

> Ah Moon of my Desire, who know'st no wane,
> The Moon of Heav'n is rising once again:
> How oft hereafter rising shall she look
> Through this same garden after me — in vain.

CHAPTER 11

THE ART AND CRAFT OF THE SHORT STORY

Katharine welcomed the Australian Broadcasting Commission's invitation to give a broadcast talk on the "Art and Craft of the Short Story", both as a supplement to her meagre income, and as an opportunity to set down her own ideas about an important aspect of her own work.

Interviewed by the *British-Australasian,* after winning the Hodder and Stoughton prize for *The Pioneers,* she admitted that the short story fascinated her, but the more insistent work of journalism had prevented her giving full play to her imagination. She had found compensation in the study of modern literature, the works of French, German, Russian and American, as well as English authors. "Guy de Maupassant is my favourite short story writer," she was quoted as saying at that time, "and Meredith is the novelist I admire most".[58]

It was not until long after her first success as a novelist that Katharine achieved recognition as a short story writer. On 9 October 1924, Leon Gellert wrote to tell her that she had won the *Art in Australia* short story competition with her entry, "The Grey Horse".

> I was delighted with your story and cannot remember a better one published in Australia. Strangely, yours was the very last story to be read by me. It was my job to tackle them all first. It took me three days and more. We were very surprised to find the author was a woman as it was the only one which deceived us by its style.

Leon Gellert went on to suggest that it would be necessary from the paper's point of view to make two alterations to the story of the mating of the grey stallion, explaining that he would not willingly alter a single word, but he had "endured such disgusting comments (in a letter from subscribers) with cancellations of subscriptions that the other Directors get 'nerves' ". Perhaps to show that he did not share the scruples of colleagues, he quoted in full the reactions of Hugh McCrae to the story:

> The Katharine Prichard story sets whole carillons ringing in the blood. Her pen rips up the country like a phallic beam of sunlight; the buds burst and the animals quicken as they did in Genesis. But, at certain points, the writer seems to contradict herself; for instance, Bill Moriarty's envious exclamation, while he rubs his hand over the shoulder of the stallion, "I wish it was me old man; I wish it was me. *It's all I'm fit for really.*" This remark is discounted by the fact of his having fathered (and apparently after a celibate life too!) one "small puckered red creature" killed by its first summer upon earth. How much more ironical if he had begotten beauty and strength; and *then*, been refused by his wife. The writing of the story and its fiery motif move triumphantly together as the words and music of a song.

Leon Gellert did not agree with Hugh McCrae's interpretation, and assured Katharine that for him the superb irony of the story was that the man, Moriarty, was weak; had failed as a stallion. Katharine replied confirming Gellert's interpretation, but making it clear by her comments that neither was completely correct:

> Is any man pure stallion? I think not — and my husband agrees — knowing both kinds better than I do.
>
> I did not wish to suggest any uncanny dovetailing of affinities . . . I don't know that Moriarty was "weak". Rather an ordinary countryman befogged by his complexes. "Weak" or "strong" are words that do not weigh for me. They are too absolute for truth.

When "The Grey Horse" was reprinted in *Kiss on the Lips,* the first collection of Katharine's short stories, the offending phrases were put back where they belonged.

Katharine dedicated *Kiss on the Lips* to Louis Esson, whose early plays she had admired and whose opinion as a critic carried more weight with her than any other: she had accepted his mild disparagement of *The Pioneers,* welcomed his enthusiasm for *Working Bullocks* and *Coonardoo* and revised the title story of *Kiss on the Lips* on the basis of his criticism of the manuscript.

Louis wrote thanking her for the dedication, full of gratitude, modesty, praise and selfless joy in her success:

> It is surprising that I should be immortalised in this delightful way. It is not your fault that I don't deserve to be: for I seem to exist in your literary imagination not at all as I really am, but as I should be, a kind of platonic idea of a literary man, a light-weight Aristotle, or a Presbyterian Anatole France . . . According to my literary ideas *Kiss on the*

> *Lips* is a rare and beautiful book. Nothing finer has ever been written in Australia or by an Australian. All the stories are good, mighty good, and some, I fancy, look suspiciously like masterpieces. Even the lightest hold their place and balance the boat. I think you vastly improved *Kiss on the Lips*. In the M.S. version it seemed to over-step the modesty of nature. You have a vision of humanity that is Balzacian in its intensity. As Baudelaire said of him, "even his scullions have genius". People do not seem as wonderful as that to me. But in the world you reveal there is life, light, colour, things have meaning, and the destiny of man is not altogether trivial . . . I should like to open a bottle of wine and propose the toast of the First Lady in the Land, our Lady of Letters, Katharine Susannah — why not? I will have it on Saturday night and imagine you are there.

Even though she knew that, on this occasion, Louis' sternly impartial criticism was tempered by gratitude, Katharine treasured his good opinion; copied the letter and kept it as a testimonial to success, among the press cuttings pronouncing their insubstantial verdict on her work.

In contrast to Louis Esson's gently veiled suggestion that Katharine's was a romantic view of life, Aidan de Brune saw her as a realist with poetic vision:

> Sometimes she is brutally and shockingly frank in her treatment of sex themes. Like D. H. Lawrence, she sees poetry in physical reproductive power in man and in beast . . . The power and cruelty of life have obsessed her. She is a fierce realist, but something more; she is a great poet who writes in prose.[59]

Three more collections of short stories followed *Kiss on the Lips* throughout the years: *Potch and Colour,* in 1944; *N'goola,* in 1959 and *Happiness,* consisting largely of stories reprinted from the earlier collections, in 1967.

The broadcast on the art and craft of the short story was both a challenge and an opportunity to Katharine. She shared many writers' suspicion of literary theorists and was determined that her own material would be thoroughly prepared.

There are thirty-four pages of notes for that twenty-minute broadcast: jottings from her own bookshelves: Emerson on literature, Carlyle, Chaucer; pencilled quotations; comments and queries on the work of Mark Twain, Daudet, Stevenson, Kipling and Henry James, scribbled in the reading room of the Public Library. "Do not remove — returning. K.S.", she had written at the head of a page quoting Canby in *Pure English:* "Correct English may be very bad English. There is a dressed and formal diction, as colourful as a concrete walk . . . The writer of pure English chooses his words with a consciousness of life in every syllable."

Katharine reread the Australian stories of the past and the present day; noted down authors and titles, from Price Warung's *Tales of the Convict System* and Barbara Baynton's *Bush Studies* to the stories of her contemporaries: Vance Palmer, Miles Franklin, Xavier Herbert and young Australian writers like Dal Stivens and Douglas Stewart, making their first appearances in *Coast to Coast*; copied brief phrases, or pages of narrative to illustrate the authors' style.

The broadcast was transmitted from Perth on 16 February 1940:

> Most writers, nowadays, agree that the technique of the modern short story cannot be defined or classified. It's as elusive as the fires of genius which generate new art forms and methods of expression.

She went on to trace the history of the short story's development and differentiated between the forms and models of the craftsman and the liberty demanded by the artists:

> The master craftsman ordained; but the great artists have always been iconoclasts. They have said what they had to say in their own way, and with the passion that moved them. Few of them have not been innovators, either in form or content . . . It may be advisable to know all the rules, in order to break them. One learns the technique of a craft as one learns the grammar of a language, and then forgets it. The forgetting may not be as absolute as we imagine; but technique ceases to be a fetter . . .
>
> For myself, I dislike all subterfuges and tricks of the trade for gaining effects. I think that you must deal honestly with your subject. Tell others about it as it affects you. Otherwise the story will be betrayed: lose its innate virtue. "We are betrayed by what is false within."

"The Grey Horse" and "The Cooboo" are generally regarded as the best of Katharine's short stories. She herself wrote to her American publisher to say:

> I've just been correcting the proofs of *Kiss on the Lips*— as the collection of short stories is to be called — and hope you may like them. Some of them, "The Grey Horse", "The

> Cooboo" and "Happiness", more nearly conform to my standard than anything I have done.

She was immensely proud of the inclusion of "The Grey Horse" in an anthology of "The World's Great Short Stories", although Professor Allan Edwards preferred "Happiness" and "The Cow", and singled out an experimental story, "The Curse", for special comment:

> It's more like a poem than a story: a passage of brilliant description, full, elaborate, lush, will be followed by a passage of dialogue terse in the extreme, anonymous, almost bodiless, like the disembodied questions and answers of "Public Opinion" . . . It's almost like a ballad, crossed by an imagist poem.[60]

A copy of his lecture notes had been sent to Katharine in advance. She worked carefully over her reply:

> Astringent criticism from a critic whose standards one respects is always helpful . . . Edward Garnett, it was, who gave me his blessing and said "Go your own way. It's the only way for you to go!" And Austin Harrison, the editor of the *English Review* warned me against becoming "cerebral". So many English writers were at the time — and still are, it seems to me.
>
> I wanted to interpret my own country and people — to submit myself to them. Not impose myself on them, but be a medium for their expression.

Katharine went on to correct an explanation she had given Professor Edwards of the reasons for the aboriginal mother in "The Cooboo" discarding her child:

> A short story, I think, should not attempt a solution, but merely give a fragment of life which will stir thought and emotion.
>
> For this reason there is no attempt at solving the problem of the aboriginal mother's act in "The Cooboo". That was the way it happened. I was wrong to say to you on the 'phone, as I did, that the explanation might be "the exploitation of native women by the station owner". That was not in my mind when I wrote the story. And is not an explanation.

Needless to say, Katharine continued to "go her own way"; and continued to earn the approval of the critics for many of her short stories when objections to her political views had dampened enthusiasm for her major novels. Three stories about Communists included in *N'goola* drew similar reactions from Sidney J. Baker:

> Buried in the book (presumably so that buyers will not discover it immediately) is a clump of Communist propaganda from Miss Prichard's pen . . . The point about these particular stories is not so much that they trade in Communist cliches, but that they are extremely poor, by comparison with most of the other items in the collection. We are offered puppets instead of characters, contrivance instead of valid plot, exchanges of slogans instead of genuine conversation.[61]

The collection had, in fact, been dedicated: "To the leaders and members of the great Australian Trade Unions who defend the rights of working people, and the struggle of all peoples for peace and a good life"—warning enough to the politically sensitive shopper. It was not part of Katharine's character to go under false colours.

There was no reason why an Australian writer should not produce a *Dr Zhivago* in reverse, a Melbourne critic admitted; but he, too, found that "A Young Comrade" and "Communists are Always Young" were "poor stuff". The offending stories were as directly taken from life as "The Cooboo" and "The Grey Horse". The characters were the good Party members whom Katharine knew. The "slogans" and "clichés" were the language they used. The "contrivance" was their own story. Katharine knew that she idealized her heroes. She was as much inclined to do so in life as in literature. "All your geese are swans, Jammie," her brothers used to tell her teasingly.

Quite unrepentant, she wrote of people as she found them—as Communists, as Catholics, and as human beings. She was delighted, and a little amused, when a story which had pleased her Roman Catholic friends, "Josephina Anna Maria", was also chosen by the Russian magazine *Soviet Women*, as the best short story of the year. But in the eyes of her critics, a Communist goose was expected to remain an ugly duckling. With that view of reality Katharine could not agree. She found her justification in Remy de Gourmont's words: "The only excuse a man has for writing is to express himself, to reveal to others the world reflected in his individual mirror."

Katharine herself added:

> The writer of a short story, it seems to me, should put an incident, or a character, under his microscope and describe them, at some moment of crisis, with remorseless sincerity.

CHAPTER 12

OUR WORK IS WHERE IT BLEEDS

Ah love the Earth is woe's
And sadly helpers needs
Until its burden goes
Our work is where it bleeds.

— Bernard O'Dowd

Katharine first glimpsed the vast, sprawling story of the Western Australian goldfields during the days with Jim at Larkinville. Yarns by the camp-fire with men who had tramped into Coolgardie with the first teams were Katharine's own find at the Larkinville rush. The big story was there, she knew, as elusive as gold itself, as demanding as gold hunger; a story lost in the abandoned diggings and derelict mines, along tracks leading nowhere. In Boulder, industrial heart of the Golden Mile, on the outskirts of Kalgoorlie, Katharine found the deep lode of the story that led to the present; it was there waiting for her; waiting to be found; waiting to be written.

Her broadcast on the short story brought some respite from financial anxiety; paid well compared with the fees offered for creative work. A series of eight talks, "Katharine Susannah Remembers", about experiences in London as a young journalist, followed.[62] On the radio Katharine spoke with a wistful, dream-like fragility which gave her words an air of romantic nostalgia for the past, although that was not at all her intention. She detested the microphone and faced up each time to that "horrid little machine" as nervously as if it were her first performance. "Like a little high-bred filly that got all of a sweat if she was expected to do anything", Jim used to tell her. Preparation of the broadcasts took time, too, and although they provided a more regular income than Katharine had known for years, it was clear that this was not the answer.

Katharine was forced to recognize that *Moon of Desire* as a money-spinner was a bad joke. She could expect no more than

£85 in royalties on an edition pared to a bare two thousand copies by wartime paper shortages in Great Britain. And that crumb, the reward for a year's work, was nibbled away by commissions and taxes. Film prospects were still like a silly dream. The house at Greenmount was under mortgage. Interest payments gnawed into the few pounds which months of work earned. There seemed no way to buy time for the work fermenting in her mind.

In desperation Katharine wrote to Hartley Grattan, during his visit to Australia in 1940, asking about the Carnegie Fellowship under which he had travelled. Grattan suggested that if she could present a good case to the Carnegie people they would probably grant an application for a trip to America, pointing out that a good deal of money, "wrung from the workers if you like", had been provided by Carnegie and Rockefeller for Australians' benefit. But Katharine did not want to go to America: on those terms it would have been impossible for her to apply. Her first visit to the United States had chilled and disillusioned her. It was time she needed. Time to think. Time to write. Time to grow back into the goldfields of the nineties. Time to make men and women of the half-formed shadows in her mind. At Hilda Esson's insistence, she turned to the Australian Government for help.

Katharine applied for a Commonwealth Literary Fund fellowship. Supporting her application, Professor Walter Murdoch wrote to the Secretary of the Commonwealth Literary Fund in Canberra, stating:

> Mrs. Throssell is the most famous of living Australian writers, and probably the only one whose name is known to lovers of literature throughout the English speaking world. She is certainly the only contemporary Australian novelist who has won a high reputation both in Britain and in the United States. She has done more than anyone else to give Australia a place of honour with the reading public of each of these countries.
>
> She is an artist to the finger-tips, and has never allowed herself to turn out work less good than the best she could make it; she has never won success at the cost of her artistic integrity. For this reason, though she has achieved fame, she has not achieved affluence; and in these times, so difficult for all who live by the pen, she is feeling the need of assistance. I can sincerely say that in my opinion she deserves all the assistance her country can give her.[63]

On 5 April 1941, the fellowship was granted. Katharine wrote full of enthusiasm to Hilda who had hustled her into the application:

> Cheers! A telegram to announce that the Fellowship grant will be coming my way. Last week I wrote, asking when a decision was likely to be made. This evidently is in reply. Actually, as I explained, I would have to drop the goldfields material and get on to immediately remunerative work, if a decision was not made soon. Had several days on it, last week and the week before — thoroughly enjoyed myself, and am going to put all I've got into this job. It's thrilling material really — but an enormous canvas I've got myself to work in. From 1892 to the present. A three generation book, and I would like to take three years for it. That seems impossible. At any rate, it's marvellous to have the prospect of working without having to stop a thousand times to scrounge round for a few quid to keep the pot boiling. Do hope I'll be able to make something worth while — and for all time. It will be difficult to concentrate — with the state of things as they are in the world today. But somehow it must be done. I feel that it's now or never for my literary reputation. And the first chance I've ever really had. Have done a lot of reading already — and yarns with old prospectors. The first part well under way. Must go up to Kalgoorlie again, quite soon to get the atmosphere again and check up on various phases . . . Of course, I get drunk with work, when I start. Too long hours and too intense about it I suppose. Must put myself on rations and try to take some exercise and rest! But fancy being able to have the washing done. That always crocks up my blasted machinery. Have been feeling so ill and weary recently; but this should make all the difference. Knowing I haven't got to bust myself to make ends meet.

Within a couple of months Katharine was back in Kalgoorlie, staying with a miner and his wife: "They let me do as I like," she wrote.

> Marvellous to have no washing up and cooking for a while. I hunt out "old-timers", yarn to miners and prospectors — and all the time with the drone of the mine batteries in my ears: talk about shifts and winzes and plods, going on.

She described her visits to the historic and less reputable pubs for a pot with some of the old girls of the fields, delighted by the frankness of their reminiscences: "That was when I was married to me first husband. Never marry again girls, I say. The second, he was a bugger!"

Katharine revelled in the opportunity to steep herself in the atmosphere of the goldfields and, even for a short while, to concentrate on her own work. In June 1941 she wrote to Hilda:

> I've been working very hard on the new book and enjoying myself thoroughly, talking to all manner of folks and living in the very atmosphere that is going into words. It's a colossal subject though — and will take more than a year — two at least to get what I'm after out of it. I'm feeling well and having nothing to do but write. Isn't is marvellous?

But Katharine's release from the affairs of the world and family anxieties was not to last. The German invasion of Russia in June 1941 transformed the Communist Party's attitude to the war. The war became a "People's War of Liberation". For the Australian press and public, too, there was some quick rethinking. The USSR became an ally. The "Red menace" became the "heroic Red Army". Fears that the Russo-German Non-Aggression Pact might lead to Soviet support for the Axis evaporated. With the assumption of office by a Labor Government under the prime ministership of John Curtin in October 1941, the Communist Party gained confidence in the prosecution of the war and moved to a position of full support. Katharine had known John Curtin as Editor of the *Westralian Worker,* and regarded him as a friend when she first came to live in Greenmount. He was a man in whose leadership she felt she could trust.

Personally, too, Katharine now felt herself deeply involved in the war effort. In September, I had commenced military training. Katharine hated to see me in the new recruit's raw, tan boots, oversized, khaki tunic and a slouch hat as stiff and uninitiated as a boy scout's; but she knew that preparation for war was inevitable.

It was still a European war in October 1941, when Katharine was asked by the Australia-Soviet Friendship Society to undertake a lecture tour of the eastern States. She dropped her work on the goldfields novel and for four months travelled throughout the east.

> I was to speak on the need for better political relations with the U.S.S.R., advocate an exchange of diplomatic representatives and the setting-up of embassies in Moscow and Australia. As I was no longer an illegal person,[64] this I did speaking freely everywhere, from Sydney and Newcastle to Brisbane, along the south coast to Wollongong and Port Kembla, taking in Melbourne and Adelaide on the way home.[65]

But by the time Katharine reached Adelaide, the Japanese attack on Pearl Harbor changed Australian perspectives on the war. In her notes for the Adelaide address she wrote:

> The threat to our own lovely and beloved country makes us feel more deeply for nations whose peaceful populations have been massacred and whose homes and towns have been devastated by the cruel and brutal enemies of mankind. We must do all that we can to help those who have suffered, and to defend Australia to the limit of human effort.

She reminded her audience that some people had been talking for years of the danger from Japan and urging the Government not to strengthen the Axis powers by trade agreements and acts of appeasement:

> We realize now that the workers of Port Kembla were right when they refused to load scrap iron for Japan — and how criminally culpable were the financial interests which have profited by the arming of a hostile power which many years ago — in the Tanaka Memorial — avowed its aggressive ambitions towards China and Australia.

Indeed, although the Left had shared Australia's European orientation before the war and regarded European Fascism as the main enemy, the dangers of Japanese militarism had been recognized. Katharine herself had joined the protest against the Japanese invasion of China in 1937 and supported the unions' boycott of Japanese goods. She wrote then: "If Japanese imperialism is permitted to vanquish the Chinese people . . . its designs for the conquest of other territory, including Australia, will be assured. Boycott Japanese goods!"[66] Now, three years later, that gesture seemed so small a price. The polemics had become unwelcome prophecy.

Ill-prepared, and weakened by the absence of Australian troops and airmen in the Middle East and England, Australia joined the United States and Great Britain in declaring war on Japan. The surrender of the British garrison in Hong Kong, the retreat through Malaya, the fall of Singapore in February 1942, the Japanese bombing of Darwin and the landing in New Guinea soon after, left no illusions.

I was in Greenmount on weekend leave when I told Katharine that I had decided to enlist for overseas service in the AIF. I knew her horror of war, half expected that she would refuse her consent, as I was still legally a minor. She had known what I intended, I am sure. Her own decision had been made long before. Katharine's love for Australia was a deep personal emotion, as real to her as a woman's love for a man. The almost mystic, spiritual identification with the land itself that is the soul of her poetry, stories and novels, was part of her. Australia was under enemy attack. In the first, bleak days of 1942, when invasion seemed probable and defeat more than a nightmare possibility, the decision was an easier one than that faced by later generations of young Australians conscripted for service in foreign wars. For Katharine, I think, it was a more precise anguish. She had a practised sensibility to others' pain, the torment of creative imagination trained to project with intensified reality the image of what might be. She was concerned that I would think I had to live up to my father's name, chase honours by rash heroics. I assured her there was little room for death and glory in a linesman's work. It was mainly plain, hard bullocking. But she fought my imagined battles in the nightmare memories of the First World War, while I bludged and sweated; waited the Army's pleasure, and longed for the girl I loved, as a soldier always has.

As soon as she returned from the lecture tour of the eastern states, Katharine wrote to Mr H. I Temby, then Secretary to the Commonwealth Literary Fund:

> I arrived in the West again on January 15th, and have been settling down to work again. Although I carted my precious m.s. everywhere with me, in order not to lose psychological touch with it, there was no time to do more than think out various phases on the long train journeys. Now, it is really thrilling to get back to it, and actually I think my mind has been refreshed by the break. I dislike public speaking, very much, all the same, and was glad to have a fortnight's rest in Melbourne with my sister before coming home.
>
> These are difficult times for a creative writer, of course. Almost impossible to insulate against the urgent needs of our people and country, at the moment, and although I hope to keep my normal routine of writing from dawn until midday, I suppose there will be breaks.

When the year of the fellowship expired, the novel was still unfinished. Katharine wrote again apologizing that her work was not completed.

> I had hoped to have the first part of this long novel finished by April. It runs to from 60,000 to 80,000 words, which would have been the first volume of what I had planned as a trilogy. But while Part I is practically all done, in the rough, and a good deal of Part II, as well as an outline of Part III, I am still working on Part I — and it may not be finished by the end of this year. This is not because I have not tried to concentrate on the book, but because it has

> been necessary for me to do so much other work, which I believe to be of importance in our present situation . . . Apart from the time, thought and study required to deal adequately with so many subjects, you will understand how devastating it is to be taken from creative work again and again, and to return to it with despair at ever being able to work without innumerable demands on one's energy.

She had in fact made remarkable progress with the first of the goldfields novels in so short a time, but the rough draft was no more than a skeleton. Even without the distraction of other claims upon her thought and time Katharine worked slowly; filling out the details of character and place which gave life to her people and made the scene in which they lived and worked a vivid reality; collecting the documentary facts and figures which were to make the trilogy as much a social history as fiction; reordering the ebb and flow of the narrative to achieve the subtle rhythm of the novel's development; weaving together the complex threads of many lives in the carefully contrived disorder by which art seeks to simulate the strange chances of life; rewriting, revising and revising; seeking the words that would make the comedy and tragedy of ordinary lives remarkable to those who might, some day, read them.

Now there were other priorities. All Australia was galvanized to resist the expected Japanese assault. Against Churchill's wishes, Curtin had ordered the 7th Division of the AIF to return to defend Australia. The Communist Party, having made up its mind to support the war effort, used its influence in the unions to support the campaign for maximum production. The Trade Union Congress accepted industrial mobilization. Katharine regarded herself as being under orders "for the duration".

There was a real fear in Western Australia that the Japanese bombing of Darwin was the prelude to invasion, and indeed it is now known that some senior Japanese Army officers had proposed such a course. The young militants of the University Labor Club and the Eureka Youth League prepared themselves to fight a guerilla war; learnt how to make "molotov cocktails" and practised partisan tactics with imaginary weapons in the bush. To some it seemed a foolish game; but it was a game which could so easily have been played with the deadly reality that the young men and women of the Maquis learnt in occupied France.

Sir Norbert Keenan, a former member of the Western Australian Legislative Council, asked Katharine to discuss what could be done if the Japanese made an attempt to land near Perth. Old and disabled by an injured leg, he lived in the heights over the Swan River. He told her:

> I have been deprived of my revolver and any weapons of defence I might have used. So have many others. I have some influence with my friends and the people I represent, and I think you have influence with your friends and the working class. I'm going to advise my people that they should not offer any resistance if a Japanese raiding party comes up the river — because it would be useless.

Katharine replied, "Well, I'm going to advise my friends and the working people to resist to the utmost with anything they've got — if it's only boiling water and those irons on your hearth!"[67]

For the first time since she had been befriended by the Prime Minister, Alfred Deakin, as a young woman, Katharine found herself approved by the establishment. She visited Canberra on her return journey from the eastern States and was delighted to find herself recognized by Government members and invited to take a place in the distinguished visitors' gallery on the floor of the House of Representatives; thrilled to be asked to dine with Dr and Mrs Evatt and amused to find that he already knew of her movements:

> I started to explain where I had been and what I had been saying on the lecture tour. Dr. Evatt stopped me. "You needn't tell me", he said. "I've been kept informed by the Security lads of all your movements; had an almost hourly report on where you were going and what you've been saying."[68]

There was no home leave when the troops in camp near Fremantle were ordered to make ready to sail. Our destination was unknown. The sailing time was secret; but somehow the word got around. There were a few women and children scattered along the South Mole waving goodbye, too far away to recognize as the ships drew out. Katharine was there, she told me. Someone had rung to tell her we were sailing. She followed the ship to the end of the breakwater and watched until it was out of sight.

None of us knew then that the tide of war had turned with the defeat of the Japanese fleet in the battle of the Coral Sea in May 1942. We landed in Milne Bay two weeks before the Japanese marines were held by the AMF and defeated on land for the first time by Australian forces in August-September 1942.

Katharine's letters arrived with surprising regularity. She wrote lightly, reassuringly; told me of the familiar, ordinary things of home, the doings of friends and family, the books she had read and the plays she had seen; wrote of the trials of rationing and shortages; discussed my soldier-verse; triumphed over the victory at El Alamein; fussed about food and sent me cigarettes, "to keep away infection". There was nothing in her letters of the paralysing anxiety she endured during those long days; but she told me years later of the soul-ache my imagined dangers had meant to her: "When you were in New Guinea, I felt if I relinquished for a moment my intense protective instinct, something might be harmful — but it couldn't happen while I was on guard."

Katharine could laugh at her foolishness, but if she could not quite believe in her "movins", the magic words which the aborigines used to ward off harm, she yearned with every instinct to make them true. She half blamed herself when I went down with malaria:

> How that damned mozzie beat me, I can't think! T'any rate have renewed all the appropriate magic words and put an extra curse on any of his tribe who might be inclined to touch you.

Katharine was asked again to lecture to the University of Western Australia. She explained to the Commonwealth Literary Fund that she had tried to arrange for someone else to take on the task, but she felt as though she owed it to Bernard O'Dowd and Furnley Maurice to pay them that tribute. This time there was no objection from the Professorial Board. She told the students that she had selected O'Dowd and Furnley Maurice as her subjects because their work had the qualities which distinguished the finest poetic expression of our time and because it was an expression of Australian thought and feeling in relation to the realities of our lives; was not limited to lyrics about love and nature; did not try to escape by introspective reveries or exotic imitations of past masters. "Poetry Militant" was an appropriate theme in the years of total war; but Katharine found some satisfaction in dishing out, in her turn, a taste of the stuff that fastidious academic palates despised. "The conventional attitudes of a poet in theme, form and diction were more or less taken for granted thirty years ago," she explained.

> Into this atmosphere of intellectual lotus-eating, stormed O'Dowd with a voice and a theme which were new and vigorous.
>
> Nowadays we are accustomed to the controversy as to whether poetry should concern itself with politics, whether

> poetry with a purpose is in fact poetry — despite Wordsworth's defence in the preface to the *Lyrical Ballads*.
>
> O'Dowd delivered his address on Poetry Militant in 1909, deriving his authority from Whitman. But at that time O'Dowd was a voice crying in the wilderness. There were of course in Byron, Wordsworth, Shelley indications that political causes could generate great poetry, but lyrical prattle about nothing in particular was still considered more befitting a poet than an expression of all that constitutes a mature and adult mind in relation to existence. We can not exclude the foundations on which our lives are built — the means whereby we live and have our being. To do so is simply to be intellectually infantile.

Katharine defended O'Dowd fiercely from the critics who considered him merely a social reformer, more propagandist than poet. She denied that he was a poet trying to write propaganda in verse form. His poetry, she believed, was the overflow of personal emotion. She suggested that his convictions made him a poet, the fire of whose spirit burns through his verses; whose vision and passion had influenced not only his generation but the future development of Australia. She quoted her favourite verses from "Young Democracy" and "Australia". Their patriotic fervour echoed the spirit of a nation fighting for survival.

> Last sea-thing dredged by sailor Time from Space,
> Are you a drift Sargasso, where the West
> In halcyon calm rebuilds her fatal nest?
> Or Delos of a coming Sun-God's race . . .
> A new demesne for Mammon to infest?
> Or lurks millennial Eden 'neath your face?

She challenged her young audience with O'Dowd's own question:

> When millions trampled in the muck,
> Succumb to want and crime,
> Are ye who read content to suck
> Sweet juices from your time?

Later, Katharine gave her thoughts on O'Dowd more fully in articles and broadcasts in which she described how she had met O'Dowd: "A tall, thin, pale young man, shabbily dressed, and ginger haired, with a walrus moustache, but so keen and alert that he seemed consumed by an inner fire".[69] She quoted from his dissertation on Poetry Militant claiming that "a real poet must be an Answerer, as Whitman calls him, of the real questions of his age"; explained his choice of an early metric form and made her appraisal:

> Disciplining his expression to this form, O'Dowd pours into it the fury of his wrath at social injustices: but he does so with a curious blending of mysticism and materialist philosophy, of humanitarian idealism and revolutionary spirit, of intense nationalism with a zealous internationalism.

It could have been her own literary testimony. Katharine's real tribute to Bernard O'Dowd was that, long after his own zeal was tempered, when he confessed himself "an extinct volcano", her work continued to be dedicated to "those who mount their hidden Calvaries to save the human race".

CHAPTER 13

THOUGH LIFE FLOWS STRANGE

Though life flows strange through many lies,
Shall men,
Who bleed for ancient things forsake the new?

— Furnley Maurice

Greenmount seemed isolated from the great events which stirred the world in the Australian summer of 1942. The peace and solitude that Katharine usually found there was an illusion while Australia fought back from Port Moresby along the Kakoda Trail and the German armies recoiled from Stalingrad. Katharine found it impossible to lose herself in her work. Her facility for picking up creative work in the midst of conflicting demands upon her time and energy eluded her. In January 1943, she decided to move to Sydney, at least until I returned from New Guinea.

Katharine shared an apartment with a woman journalist friend, and a couple of cats, on the top floor of a block of flats opposite the William Street studios of the Australian Broadcasting Commission, and later found rooms of her own in the same building. Sydney, even in wartime, provided the stimulus of contact with fellow writers which Katharine had missed in the seclusion of Greenmount. There were old friends: Louis Esson had left Melbourne and now in the "Celtic twilight" of retirement from active writing devoted his time to the Fellowship of Australian Writers, and cricket. Christian Jollie-Smith practised law in the city and lived alone over the habour at Watson's Bay, where she played the piano, her heart's own love, to Katharine at weekends; Hugh McCrae had abandoned poetry to write his bitter-sweet love letters to the world. Katharine found she had more in common with younger writers like the Communist journalist and poet, Len Fox; John Thompson, poet and broadcaster, and George Farwell, journalist, playwright and radio commentator, who often called on his way to the ABC, across the road; and Miles Franklin, the never-say-die warrior of earlier literary battles.

Here, too, were the headquarters of the Communist Party of Australia. Membership had more than doubled under the pressure of illegality.[70] With the impetus of an electoral alliance with the State Labor Party of NSW and the Soviet victories in Europe, the Communist Party had become almost respectable. Marx House in the centre of the city became the head office of a business machine as neatly efficient as any of the private enterprises with which it rubbed shoulders. Katharine became a member of the Central Committee, the Party's main policy body, in 1943. Paradoxically, being close to the centre of political activity meant that Katharine was relieved of many of the minor organizing chores which had come her way in Perth. She was still called upon to speak, contribute articles to the press and attend meetings.

A major share of campaign organizing in the 1943 Federal elections, which resulted in a landslide Australian Labor Party victory, was credited by some authorities to the Communist Party.[71] Katharine, too, spoke up for Labor and found herself unexpectedly in debate with the Leader of the Opposition. When the *Daily Telegraph* ran a series of articles on the beliefs of eight Australians from different walks of life (with a prize of six War Savings Certificates for the best reader's letter on his personal credo), Katharine was amused to find her statement, "Our future rests on Socialism", printed opposite "We must retain Capitalism", by R. G. Menzies, MHR. Katharine made her statement a plea for the implementation of the socialization objective of the Australian Labor Party:

> I believe that this objective, cited in the platform of the Australian Labor Party as "the socialization of industry, production and exchange" will present the only basis for effective reconstruction after the war, and that no scheme of reconstruction will be of any value which has not this foundation.

She asserted that the ALP had lost sight of this objective for some years, but insisted that it could be achieved by constitutional means, although it was bound to be violently opposed by "pro-Fascist forces" in Australia:

> They sought, and still seek to discredit our Soviet ally. They have attempted to wreck the Curtin Government which, at the most critical period in our history, saved Australia from disaster and united the people for increased production and personal sacrifices to win the war — and the peace for reconstruction.[72]

Life in Sydney gave Katharine access to the theatre and concert programmes she loved, books unavailable in the libraries in Perth, and time to take up the study of the Russian language begun during her visit to the Soviet Union in 1933. So, at fifty-nine, she enrolled in Russian classes at the University of Sydney; found the first-year lessons too elementary; tried second year and was delighted when she scored 94 per cent in her first examination. "It was quite simple really," she wrote. "I should have got 100%."

Katharine had for a long time been concerned that there was no opportunity in Australia for radical writers to find a publisher for their work. Early in 1943, she joined with George Farwell and Bernard Smith in editing a new literary magazine, *Australian New Writing,* although she confessed that she "left most of the work to the other two". Introducing the first issue, the Editors explained that they believed it was high time that Australian authors faced up to the present day, instead of writing of sentimental falsehoods, murders, lovelorn blondes and the upper-class unemployed. "Bedtime stories for grown-ups," they declared. They referred with pride to the democratic tradition of Australian literature in the nineties, quoting Bernard O'Dowd's vision of the democracy to come:

> That each shall share what all men sow:
> That color, caste's a lie:
> That Man is God, however low,
> Is Man, however high.

Although the Editors reported an exhilarating response to the first issue from all over Australia and New Zealand, battle areas, war plants, universities and coal mines, and despite guarded approval by the *Sydney Morning Herald,* the fourth number did not appear until 1946, when, like so many attempts of the same kind, *Australian New Writing* died.

When Katharine heard that I had put in an application for the diplomatic cadetships newly announced by the Department of External Affairs, she was thoroughly convinced that I could be far more use in Canberra than maintaining telephone lines in New Guinea. She wrote for my twenty-first birthday advising me to cash a small life insurance policy:

> The chances are you will need this fund to draw on, when the Department of External Affairs' job materializes. Nothing else but my love — and gratitude that life gave you to me — can I give you befitting this great occasion, my darl-

> ing. Every night, I think of you, sleeping on the balcony and looking out to the stars — begging only that you may be safe and well, and know something of the fullness and satisfaction of being a man.

I spent the day on kitchen fatigue peeling spuds, and enjoyed little of the "fullness and satisfaction" of the occasion.

Katharine's letters were filled with the expectation of my return. She planned her celebration, hoarded food, bought herself a new hat so that she would be "a credit to me" and found all things celebrated with her: "Such a lovely sunny morning, and the cathedral bells making a carillon for the Tunis victory"; told me of the crowded press of events in her daily life:

> It's afternoon again, and I'm just back from speaking on the Anglo-Soviet Treaty. In the Domain, with amplifiers attached — which made my voice sound like I don't know what! John Dease was speaking too and Canon Garnsey, so I was in quite distinguished company and there was a great crowd. Such a cold afternoon too, and the ground soaking after weeks of rain. I marvel how people can stand like that and listen to speakers for hours on end. Though I've done it myself when I was younger and stronger. These days, I slip away as soon as I can.

She turned again to the still unfinished novel of the goldfields: "This week I've been working on the book — been quite absorbed with it — which is a good sign!"

One of the Sigs on duty in the radio tent first told me that the ABC had announced the names of nine men appointed diplomatic staff cadets in the Department of External Affairs — mine was among them: "You're in, mate! Home and hosed! Half your bloody luck!"

Katharine wrote at once confirming the announcement:

> One completely fou de joie mother of yours! My first word was telegrams from Victoria — Henrietta and Hilda. I rang and got the good news confirmed. Then bolted for the telegraph office to send you a wire.

When the troop train arrived at the Sydney Central Station a week or two later, six hours behind time, Katharine was there at the end of the platform to meet me. I did not know myself when I would be arriving. Troop movements were still secret. Somehow she had heard there was a train expected from Brisbane.

Katharine had worn a coat the colour of spring wattle so that I should not miss her. She stood in the centre of the platform near the barrier, searching the tanned and atebrin-yellowed faces of men in khaki and jungle green, who streamed towards her. Her friend, Doon Stone, told me:

> She waited on the station platform, from daylight to midnight, for three days. She had the most fanatical fixation that she must be there to meet you. So there she stayed, cold and exhausted and alone, until you arrived.

With relief from all the anxieties that had preyed upon her while I was in New Guinea, Katharine felt again the tug of the goldfields story and somehow contrived to write among the distractions of the city and the realities of the present: the war, the potboiling chores still necessary to earn her living; the political commitments she had accepted; friends who called unendingly to talk of art and literature, of world affairs and industry, and the personal problems of love, marriage, children and the state of their health — friends among the men of power in industry and radical politics; those whose names were to fade into obscurity; young writers who later achieved recognition; the known and once-famous, who drifted with the years and disappeared; the unimportant, insignificant, unaccomplished men and women who earned Katharine's affection by simply being what they were. Katharine wrote:

> Bill Harney came in to see me the other night too and was full of another book. Sang and recited some priceless folk songs of drovers and combos — there was one about a native girl, seduced by a Chinaman — which the abos had turned into a corroboree — I can't remember exactly how it went. But it was something like this — with the gin chanting shrilly:
>
> "Poor feller me, poor feller me.
> Pingerrie Jo, he catchee me.
> Poor feller me, poor feller me!"
>
> The men repeating the lament from their point of view! But the name wasn't Pingerrie Jo. I just can't remember it. B.H. was going North next day. A wonderful chap, really — a natural genius — if ever there was one, as far as his writing goes. Rough and ready, but genuine in his poetic feeling and expression. A literary find. Really one of the men our country has made, and expressing himself without any airs and graces. It wouldn't do for all of us to write like that — but it's grand that he can.

Katharine came to know Bob Wells, leader of the Miners' Federation, at the time, through the help that he gave in checking the technical details of underground mining in the manuscript of

Wasting Assets, as the first volume of the trilogy was originally called. She read him parts of the book; accepted his suggestion for a minor change in terminology, and was delighted to find him rapt in the story's development. Bob called often after that to talk to Katharine. She was absorbed by his discussion of the coal miners' problems; learnt to admire his dedication.

> "He's a fine chap," she wrote to me. "If you had an elder brother I'd have liked him to be like Bob, which is about the nicest thing I can say of him."

Not long before, Katharine got hold of Zola's book of the French coal mines, *Germinal,* and was swept away with enthusiasm for its vigour. "A marvellous book!" she wrote:

> So powerful and with a realism which takes one's breath away when you think when it was written — so many years ago, it seems all the more remarkable, although it would be hopeless for anybody to write like that now. Of course, most people, I suppose, are shocked by the sex aspect of the book. But this crude and brutal treatment derives from the conditions people were living under. My translation was by Havelock Ellis, and well done — dare say the original has difficult argot. There is a note to say Zola was not "a literary stylist" and that the book raised a howl of frantic rage. I can imagine it would — by its revelation of the life of coal miners and their families in western France, and also the working class philosophy underlying it.

Katharine confessed that she'd give anything to have written such a book:

> I'd much rather write like that really, with all the flow and piled up accumulation of words and ideas, than with "literary style" — the careful elimination of every unnecessary word and detail.

With Bob Wells' introduction, Katharine visited Newcastle and Cessnock; talked to miners and their families; drove through the coal-mining towns; sat in at a meeting of miners and met, disapproving, Bob's glamorous fiancée: "bloody fingernails and all. Wouldn't like you to marry such like," she wrote. "T'would be disastrous for a bloke with important work to do . . ."

For a while Katharine toyed with the idea of a book on the coal mines, but the goldfields were her territory and she put aside the idea of any diversion until the trilogy was finished. Nevertheless, the work of the coalmines continued to interest her, and when the coal strike of December 1944 dragged on, threatening a breach between the Labor Government and the unions, Katharine visited Cessnock again to see for herself the cause of the trouble. "Went to a miner's wedding and talked to lots of the boys," she wrote. "You get an entirely different slant on the whole situation, hearing their side of the case."

She spoke of the miners' exasperation with delays in repairs of machinery, the strain of work underground, their exhaustion after years of intensive work for increased production during the war, their determination not to submit to the garnisheeing of wages. "I'm very concerned about the situation," Katharine concluded.

It was a foretaste of the disenchantment of the Left with the Labor Government, which reached its nadir in the ironworkers' strike almost a year later, when the war had ended.

New editions of *Coonardoo, Working Bullocks* and *Haxby's Circus,* the publication of *Potch and Colour,* and a translation of *The Pioneers* into Afrikaans for broadcasting in South Africa, provided some financial relief, but Katharine still found it necessary to pick up what ready cash she could from the occasional ABC broadcast.

In recognition of his early promise as a dramatist and poet, Katharine spoke on the ABC about Louis Esson, shortly after his death in November 1943.

> Louis Esson brought to Australian literature a scrupulous intellectual integrity which had far reaching effects and will always be associated with his work. It was reflected in his poems and plays, in their relation to reality, and in his attitude to life. Nothing on earth would have induced him to lower his standard in writing, to strain a point for dramatic purposes, or to compromise in his criticism of poetry, prose, or the drama.

She spoke of Louis Esson's poetry, comparing him to Villon who sang the zest of living among thieves and vagabonds as well as among those who love "far forgotten forest places, savage splendour, silent spaces". Katharine regarded "The Splitter" as one of the finest things in Australian literature; quoted it to her audience, who in those war years had cause enough to recognize its prophetic imagery:

> Back in the bush
> Unbroken, the splitter
> Hews stroke on stark stroke.
> Thro' black butts and blue gums.

Man, the Destroyer!
Man, Master-Builder!
The axe flashes.
Savage blows shatter
The dawn world enchanted.

Katharine grieved for Louis, as a friend and as a fellow artist whose genius had withered. She concluded:

> Latterly, Louis had become discouraged and disinclined to write at all. Of what use when there is no theatre for the production of plays by Australian dramatists? Discouragement has destroyed the finest genius, and those of us who value Louis Esson's work realize that another man has been wasted who could have brought distinction to the theatre in Australia.

Katharine spoke, too, of Furnley Maurice, once regarded by Hartley Grattan as one of the most significant Australian poets of his time. Katharine loved the lyricism of his early verse; shared his joy in quietness and solitude; delighted in his revolt against the barbarity of the First World War. She read some of the verses that she loved, largely leaving his words to speak for themselves:

Though life flows strange through many lies,
Shall men,
Who bled for ancient things forsake the new?

Shall courage give its bodies and its souls
For nameless causes without pride or gain,
While dotage minds its money and plays bowls
And wears the decorations of the slain?

Hilda Esson wrote to Katharine not long after her broadcasts on Louis and Furnley Maurice:

> There is something strange and fascinating beyond words in your talks on literature . . . Your lovely lyrical chanting of the words was very successful. But above all I felt as I listened, the great commandment to the artist is, first and last, to have passion! In your almost ethereal beauty of thought and expression there is that passion that makes everything you say almost unbearably vivid and moving. You make everyone else look prosaic and flat-footed and boring.

The qualities that Katharine recognized and admired in the work of other writers often reflect more of her own true values than her personal assessments of her own work over the years, although she placed more importance upon recognition of the achievements of her fellow writers than on a cold, critical impartiality in the exposure of their faults. She knew the blight of public contempt; preferred to compromise her own literary standards rather than damage another writer's reputation to gratify a sense of her integrity as a critic. "So often I have perjured my literary conscience for a friend," she confessed in a letter to me the year before she died.

She could genuinely admire the honest impartiality in Louis Esson's literary criticism, and had herself tasted his displeasure; but could not herself adopt the role of dispassionate arbiter of aesthetic merit. She was prepared to give an honest opinion in private, but even then in such gently guarded terms that as often as not a young writer remembered only the kindness.

Katharine valued Miles Franklin's friendship; admired her grit and determination, the wry cynicism with which she saw herself and the people about her, though they had little in common apart from a "temper democratic: bias Australian". Katharine had reservations about the garrulity of Miles' characters, but she put aside her critical faculties when it came to discussing her work before a radio audience, explaining: "Tributes to writers who are dead always sadden me. I know how much better it would have been to appreciate their work when they were alive."

Katharine could give genuine admiration to *All That Swagger*, Miles Franklin's saga of the pioneering days in the country around present-day Canberra, which had won the *Bulletin* prize in 1936.

> It is a grand book, and will take its place among the classics of Australian literature. It has the honesty, simplicity and vision of the past and future which make for immortality.
>
> In it, I think Miles has realized those dreams of a little girl who wanted to become a great writer. Her work may not have brought her the wealth and glamour, sometimes associated with the career of a successful novelist. But those who are familiar with her books recognize their high quality.

Never one to let an opportunity go by, Katharine slipped in a plea for reprints of Australian books in cheap editions — so that everyone could know and appreciate the work of Miles Franklin.

"You're my only fan of any tonnage," Miles grieved; and in gratitude once almost confessed her secret. But Katharine declined to guess at the identity of "Brent of Bin Bin", by then a pretty open secret in the literary world. "Miles is a very dear friend of mine, and I wouldn't dream of asking her," she said teasingly. "The minx in her takes a mischievous delight in keeping us guessing. So be it."

Searching for words to describe Katharine as others saw her during the war years in Sydney, I appealed to Eleanor Dark, who replied:

> I feel it very difficult to put into words, perhaps because the spirit so dominated the flesh that one felt her rather than saw her. To say that she looked frail, strong, reposeful, alert, tired and vigorous seems contradictory, but valid too. And to describe her as a slender, handsome woman with dark eyes that contrasted strikingly with the backward sweep of her white hair and a smile full of kindness and humour seems to convey so little . . . For me — and probably for most people who knew her — it is less a picture than an impression of qualities that remains. One does not look at sympathy, perception and courage.[73]

Katharine recognized the claims that the past made upon her; paid her tribute to those who had bled "for ancient things"; but it was to the future that she looked. Literature she saw as a foreword to the new world which she believed must arise from the defeat of Fascism by the democratic alliance.

Katharine explained her view of literature for the Australian people in an address at Marx House on 31 October 1943, before an audience which shared her goals, accepted the language of Marxism without the conditioned resistance of the general public and found no fault in an authoress crossing the boundary of art into the preserves of politics. To this audience Katharine could speak without inhibition. In the restricted circle of a Communist Party meeting, Katharine could exercise freely her right to criticize the Communist approach to literature, to correct errors and to suggest to fellow Communists a more productive attitude — a freedom which she denied herself in public, under the strict Communist Party discipline of that time.

She claimed that literature, in common with all the national possessions of the people, had been captured by the capitalist system; that the production of literature depended upon publishing houses and circulating agencies based upon profit. The people had been deprived of access to literature opposed to the capitalist system. Instead they were given books which provided a way of escape from the dullness and dreariness of their lives; a drug which helped them forget that truth is stranger than fiction. Katharine warned that no national culture could exist in isolation: it must draw on the literature which great minds of all ages and countries had created:

> We must realize that it is not only the development of a national literature that is required, but a broader cultural level for our people based on a knowledge and understanding of the great literature of other countries.

As to the role of Australian writers, she believed that no more should be expected than that they should present the realities of life in Australia of their day. But, she added:

> For those who are Marxist, of course, this is not enough. They see more clearly the need to direct the attention of the people to the most vital phases of the class struggle. And what magnificent material lies to our hand. "Humanity's leap from the realm of necessity into the realm of freedom," as Lenin says. And yet it is not enough merely parroting the slogans of the Communist Party, or dragging in Communist morals by the scruff of the neck. The ulterior motive must never obtrude in a work of art: it must be so part and parcel of the whole that it is swallowed in a gulp as it were. The reaction of the reader to the writer's theme is the test after all of his power . . .
>
> And a writer has to live if he or she is going to work, eat and pay rent and be clothed. Any Australian writer who wants to write for the Australian people, above all who wants to be associated with their struggle for Socialism, must try to exist on much less than the basic wage, and in earning that even, waste time and energy in writing not what he or she wants to write, but what Capitalist publishing houses will buy.

Katharine put forward to the Communist Party a three-point programme for the development of Australian literature: an educational system which would give the people cultural opportunities; publishing houses and cheap editions; the encouragement of writers whose interpretation of Australia was reinforced by an understanding of Marxism. In a pencilled footnote to her address she added her personal plea: "Time to do this work."

CHAPTER 14

THE WEAVER AND THE WEFT

Hearken, oh Earth; hearken oh Heaven bereft
Of your old Gods. These ageless fates are left,
Who are at once the makers and the made
Who are at once the weavers and the weft.

— Lucretius

The goldfields trilogy spans a period of fifty years, from the end of the nineteenth century to the year after the Second World War. Three generations of men and women move through its 1185 pages. It traces the development of goldmining in Western Australia from the discovery of the first nugget to the emergence of a national industry; examines the growth, decay and regeneration of the goldfields' community from the hardships of the pioneering days through industrialization, economic depression, recovery and reconstruction; proclaims the heroism of the ordinary man and gives voice to the dreams of those who dedicated their own lives to making a better life for others; tells the story of Sally Gough: tragic, heroic, indomitable.

The goldfields trilogy is a chronicle of the growth of industrial organization among the working miners, from the rough justice of the "roll-up" on the rushes of the nineties, the Alluvial Diggers' Rights Association's action to protect the prospectors' claims to alluvial gold found on the leases of the mining companies, to the inter-union registration conflicts and the first stirrings of political action in the boycott of Japanese goods before the Second World War. Its ethos is mateship. Its tradition is the tradition of Eureka. It speaks the language of the prospectors of the west and the miners of Kalgoorlie, the good union men and the militants among them. Its aspirations are their aspirations. The bush philosophers, the professors of the outback, ready to quote a verse of Lucretius or a yard of political theory and to offer their comments on the price of gold, the Government of the day, or the international situation, are close to the heart of the story; but its heroes are not the handful of men and women who have found their way to the political solution that Katharine herself believed in. It is the woman, Sally Gough, staunchly loyal to her friends and family, torn by love, grief, doubts and despair, unbroken by all that life can do to her, searching for answers to injustice and the tragedy which war twice brings her — it is Sally and her friend, Dinny Quinn, enduring as the harsh land they both love, who are the trilogy's true individual heroes.

Katharine worked on the trilogy for some ten years between 1940 and 1950, although her interest in the goldfields first developed during the Larkinville rush of 1930, and there were jottings for a goldmining story in notebooks as early as 1916. Work on each new volume of the trilogy was commenced before the preceding volume reached the public. The work was continuous but, although the three books are taken here together, there was no time when they could become Katharine's sole preoccupation, apart perhaps from the few months in Kalgoorlie when the Commonwealth Literary Fund fellowship was first granted. Her life continued to follow the mainstream of the world's turbulent history in the years of the Second World War and afterwards when the victorious alliance withered. Her thought and energy were swept up in the currents and eddies of Australian radical politics; shattered again by personal tragedy.

It was not only financial necessity that led her to turn from her work on the novel from time to time, but also, I think, the habits of mind, duty and conscience, which demanded contact with the here-and-now. She could not give herself to the causes of the nineties and ignore the causes of today. It seemed to her self-indulgence to devote herself solely to past battles. She lacked the ruthlessness to put aside the present. But perhaps it was the very depth of her involvement in the life of her own day, which seemed at the time so wanton an invasion of her creativity, that gave fullness to her understanding of the characters and times of the past of which she wrote. In a different time and place, she shared their struggles; scrounged around for a living; found inspiration in the ideals of the common good; frustration, despair, determination, in a wilderness of unconcern; suffered the anxiety of failure, the mirage of success, grief, despair, sacrifice, joy and exultation; knew the necessity of unyielding effort.

Katharine wrote from her own experience, and the experience of others, transmuted in the crucible of her imagination into lives of her creation. She detested concoctions of plot and the invention of grotesque or fantastic characters; took pride in the authenticity of detail in her work, though none of her people are merely photographic reproductions of reality. The yarns told by the old-timers which are so much a feature of the trilogy may be very much as she heard them. To Katharine they were pure folklore, part of the custom and tradition of the fields, though they too bear the craftsman's polish; the artistry which makes a stone a gem.

The narrative of the novels weaves together the threads of many lives; draws upon her observations of scores of different personalities and life-stories remembered over twenty years, recorded in her notes and reborn in the form of Sally Gough; her husband Maurice, falling from failure to failure, pathetic, defeated; their sons: Lal, the Light Horseman, full of life and the joy of living, killed in the second battle of Gaza; Dick, the gentle, favourite son, broken by the war and his wife's desertion, killed in the mines; Tom, the quiet, self-sacrificing rebel, "dusted" after twelve years' work underground, coughing out his last years of life; Den, the youngest, in love with horses and the land, who died of pneumonia on the mortgage-racked dairy farm to which he had escaped.

There are the grandchildren in whom Sally found consolation, joy and sometimes disappointment; each one a distinct and evolving personality, growing, as a child does, through the enthusiasms and illusions of youth to the realization of its own individuality: Daphne, the gay, fun-loving girl caught in the pit of an unwanted pregnancy; Dick, the ambitious, self-seeking egoist willing to disown his family to get on in the world; and Bill, the young Communist, earnest, dedicated to his beliefs, anxious to avoid emotional entanglement, in love despite himself with the vivacious stepdaughter of Paddy Cavan.

There is Paddy Cavan, himself, the half-illiterate Irish urchin who followed the rushes of the early days; tramped in with the first teams to Coolgardie; scrounged and thieved and lied for a living; saved, hoarded and sweated; learnt to buy and sell shares; traffic in stolen gold; plant incriminating evidence on an inconvenient rival and silence his opponents — Sir Patrick Cavan, self-made man, man of wealth, mining magnate. And Frisco, Francisco Jose de Morfe, the romantic, devil-may-care adventurer who made and lost fortunes; considerate, unscrupulous; the lover who at last, blind and helpless, won Sally's love — and lost it in the arms of a fat, naked, middle-aged widow. There are Dinny Quinn and the cavalcade of his mates, the old-timers who had been on the track together from Southern Cross to Coolgardie, Hannan's, Kurnalpi, Kanowna, the fabulous golden hole of the Londonderry, and the disastrous rush to Lake Darlot, where Sally went down with typhoid fever and was brought back a hundred miles through the bush by the aboriginal woman Kalgoorla. And there is Kalgoorla, symbol of the ravished land, buried at the foot of the Boulder Ridge among the dumps and pot-holes of an abandoned rush with the poppet-head of a deserted mine as her memorial and the winged seeds of the wild pear, the kalgoorluh, as her only tribute.

As the novels of the trilogy developed, Katharine evolved a new method of writing to handle the immense cast of characters thronging the scene of her story. She had set out to deal with the march of events through five decades; the history of the goldfields within the context of Australian history and the echoes of the great upheavals in the world beyond: the Great War, the Russian Revolution, Depression, the Spanish Civil War, Nazism, World War II, and the first chill of the Cold War. There is nothing to suggest that she deliberately sought a new approach to her subject. There is no evidence in her letters and notes of an attempt to invent a style appropriate to the broad canvas she now chose. Rather, her technique was adapted to the nature of the material itself. That vast, arid territory, laced with eager, ant-trails of men scrabbling in the earth for gold, the frenzied activity of the rushes, called for new words, new vision.

The solitude of an outback cattle station, timber forests in the south-west, the symbolic microcosm of a travelling circus and the tragedy of family life in the Depression were of little use in this new setting. *Coonardoo, Working Bullocks, Haxby's Circus* and *Intimate Strangers* dealt with individual men and women. They were confined in time to the span of a single life; concerned only indirectly with the community in which the men and women of those novels lived and worked. Katharine had explored some aspects of the goldfields in the short stories collected in *Potch and Colour,* but they were camp-fire yarns which required a concentration of atmosphere and events, separated from the fuller background, like fire-lit portraits against the darkness.

Katharine had set herself a double objective. In the introduction to the first volume of the trilogy she explained: "In this story of the goldfields of Western Australia, I have tried to tell, not only something of the lives of several people, but to give also the story of an industry." The two objectives had to be reconciled, accommodated within a single, harmonious whole.

Although the method of the trilogy was consistent with the approach that Muir Holburn and Jack Lindsay later described in her work,[74] the unity of man, work and nature, it was now extended to embrace the working miners as a group and their industry as a subject in itself. In addition to the intimate involvement with her characters which Katharine had already achieved in earlier novels, she now found that her subject also demanded a panoramic view. She had to find the way to disengage the readers from emotional entanglement with the individual lives of her characters; to step back and look broadly at the movement on the work-torn chessboard of the goldfields.

Katharine knew literary theories. She was thoroughly familiar with the rules by which the theorists sought to define literary forms: "I couldn't bear not to know the tools of my craft," she wrote, looking back on her life's work.

But in the trilogy, content was more significant than form. Authenticity of character and accuracy in detail were important to her, and the techniques by which these could be achieved. She explained to me that: "Observation of conditions, atmosphere, environment, which affect a situation: the revelation of character in detail, the use of dialogue to give the natural flow and at the same time the essence of each character, have to be so sensitively wrought and interwoven, these days. Aldridge does it perfectly in *The Diplomat*. One feels the mature and shrewd mind, the experienced writer in his use of words, although occasionally, I was startled when he describes a man as having 'careful ears', for example. Still, that description could be an impression of character. I know I've often been struck with it: in the back of a man's head — and neck!"

There were no models for the work she attempted, although Katharine had her own literary heroes. She had been thrilled by the work of the Polish writer, Vladslaw Stanislaw Reymont, the Nobel Prize laureate for literature in 1924, whose reputation rested largely on the four volumes of his great novel, *The Peasants:*

> I remember how entranced I was, reading *The Peasants* for the first time. Its vigorous naturalism, beauty of style, and the intimate sympathy with which the life of these Polish peasants was given, seemed to me to have created one of the most perfect things in literature. I still place *The Peasants* among the novels to which I render absolute homage.
>
> Some critics have denied that it is a novel in the orthodox sense of the word. But this criticism, in my opinion, is

> pedantic, and out of tune with developments in literary technique. The narrative of *The Peasants* flows as smoothly and inevitably as the slow rivers which move through the Polish plains. It is sustained by graphic characterisation and by the drama arising from the characters themselves.[75]

Katharine faced different problems: how to achieve the readers' intellectual participation in the substance of history, their awareness of setting and philosophical content, at a distance, as it were, from the personal torments of her characters. As the German playwright Bertolt Brecht had done, Katharine introduced documentary material in the novels of the trilogy for a similar purpose. Fact is interwoven with fiction, fiction with fact. From the statistics of gold production, quotations from official reports, flashed on the projection-screen of the novel, the fictitious characters gain authenticity. They live side-by-side with the historical figures of the day. And they, the dead men of history, gain vital shape by association with the living personalities of the novel. History becomes life, and the life of the people of the fields is moved, as it was in their own time, by what has become history.

Some of the perspective of time, the sense of a future as yet unrevealed, is achieved, too, by the use of reminiscence: the assumption by the main characters of the novels, Dinny and Sally, of the role of narrators; as if they had briefly stepped out of the present time in which they are involved to look back from their own future. The device is used quite freely in the first volume of the trilogy, rarely in volume two and not at all in the final volume. Dinny and Sally had reached their own time. Their lives could be closed; and the "gentle reader" could know that the end had come.

Reminiscence is also used, in a quite different way through the yarns of the old-timers. Like the chorus of classical Greek drama, they set the scene, introduce the characters and comment with wisdom or ribaldry on the action. They prepare for a change in the mood of the story's development; provide a coda to the conclusion of the first volume, a prelude to the opening of the second, or merely give relief from the workaday life on the fields. Yarns by the camp-fire in the prospectors' camps, or on the veranda of an evening, were so much a part of the way of life of the old-timers that they are inseparable from the environment of the trilogy; their use as a stylistic device is unobtrusive, integrated in its total fabric. There are scores of such yarns. Short stories in themselves, they constitute the folklore of the goldfields. They establish the tradition of mateship, fair play, the irreverent mockery up the up-jumped Jack-in-office, the rough, bush courtesy to women and the humour of the outback:

> Tom Doyle was still Mayor of Kanowna and full of pleasure and pride in this position.
>
> Dinny liked to tell how, bursting with importance, when he was first elected, he had broken the news to his wife.
>
> "Glory be to God, Kate, I'm Mayor of this town now, and y're the Lady Mayoress," said Tom.
>
> "Tare 'n ages," gasped Kate, "what relation does that make me to the Queen?"
>
> They gave a great party to the people of Kanowna. A ball it was called, and Tom, having been told how things ought to be done, borrowed a dress suit for the occasion . . .
>
> There was Tom half-full, sweatin' like a pig and prancin' round with the Warden's lady when he slips on the floor the boys'd polished-up with candle grease, and whack — crack — down he came with a wallop and the lady on top of him, and there's a great split in his pants. Kate rushes over and says she'll sew 'em up. Hustles him into the ladies' room and makes Tom peel off while she does the trick. But the women troop in after the dance, so she shoves Tom out by another door she thinks leads to the back premises. But it's into the ballroom she's shoved him, and there's Tom standing like an old rooster, with bare hairy legs, minus his pants, for all the town to gape at.
>
> "For Chris' sakes, let me in Kate," he bawls. "I'm in the ballroom!" The crowd roared, laughing so as Kate couldn't hear for a bit — and Tom had to stand there with his long legs shakin' under him, until she chased the women away, let him in and dressed him up again.

Phrases are repeated, echoed and re-echoed by character after character with the persistence of rumour in a community where existence depends upon gold: "Kalgoorlie's done!" Fear of the petering out of high grade ores haunts the men of the mines. And, like a counterpoint to the catch-cries of disaster, the old-timers repeat their confident chorus that the gold is still there in the underground lodes and the vast, unexplored country of the west. Their hope is a reassurance as strong as the faith that keeps a man slogging, shifting dirt day after day without sight of a colour, knowing that the next day might bring him luck.

It is through repetition that the ethic of the goldfields is established. The fact that a man "tramped with the first team along the track to Coolgardie" is a mark of distinction. It is a boast often made, an introduction, almost a form of address among the pioneers. The underground miners' justification of stealing gold from the company mines is asserted and reasserted in the way the goldfields community has of making its own morals in the matter. There was nothing wrong in a man bringing up a few pennyweights or ounces now and then, they tell themselves over and over again: it was the big fellows who made a racket of it, fleecing their shareholders of millions. The repeated self-vindication, the rationalization of their theft, demonstrates the transformation of public morality under the pressure of industrialization. The men who could be trusted to leave untouched the bags of rich, gold-bearing ore stacked, unguarded, in a tent made of sacking on the old Hannan's rush, now found the odd pickings from the mines of anonymous shareholders fair game.

Doon Stone, on leave from the WAAAF, was staying with Katharine in Sydney when she was asked to read the manuscript of the first book of the trilogy. She recalled:

> It was Friday evening and I was all for starting in at once to read the night through, but Katharine was casually adamant that I could read it tomorrow.
>
> The next morning saw me flat on my tummy on the carpet with the open script and there I stayed throughout the day . . . 'till Katharine came drifting into the twilit room from her afternoon siesta and we drank our sherries with a rising excitement as my tumbling words of enthusiasm lighted again reflections of the fires that had inspired her.

Katharine was dissatisfied with *Wasting Assets* as a title: too negative, she thought. Before the typescript was mailed to Jonathan Cape she amended the title to *The Roaring Nineties;* changed her mind again and decided on *Mirage.* And finally yielded to Cape's preference for *The Roaring Nineties.*

In October 1944, Katharine's work was completed:

> It is finished, parcelled up and all. Feel it ought to be forcibly removed from me now. I will peck and pore over odd bits, tidying up, a stray hair here and there. ('Scuse the mixed metaphors!) Maybe the thing will have to be cut. It would be more popular so. But on the other hand, I haven't written for popularity; but to give a complete picture of the time and the people — in so far as it could be complete within the compass of such a novel. And a writer, at my stage of her life, is entitled to make her own terms as to how she will say what she wants to. Sure, it's a conscientious job—but I hope also has the thirra[76] which redeems a conscientious job from mediocrity.
>
> La! La! time will show.

The Roaring Nineties was published in 1946 and subsequently translated into twelve foreign languages. The London *Tribune* devoted a full page to Jack Lindsay's careful analysis of the book:

> In the present novel she carries her naturalist method to a still higher level, and, I think, vindicates her position as the most important Australian novelist, the main exponent of the school of critical realism . . .
>
> I can pay Katharine Prichard no higher compliment than to say that her vastly complicated naturalistic picture does become art, does reveal itself unified by a poetically conceived Theme. The theme is that of Gold, gold the metal, gold the symbol, gold in the last resort a dynamic identical with the restless human energy, destructive and integrating, which is transforming the earth.

Hartley Grattan gave his verdict:

> Katharine Susannah Prichard who, with the passing of Henry Handel Richardson, is now unquestionably the most important fiction writer of Australia, collected some of her vivid short pieces under the title *Potch and Colour* (a title borrowed from the opal miners) (1944), and then in 1946 brought out simultaneously in Australia and England *The Roaring Nineties*, the huge, vigorous, immensely vital, extraordinarily populous, and sociologically sound first volume of a trilogy on which she had been working for a decade at least. It deals con amore with the great gold-rush to Coolgardie and Kalgoorlie in Western Australia in the early Eighteen Nineties. This is unquestionably the most important Australian novel of recent years.[77]

Katharine could be satisfied that, indeed, the thirra was not lacking.

CHAPTER 15

LET THE DREAMERS SAY

> The dreamers wait. What can the spirit urge
> Against the madness of this sorry day?
> How can the timid form of Peace emerge
> Unless the Marshals let the dreamers say?
> And they are few and most forsaken, Lord,
> Who slaved and suffered for their human hope,
> Though Thou shalt give the Martyrs to the sword
> Preserve the future from the hangman's rope!
>
> — Furnley Maurice

There were no doubts about the title of the second volume of the trilogy. It was *Golden Miles* from the first. The title made itself. There could be no other name for the book set in that fabulous stretch of gold-bearing earth between Boulder and Kalgoorlie. Katharine started work on the novel as soon as Cape had accepted *The Roaring Nineties*. On 9 April 1945 she told me:

> Yesterday I wakened early and started to do a bit of *Golden Miles*. Stuck at it all day and at 11.30 thought it was time to stop. It's hard these days, to get consecutive time. Every week, I promise myself to make no engagements — and every week things turn up that have to be done — so that often I don't do four hours steady work. Must organize better — as my friends in the S.U. would say! Very useful idea. Whenever I get into a jam, I say to myself: "Organize it, comrade!" And things go better.

But Katharine's best efforts to organize made little difference. There were innumerable minor interruptions, and some major upheavals in family affairs to break the flow of her concentration. From Sydney, she wrote:

> And yesterday I got stuck into Vol. II, after George went.[78] Stayed two hours and me champing on the bit! Nice of him to come in for a yarn after his broadcast, but half an hour would do me, and everybody's a darned nuisance when I

> want to work. However, when I did, I just got underground, and stuck there till quarter to twelve.

Despite the intrusion of her hundred and one other interests, Katharine wrote and revised, worried at the problems of character development, corrected, discarded and started again: "Sunday night and I've been working all day — done a bit of psychological development over half a dozen times, at least — and it isn't right yet," she told me — and went on to describe how she'd been picked-up by a drunken sailor while she was waiting for a tram.

> Must have been my yellow coat and pink roses . . . I told him to go to the British Centre, and he'd find some nice girls to talk to him. But says he: "I like you. I like your face — never mind about the girls!" So there, darling! And the poor lad wasn't so drunk! !

All of her work on *Golden Miles* in Sydney was written from notes made in the goldfields. Her friend, Doon, brought up in the busy, booming town of Kalgoorlie, helped with advice. Katharine read her a chapter of the book dealing with the men's work underground and was encouraged to find no inaccuracy in the complicated technical jargon of the miners: their talk of "winzes", "drives", "rises", "venturas" and "boggers". She worried over the techniques of drilling, firing, transporting the ore from the work-face to the surface; the organization of work fifteen hundred feet underground; the hazards of bad air, flooding, rock-falls and explosives misfiring. Every detail had to be correct. Doon recalled:

> Katharine would sometimes read passages from the M.S. to me, with such a wealth of fire and expression that we seemed spirited away from the Darlinghurst scene back to the days when, as a rough and tumble kid of nine I roamed the "Block" and tobogganed down the dumps in fruit case sleds. This was a gold-fields era that was indelibly stamped upon my memory, and some of the atmosphere of *Golden Miles* was directly derived from my own and my family's life.

Work on *Golden Miles* came temporarily to a halt when, at the end of 1945, I was posted to the Australian Legation in Moscow at two weeks' notice, stole a weekend honeymoon and left my poor little bride with Katharine, to follow me when the Department of External Affairs could find her a sea passage. Katharine blamed a lecture tour in Tasmania for adult education and the

Commonwealth Literary Fund for the interruption in her work, but I dare say my own affairs were really more responsible. "Shouldn't have stopped to go to Tasmania, perhaps," she explained. "But presently will be finding the thing chewing at my brain again, and make up for lost time."

No wonder she found the heat and dust of the goldfields eluding her when her mind was in Moscow, mid-winter:

> Oh my darling, take care of you! Nina[79] says you should put a little grease on the end of your nose in frosty weather. And never forget to keep the ear-flaps on your cap down. Because you don't know when the frost is likely to nip them.

My wife, Bea,[80] became as dear to Katharine herself as she was to me, during those weeks before she could leave to join me. There were interminable delays: outfitting, packing, searching the clothes-rationed shops of Sydney for fur gloves and the sheepskin coat they wanted to send me. Katharine worried over Bea's health; tried to convince her that she wasn't going to be "an ordinary sort of mother-in-law"; gave her £150 for the journey (from her advance royalties for *Roaring Nineties* — of £100). When at last the ship sailed, Katharine felt that Bea had become a daughter to her. She wrote:

> The fledglings have flown — and my nest is empty. But there is still my work, and I suppose, most of all, I am a creature of that. Belong to the creative force which possesses me: can forget everything else when I am writing. Maybe when I'm too ill or old to write I'll be lonely and miserable. But I don't think so. Can always forget myself, and realize that what happens to the outward and visible K.S. doesn't matter — so long as all that I've worked for goes on — including you darling, and Bea, and your life together.

Later, Katharine told me that she had cried for days after Bea left, unable to put from her mind the despondency that haunted her.

The foreclosure of the mortgage on the old house at Greenmount and a threatened forced sale of the property sent Katharine hurrying back to the west. She wrote to Jonathan Cape on 4 March 1946:

> I may have to go West for a month or two soon. The mortgage on my home there, foreclosing, and all the disposal of books and pictures there to be coped with. This mortgage

> was one of the desperate things my husband did when I was away from home so long ago . . . and the last straw I think to his anguish of mind. It will be difficult to say goodbye to the dear place but I will not allow myself to be sentimental about possessions. A corner, somewhere to work and rest in is all I will ever need now. Hope to take the M.S. of *Golden Miles* with me, and get a good friend on the goldfields to read it for any inaccuracies. May stay in the West for a while to prepare for Vol. III; but am trying to arrange not to be disturbed until a rough draft of "G.M." has been done.

Katharine was penniless. She confessed that she had £170 in the bank when she had made her gift to Bea. She gave £10 to a cousin and her last £2 to a girl, stony broke and in desperate need of money. But a good friend in Sydney, who had been told of Katharine's concern about the sale of the Greenmount house, took over the mortgage; Angus and Robertson paid up an overdue cheque; *The Roaring Nineties* went on sale in London and publishers in Paris promised 36,000 for a French translation, in blocked francs.

Despite the brave face she had put on the prospect of the sale of the old house, Katharine was full of joy in the peace of the place. She wrote:

> Home again! And you've no idea how heavenly it feels to be in our little kipsey again. Everything much as we left it — except trees and shrubs grown old and straggly. I've just been wandering around, looking at books and pictures and feeling rested, after a bath and sleep and meal, and strangely happy to be there! I thought I'd be a bit sad and mopey perhaps; but amn't, knowing you're well and happy . . . A hot still night, but a little breeze coming through the dining room door, as I sit in the famous Hamlet chair and look out to the dark trees over Greenmount.

Katharine decided to stay at Greenmount, at least until she had completed the remaining two books set in the goldfields, although she had found it easier to earn a living in Sydney. The odds and ends of jobs, like judging competitions and talks for the ABC, had been well paid and she found that they helped amazingly with the budget: but costs were lower in the west and Katharine hoped that things would even out. Within a few weeks she was back at work on her manuscript, and wrote to me:

> Feel it's much better to be working on my W.A. material here. So many people, miners and miners' wives, handy to plague with questions. Next week, I'll be doing some reading

> at the Library. So far have avoided letting many folks know of my return. But the news seems to be getting around.

Within two months the first rough draft of *Golden Miles* was finished. Katharine knew that the whole book would have to be worked over strenuously before her work was done, but it was a relief to her to "have the scaffolding up":

> Of course, I shouldn't be doing this work on Sunday which is reserved for correspondence — and there's piles of it to be attended to, but the temptation was too strong, this morning, and so I just wrestled with Sally and her final remarks. She was most obstreperous: kept wanting to air her views and they have to be held more or less in reserve for Vol. III. Have you met her yet? My copies haven't arrived from London, and the Australian edition is not out.

Katharine expected an Australian edition of 10000 copies of *The Roaring Nineties* but income tax cut royalties on the English edition to £75 15s 0d and the first batch of reviews, disappointingly unenthusiastic, had only just arrived when, without warning, the tragedy that Katharine had feared when Bea left Sydney struck us.

She had written her usual loving letter to Bea, pleading with her to take care of her health, reminding me to boil the milk and water at the house in the country where we were staying. "Take care of you darlings: very great care, please," she wrote.

Bea had been off colour. "Moscow tummy", we thought. Nothing much: a bit of a cold and a headache. The next day she could not stand. She was taken to hospital; but despite everything the doctors could do, she lapsed into unconsciousness. Perhaps a week later, Bea died of poly-neuritis.

Bea's death was devastating to Katharine, not only in sympathy with my grief, but because of her own love for the frail, gentle girl who had become so dear to her. The memories of her anguish at my father's death flooded back, overwhelming her senses. Her letters poured out her love and sympathy; comforting, consoling; aware of the utter emptiness of anything that could be said; striving to reach out across the thousands of miles that separated us and take some of the pain upon herself. Every few days she wrote, trying desperately to bring some sense of normality into her letters; breaking off into the heart-cry of her yearning to ease my loneliness and despair; afraid of what I might do; helpless to protect me, except through the words of comfort that she wrote.

Grief and anxiety brought Katharine close to collapse. Her friends Cecilia Shelley, Kal and Helen McIntyre, "my bodyguard" she called them, surrounded her with their thoughtfulness and care. Her doctor warned her that she must avoid over-strain. She promised, for my sake, to be religious about resting. When grief and worry kept her awake, she recalled the Buddhist prayer which she had made a mantra to send her to sleep again: "Om mani padme hum, the sunrise comes! The dewdrop slips into the shining sea". "Don't think I'm turning mystic, darling or anything like that," she assured me.

> But I have found these Eastern ways of tranquillizing the mind, do have physical results. It's a good idea too, to have some lighter reading, or poetry, to read for a while before you're going to sleep. I always do this now.

As she rested, carefully shepherded her emotional and physical resources, Katharine gradually drew back from the needle-point of pain to the widening vision which her browsing allowed.

I had been granted compassionate leave to return to Australia when Katharine turned once again to her work on *Golden Miles*, ". . . And not so early on the Sabbath morn! Having a spot of Vol. II that I wanted to put my early morning thoughts on to, so soon after dawn I was scribbling, with a pallid cuckoo calling, and the wistaria outside my window a joy to behold", a sure and certain sign, she assured me, that she was feeling better.

She hoped to complete *Golden Miles* before she came to live with me in Canberra in May 1947. "Am feeling v. fit," she wrote, after convalescing from an appendix operation which had delayed her departure at the last moment.

> So much better than for a long time, and have been working on my type-script. Hope to get Jonathan's copy away before I leave here. Sent several chapters rather technical to Bob[81]; he says he can't fault them. And Celia has just survived the reading aloud. A great help to me to do this — gives the bird's eye view of the whole canvas. And I've cut quite a lot as a result. But Celia thinks *Golden Miles* is even more interesting than *Roaring Nineties* which is a comfort. I'm afraid its straight left won't please some people though. Have had to be very severe with myself and weed out several bits not strictly germane to the theme.

In fact, Katharine's "straight left" was far from a direct assault on her subject; but when "Communist menace" was the current political cliché it was startlingly outspoken. Political ideas were almost unknown in Australian fiction. Judging by Australian literature, Communists might never have existed, although the "red bogey" fattened the daily press and conservative politicians terrified the voters with visions of Communist unions capturing the country. To deal with the growth of radical ideas in an ordinary Australian family, and to deal with such ideas sympathetically, on their own terms and in the language used by Party people themselves, was as outrageous in the world of the forties, as *Coonardoo* had been to the decent, white moralists in 1928. In effect the subject was taboo. Truth was the only concession that Katharine could make. Her own views were clear-cut. She had long ago reached her conclusions. But her characters were allowed to find their way through the doubts and indecision that lead to conviction. She employed in practice the theories described in her own lectures.

Dealing with the issue of conscription during the First World War, Katharine took care to reflect the family divisions which that controversy provoked, although time had veiled political passion in history. She drew on her own experiences. The conflicts within her own family are re-created in the lives of Sally Gough and her sons: Dick Gough writes to his father from the front saying, "Tell dad I'll put on the gloves and give him a go round the yard if he votes for conscription" — those same words that had once influenced Katharine to change her mind during the second anti-conscription campaign. Sally remonstrates with her daughter-in-law, Eily: "Oh my dear, how can a little girl like you influence people . . .," as her own mother had said.

Katharine's left-wing characters become a target of family fun, and savage attack. Young Tom's earnest speechmaking to the family earns him a chiaking as "the local member", and his father's taunt, "You've got the gift of the gab — even if you haven't got the guts to fight." Sally, too, protests that she's "not a public meeting", when Eily airs some of her ideas on working-class solidarity in the typically impersonal jargon of the dedicated, "politically conscious", young woman. Sally, at first, has all of the scepticism of the average woman to the star-gazing of Tom and Eily; wants them to be more like ordinary people in their ways and ideas; resents their dedication to "the almost mythical people they called 'the workers' ".

But political people speak in political language. That could not be avoided, if the subject were ever to be dealt with at all; although Katharine knew the risk she ran of having the whole novel rejected. "I'm not surprised that you had the jitters about Cape's attitude," Hilda wrote to her.

Cape had never rejected any of her manuscripts, but Katharine was prepared for him to find her point of view unacceptable. Her fears were unnecessary. Within a month Cape wrote to say that he was satisfied with *Golden Miles*. Katharine wrote to him, gratefully:

> It was a great relief to my mind to receive your air mail letter. And so good of you to write at once.
>
> I was very undecided about using the quotation from Furnley Maurice's poem[82] at the beginning of the book. It does not quite express my intention, as a text: but I think will be something of a plea for tolerance from those who may not like the political tendencies of "G.M."

Tolerance was not the temper of the time. The greater immediacy of the events of *Golden Miles*, its increased militancy and the ferocity of the anti-Communist rage boiling over from President Truman's "Loyalty Programme" in the United States, made it almost inevitable that contemporary critics of *Golden Miles* would see the book in political terms. The Communist press praised the book without reservation; saw it as "working-class history"; its greatest achievement the depiction of the strength of working people. The *Bulletin*, 27 October 1948, led the attack. "It is principally a large heap of words", the *Bulletin* reviewer proclaimed, seeing the novel as mere propaganda, thus setting the keynote for the chorus of critics in much of the daily press. There were exceptions. The Canberra *Observer* saw it, with *The Roaring Nineties*, as finally establishing Katharine Susannah Prichard as Australia's foremost novelist. The English reviews, too, were "not exhilarating". Katharine was wryly amused by the *Manchester Guardian* which found *Golden Miles* "better on the human than the literary side. The actual writing rather undistinguished but the people very much alive". "When I was a young thing, I used to like to air my literary graces," Katharine told Jonathan Cape. "But now I want to shed them and write with the stark simplicity which it seems to me distinguishes the finest literature."

Only some of the provincial newspapers and Jack Lindsay in the London *Tribune* came to the rescue:

> What would happen to the novel industry in England if it somehow, against all its good intentions, turned up a novelist with such massive, earthy and passionate (if slightly ponderous) understanding both of people and the whole setup here

> as Mrs. Prichard has of Western Australia. It's hard to imagine in our thin and rickety novel-world.

Katharine was immensely relieved to have earned Lindsay's approval, although she knew little of him at that time, and hated to think that he had found the book in any way heavy going.

She "cracked hardy" in the face of a critical press and continued to insist that *Golden Miles* was the best book that she had written: "The press has not been very enthusiastic about *Golden Miles,* has it?" she wrote to Jonathan Cape:

> But the booksellers tell me it is selling well; and my fan mail has been consoling. One doctor from Melbourne writes that you "ought to be proud to have fathered the book"! My poor Jonathan, with such an illustrious family too!!! Another bloke from South Australia says he started to read *The Roaring Nineties* when he came home from work, read until midnight, and got up early in the morning to finish it. Then read it slowly, "chewing over every word", and has read it six times since. He says, he's not of my way of thinking, politically, but when he says his prayers, being Irish, asks God to give "more power to your elbow".

But for all the brave face she adopted, sales of *Golden Miles* were half what was expected: Katharine earned £198 — for two years' work. The hostile barrage of the critics and the denigration of *Golden Miles* had its effect upon her confidence. The joy she had first found in the creation of the final volume of the trilogy was eroded by doubt: "Me, I sometimes think I'm getting tired and stale from using words so much," she told me. "Need a whole new language to say what I want to, vividly — with a freshness which will really have some effect on people."

CHAPTER 16

THE FUTURE LIVES

Only the future lives and holds us sure
To things that never were
Being completely fair.
Then for a purpose of eternal worth
Human deliverance more vast than earth
Hath known, give gladly of your body's breath
In sacrificial life that men call death.

— Furnley Maurice

Katharine learned to know the beauty of the blue mountains fringing the Canberra valley through pale lilac, evening mists; the candle-flame of the poplars along the Molonglo River in autumn; the Murrumbidgee lined with she-oaks in the deep gullies at Kambah where we picknicked on springtime weekends; the air, clear and cold as champagne when frosts whitened the grass and etched the trees in cut crystal on winter mornings. But Canberra always seemed unreal to her, a fantasy world:

> . . . like a town made by Pinocchio. All that neatness and prettiness, so far removed from the struggle for existence. It's as if the gods could "lie beside their nectar" there on some intellectual Olympus "while the bolts are hurled far below them in the valleys".

She stayed with me in Canberra throughout 1947, but the climate had cooled since her last visit. The common cause which Labor and the Left had found during the war had disintegrated with the dissolution of the wartime alliance. The rising animosities of the Cold War and the first echoes of the campaign against "un-American Activities" whispered through Canberra's discreet corridors. With my colleagues in the Department of External Affairs, Katharine was as careful as the most practised hostess in avoiding political arguments. To Jonathan Cape she wrote:

> I am in Canberra, and feeling more like a blown leaf than ever, in the icy blasts which hurl themselves from snow-

> capped ranges through the ornate highways of this most un-Australian of cities. Perhaps it will interest me, presently. As a manifestation of our way of life, it should; but of course, my mind is all in the West, at present, and I dare say I'll go back to the goldfields before Vol. III is finished.

By the end of the year, Katharine was glad enough to escape Canberra's restraint and artificiality and return to the west, writing again to Jonathan Cape:

> I'm beginning to work on Vol. III of the trilogy and will return to the goldfields in a few weeks. Ric is going to marry again early in October, and I feel I'd rather work there than here. I am pleased that the lad has found someone with whom he can be happy and have a normal life. She's a shy, quiet girl, very like his first wife, but intelligent, — a B.A. of the Melbourne University, so there's much to be thankful for. I might have had to embrace any sort of nitwitish glamour girl! They want me to live with them, but I won't do that — though have promised to visit them now and again.

Katharine stayed for a month in Kalgoorlie on her way back to Greenmount. It was stimulating to have the atmosphere of the goldfields around her again; to talk to old friends, though many had left the fields or died. She attended sessions of the Arbitration Court; went over the treatment plant of the American-owned Lake View and Star mine; travelled all day with a forest ranger through the country around Kalgoorlie. She wrote:

> The country was looking marvellous after heavy rain. You've no idea how fascinating it is. All the miles of mulga and young salmon gums, black butt and snap and rattle with native pines and — sandalwood. The ranger's job is to keep his eyes open for timber thieves — and we had one exciting dash through the bush after tracks made on an unlicensed lease.
>
> It's all the country beyond Kanowna that Sally went off into Con's Gully. The Jubilee rush, where we boiled the billy for lunch, was just Con's Gully — and a few miles further on stopped to yarn with an old prospector of 87 and his mate — well over the 70's. Great old boys! Then on towards the Camelia mine . . .
>
> Coming back, the colours of the sunset over red earth of the dry bed of salt lakes — gorgeous! (Usually they're white with salt crystals.) This one was glowing and burning almost as if it were on fire and smouldering. Purple dark of the timbered hills all round, and that orange rind of sky

> fading into limpid green — with the first stars, crisp and sparkling brilliantly.

Later, the impressions recorded in that letter were to be included in the last volume of the trilogy. But Katharine found it difficult to get back into her stride. Friends had rented the old Greenmount place while she was away, and she found things at sixes and sevens. Katharine retired to the workroom in the orchard and tried, without much success, to recover her blessed solitude.

The dry grass was high around the workroom. Katharine was terrified of fire during the hot summer months in Greenmount. Several times the house barely escaped, when bushfires raced through the paddocks. The annual weeding and burn-off was a ritual with her. Early in the morning she would be up, pulling the grass, fixed hard in the baked clay of the earth; raking it away from the weatherboard walls of the workroom where it brushed like a fuse awaiting a spark. Later, the Midland Volunteer Fire Brigade or, more often, a team of friends, lads from the Eureka Youth League, arrived to burn off, armed with knapsack sprays to reinforce the trickle of water from the garden hose. Katharine was in a panic of apprehension when smoke billowed from the burning grass and flames crackled through the wild oats that grew hip-high in the orchard. Even when the fire-breaks had been burnt, she got out of bed several times during the night and padded round the blackened stubble in her shred of a dressing gown to douse any stumps still smouldering, afraid that they might burst into flames with the westerly winds, scattering sparks into the night. Only when that blackened corridor had been completed could she concentrate on her work with any peace of mind.

> Been keeping my nose to the grindstone of Vol. III which goes very slowly. Always difficult getting back into the rhythm of the thing again. It looms and whirls all through me, but I've become so critical, I destroy most of what I write these days and seem to be working more as if I were modelling in clay, than trying to make words fulfil the same purpose.

Within a few weeks Volume III was making its own demands:

> When I waken, I'm tempted to make a note, or some correction in the day before's work — and so my pen takes charge. Have been writing every morning round about dawn, and taking a sleep in the early afternoon, if possible. Before the small boy comes home from school, when all the kids in the neighbourhood rampage on the side veranda!

Katharine worked on through the Christmas and New Year holidays in century heat, concerned only to make the last book of the trilogy all that she dreamed of. It was stifling in the workroom. The casement windows gaped, but there was no movement in the air shimmering over the corrugated iron roof. The pulsing shrill of the crickets was a ceaseless, brain-piercing scream. The heat beat against the oil-darkened weatherboards, turning the room into an oven. By mid-morning it was impossible to think: impossible to rest, in that oppressive, overpowering atmosphere. Katharine retreated to her bedroom, and dressed in the flimsiest underthings she could find, put summer aside and worked on.

Possessed by the demands of creative effort, Katharine resented interruptions to her work. She was furious when a chance acquaintance called and talked for two hours in the middle of a man dying in Volume III. She schemed to get out of organizational work which she now found too exhausting and time wasting; put off her weekly letter when there was a special episode to complete: "I had a love affair to polish off," she explained, "and couldn't leave my folks all up in the air." At last, the General Secretary of the Communist Party of Australia, J. B. Miles, for whom Katharine had great respect and affection, told her personally to concentrate on her writing and spend less time on political activities. Katharine welcomed his advice and took it as the Party's directive. She was free to pour all of her energy into her work.

Katharine had been worried about the title of Volume III. Cape still disapproved of *Wasting Assets,* to which she had reverted for the final book of the trilogy. Katharine herself was not satisfied. She felt that title and theme should be woven together in a work of creative imagination. And then, like a sign from her own pagan deities, the words fell upon the unfinished pages of her book:

> Oh, I must tell you about the title of Vol. III. Did I tell you about having discovered that the wild pear is called 'kalgurla" by the natives; was plentiful on the Boulder ridge, which they called the "place of kalgurla". I found one when I went out to Hill Station, and brought it home with me. Well, it split in the heat, and shed a shower of the loveliest thistledown with a heavy brown seed attached. Going into my workroom one morning I found it sprayed all over my papers — and there was my title, *Winged Seeds*! Do you like it? I feel it's just right. The symbolism, and derivation from the theme : was so excited at having found the appropriate name, after worrying about it for quite a while.

It was as if the integration of the title and theme of the book in her mind gave new impetus to her work. Katharine drove herself unrelentingly through the worst heatwave that Perth had known for sixty years. She found it difficult to think of anything else:

> "W.S." got me up early, and gives me no peace, these days. Always wiggling and niggling in and out of my thoughts. It's a nuisance even to eat and sleep. And yet I have to stop from sheer physical weariness. But after a night's sleep can deal with my folks again. Am more anxious about this book than the others because it must not flag, but carry interest and spiritual zest to the last gasp. The rough draft ought to be done by the end of June. And then — the serious, careful writing of the whole begins again. And I always feel better when the draft is done: know that every piece of the jigsaw has fitted into its place. The rest will follow more easily.

Katharine resisted the temptation to fly to Canberra when her first grand-daughter, Karen Han Throssell, was born, although she swore that she had felt sympathy pains and knew before my triumphant telegram that "Han" was on her way. "I must tell you," she wrote: "I was having dinner with Keith and Lin,[83] on Friday night. Kept getting odd pains. Of course, Dorothy[84] has been in my mind all this week. Coming home in the bus, the pain was so funny that I thought. 'They're just like the first labour pains. I wonder have Dorothy's begun?' Then I said to myself, 'I must remember about this.' So really, I must have been having sympathetic pains with her! When I told Sam and Annette,[85] he laughed, and said he actually knew cases where the man had 'em. So there! T'any rate, it was funny, wasn't it. Hilda always says I have an uncanny prescience about things. Sometimes maybe. Not always!"

Katharine's letters were full of the baby; advice about care and feeding; instructions on the preparation of the "humanized milk" that Truby King had recommended twenty years before; warnings about the use of a dummy or leaving the baby to cry; how to brush her hair the wrong way, "to make it curl". She longed to hop straight on a plane to Canberra to see her grand-daughter. Promised herself a trip, "as a reward of virtue", when *Winged Seeds* was finished.

The pace that Katharine had set herself was too demanding. Her health cracked from sheer physical exhaustion. She was laid out for a week with soaring blood pressure and dazzling migraine headaches which left her tired and depressed. She wrote in June 1948:

> Am hoping that by April next year I'll be free. And, then, I'm going to have a really long holiday. Feel as if I don't want to write any more! Have never felt that way before. Dare say it won't last though.

Katharine stuck doggedly to her schedule, sweeping and cleaning once a week when she could spare a few minutes from her writing; a visit to Perth and the Modern Women's Club[86] on Fridays; weeding, wood gathering and washing on Saturday; all manner of odd jobs: "After a day in town I'm always a little haywire and take it out on the chores," she explained.

She faced the long months of writing and revision ahead without exultation. Towards the end of 1948 she wrote:

> My first six chapters of *Winged Seeds* are with Clarice[87] for typing. And I'm slogging away every day on the others. Some days things go well; on others I get depressed. In existing conditions it's impossible to write this last book as I wanted to. Who would publish? And who read a book published at 11/- if I did? The tempering of the wind to make it acceptable is my chief problem. Not retracting, but presenting the inevitable, at the same time, with the reality of life on the 'fields maintained. The story must rise supreme above all other considerations, I tell myself — and hope it will.

Money had once again become a problem. Advance royalties for the French translation of *Working Bullocks* was cut from £70 to £30 by the devaluation of the franc — and even that could not be sent out of the country. "So I dare say some of my friends in France will receive 'un petit douceur' ", Katharine decided philosophically. When a translation of *The Roaring Nineties* in Czech was proposed, in an edition of 20000, Katharine donated the entire royalties to reconstruction of one of the villages destroyed during the war. Later, a separate translation in the Slovak language was proposed and Katharine felt that she had to make a gift of Slovak royalties too. She told Jonathan Cape:

> Yes I know I shouldn't behave like a millionaire if I don't earn even half the basic wage as a writer, but it gives me some satisfaction to feel I may be helping people who suffered so much. That's worth more than a few kronen, isn't it?

"I'm not broke!" Katharine assured me:

> Have always got my £2/5/0 pension, you know. And as well still have about £140 in the bank . . . I'm going to hang on to £100 so that I can always come to you, at a moment's notice, if need be.

On top of it all came a slug for income tax assessments for three years, on royalties that had already paid tax at 9s in the pound in England. "I get so demented that sometimes feel it would be better to give up writing and just live on the old military pension," Katharine fumed.

There were times when loneliness overwhelmed her, despite the comfort of her friends in the west. "I do long to see you all," she wrote.

> What a great day it will be when I arrive to see the belovedest little bit of you. Sometimes, I feel a thoroughly unkissed and unkissing old K.S. these days. Queer isn't it? But there's nobody I want to kiss — so there you are.

When I wrote in August 1948, to say that I was to be posted to the Australian Legation in Rio de Janeiro and expected to leave with the family by sea in a few months, Katharine had no hesitation. She arranged at once to make the long train trip to the east. In the post-war years, there were queues at four in the morning for tickets on the transcontinental express, but Katharine found that my father's name still had influence in the west, and within a fortnight she had succeeded in making a booking for the five days' journey to Canberra, assuring me:

> It won't be difficult to drop *Winged Seeds*. I'll leave a swag of chapters with Clarice. Have got about eight to finish. And these need a lot of thought and care. They'll be an anodyne when I return, and with nothing much to look forward to, dare say I won't hurry and scamp them as I might have done, if I'd been coming to see you when they're done.

It was a love story from the beginning between Katharine and Karen. She delighted in photographs of the baby; displayed them proudly to all and sundry; carried them with her in a wallet of special treasures. But Katharine was anxious not to intrude upon my family. Before leaving the west, she wrote to my wife saying, "You know, I think of you as Three-in-one, now. His happiness bound up with you and Karen, so I don't want ever, to disturb that basis."

Katharine gave herself wholly to that small, bright-eyed scrap of humanity. When Karen grasped her finger, gave her a wet, gummy grin, wriggled all over with pleasure and greeted her as "Ga-ga-ga", Katharine was captured completely. Utterly devoted to the infant, she became for the few months before we left for Brazil the very picture of a quite besotted grandmother; spoiling the baby unashamedly; singing the little aboriginal song that, somehow, always succeeded in quietening those black, eager eyes:

Bee-bee coondooloo, coondooloo;
Monta-lala, monta-lala.

Over and over again she sang her song of sympathy and love, until, comforted, the baby slept — or woke again demanding more.

Three months with her own family in Canberra were balm to Katharine's soul. It was hard for her to say goodbye again and to endure the weeks of silence between letters while we were at sea. She promised herself to get back to work, but her thoughts followed us on the long journey across America and down the east coast to Brazil. By the time we had arrived, Katharine wrote to say that she had done another chapter of *Winged Seeds;* was getting up her thirst for it again "like a tiger having tasted blood, as it were".

Katharine became more and more concerned about the drift of opinion away from the Labor Government as the 1949 Federal elections approached. The Liberal-Country Party Opposition campaigned on a promise to outlaw the Communist Party. Katharine believed that the Labor Party itself showed signs of yielding to right-wing pressure. Her leave from political duty was over. "As the campaign for the elections gets under way, the atmosphere is becoming very tense," Katharine told me in a letter to Rio.

> The Opposition was never more active and vicious in its attacks on the Government. And some of my friends have been having a difficult time. I know you won't approve — but I had to speak at a meeting of protest this week; an appeal for defence of the democratic rights of the Australian people. It was a hot night, and speaking in the open air, not easy for your little mother, darl — particularly as a bunch of drunken youths were trying to disrupt the meeting. However, they didn't; and I didn't get any rotten tomatoes — which is their latest method of argument.

The work went on, with all the familiar distractions — university lectures, political meetings, an invitation to the Pushkin celebrations in Moscow, power failures and blackouts which interrupted night work, and another spell in hospital with heart trouble. "It's really a frantic struggle always to get time for thought and creative work," Katharine wrote to Nettie Palmer. "But I do not regret having kept close to 'our mother the masses' from whence cometh our strength etc."

Katharine worried and fretted over the conclusion of the novel, caught between the need for a striking denouement and the dry facts of history. She refused to take liberties with events as they were for the sake of literary effect:

> I've still been tinkering with my last chapters, re-written them a dozen times, and am still not satisfied. The theme has got to be so carefully handled, and yet the logical conclusion should be boldly and simply stated. What's worrying me, I think, is whether Sally stands out as she should, monolithic, a tragic yet human figure, intrepid and undefeated. If there had been a big strike on the goldfield, I'd have got a dramatic climax, but things have been as dull as ditchwater there since the last depression, so I've got only that situation to work with. Goodness knows whether *Winged Seeds* will have any wings, or be the worst flop I've ever conceived! Maybe it's the atmosphere of these days that makes me so apprehensive. I can only say to myself, as usual: "Do your damndest, and what anybody else thinks doesn't matter!" But after all I feel it's my work that's at fault, not the conception. I'll still be slogging away for months to try to make the work measure up.

Katharine found the dramatic spark for her conclusion in the same gossamer-tipped seeds that had fallen on to her manuscript from the wild pear:

> Lances of golden light were flashing through the bush now, striking the heavy, drooping, dark green pods among the dead-looking thorn bushes. One after another the wild pears clicked and split, shedding a shower of gossamery thistledown. Sally picked up a handful and found each fragile, glistering orb of fluff loaded with a brown seed. "Seeds with wings," she murmured. "Winged seeds . . . they'll find a corner where they can grow, even in this hard ground."

The cycle of death and regeneration was symbolized in those seeds of hope falling on the grave of Kalgoorla, at one with the land, despoiled by the ravening search for gold.

Katharine knew when she posted *Winged Seeds* to Cape that she had indeed done her damndest. "Here's *Winged Seeds* all ready for posting," Katharine could write to him at last at the end of September, 1949:

> And of course I'm all in a dither about it. Will be living in a state of acute misery until I hear from you . . . Am enclosing some winged seeds. Do you think they could be used for illustration? Drifting down a blue cover should look effective . . .
>
> In *Winged Seeds* I've tried to face up to the problems of our own time — at least until '46. Developments of the last week have intensified them. How damnable the American rampage is! All that is best in the English tradition is being swept away by it; but I still have confidence in the power of the people to survive and recreate. They always have done.

Katharine in 1909, as editor of the Melbourne Herald*'s Womens Page*

'Lo I am a witch and weave a spell' : Katharine in the Lavender Fields in Devon, 1915.

Katharine's first meeting with Jim Throssell at Wandsworth in 1915.

With 'Red' Burke's bullock team in the Karri country.

TOP *Bath time on the verandah at Greenmount in 1923.*

BOTTOM *Teaching Ric to ride, 1925.*

TOP *Katharine in 1928.*

BOTTOM *Ric, Bill and Biddy with Katharine at Rockingham.*

A tribute from Hugh McCrae.

A gift of seeds for the children of Greenmount School from the children of Siberia, 1933.

BOTTOM *Katharine's pledge : 'Yours in opposition to War & Fascism'.*

TOP *Katharine in 1945.*

BOTTOM *Receiving the World Council's medallion for services to peace in 1959.*

CHAPTER 17

WITH HALF THE WORLD BEHIND ME

Must I turn aside from my destined way
For a task your don would find me?
I come with the strength of the living day,
And with half the world behind me;
I leave you alone in your cultured halls
To drivel and croak and cavil:
Till your voice goes farther than college walls
Keep out of the tracks we travel!

— Henry Lawson

In Australia, the political climate of the fifties froze. The defeat of the Labor Government under J. B. Chifley in 1949 brought R. G. Menzies into office on a private enterprise and anti-Communist election policy. A bill to dissolve the Communist Party was introduced in the Commonwealth Parliament. When the act was declared invalid by the High Court, the Government unsuccessfully sought authority by referendum for constitutional amendments to grant the Commonwealth power to pass laws for "the peace order and good government of the Commonwealth with respect to Communism". Australian troops joined the United Nations Forces in Korea and were engaged in war against the Communist Governments of North Korea and the People's Republic of China. The anti-Communist witch-hunts of Senator McCarthy's Committee for Un-American Activities purged liberal opinion in the United States and spread its influence of fear throughout the Western world. The Holy Office in Rome forbade Roman Catholics to read any books and papers supporting Communism or Communist actions. "At present things here literary and dramatic, are in a worse way than they've ever been," Katharine wrote in 1950. "The people seem cowed — afraid to say that black is black and white, white even."

Katharine found herself again confronted by the hostility of conservative opinion. The conformist majority, swayed subconsciously, or convinced by fear of Communism and Communists, saw Red conspiracy in everything. The Cold War between Capitalism and Communism had made the minds of men a prime target. It was a war of threats and passes; a war of propaganda in which the first victory was conviction.

In Perth, easy-going, sun-loving, conservative capital of Australia's largest, least developed State, isolated by the vast distances of Australia, proud of its reputation for courtesy to the stranger: here too, the bitter currents of ideological conflict stirred. Katharine's old humpy at Greenmount, surrounded by black wattles and white-flowering gum-trees, half hidden among the grape-vines, climbing roses, honeysuckle, wistaria and a wild straggle of garden, was pointed out as the place where "the red witch, that Throssell woman", lived. "Maybe there'll be more difficulties to contend with before the year is out," Katharine wrote to the family in Brazil in February 1950:

> But do not worry about me, my Nicky darling. Everybody knows where I stand, and I'm not concerned about anything that could happen to me, personally. Although you don't share my political convictions, I know you will understand that I have to do what I believe to be right. That's one thing about our relationship — mother and son, we might be — but we each recognize the other's right to go their own way. Your way may not be my way, or Dodie's either. That won't make any difference to our love and respect for each other's point of view. Above all, I couldn't bear you to be embarrassed by what I do, or say. So don't think you have to take any action if there's any interference with my normal way of life. Maybe there won't be. As far as I am concerned, my mind is quite serene. I'd only be distressed if you were affected, my darlings.

The action which Katharine feared, with the Communist Party Dissolution Bill in the offing, did not happen; but *Winged Seeds,* published in London in September 1950, could not escape a political judgment. The critics screamed "Propaganda!" and damned the book — on purely literary grounds. *The Times* pronounced that, "Australia appears to be more addicted than England to a parrot-like Communism and atheism, though it has a hopeful vitality . . ." And Lionel Hale in the *Observer* wrote:

> This contemporary record wanders garrulously among labour troubles, and in its contentiousness its characters fade away behind propagandist masks . . . whatever the writing of a novel about Australian goldfields should be, it should not become a habit. Miss Prichard has worked this vein for some time, and here finds only a nugatory nugget.

Katharine was undismayed. "I expect all the mugwumps to turn up their noses. So what matter?" she wrote.

The Australian critics were more direct: they at least avoided condescension. The *Bulletin* puts its views unmistakably:

> Dutifully promoting Communist jargon, twisted into situations to justify political theories, Katharine Prichard's characters become half comic and half repulsive, with the disquieting unreality of the tortured.

There were few who realized, as Muir Holburn did, that "the trilogy having been conceived as an artistic unity, must therefore be so considered if it is to be justly appraised". Holburn took the three novels together. He warned that: "The goldfields trilogy is of course frustrating material for the conventional critic. It may well do hurt to deeply rooted literary and social prejudices but, alas, its quality is so obvious that it cannot be ignored." He discovered the threefold aspects of life revealed in all her major books, "people and environment with work as the nexus"; found the trilogy the culmination of Katharine Prichard's work, and concluded:

> Throughout all the author's principal works we find persisting in manifold forms a governing belief that is here elaborated into a poetic truth from which the whole work springs and draws its strength. The belief is, in essence that . . . beauty and poetry are present throughout the natural and human worlds — they are immanent in deserts and withering climates and among poor and humdrum people. They thrive wherever there is mateship, love, pity, struggle in the cause of human ideals.[88]

Katharine was far from immune to criticism. She could say, all frail defiance, that she would continue to go her own way; make a brave show of having done her damndest: she could ignore clever journalist comments, or the pretensions of minor academics, but she could not yield to the literary critics, of any political strain, when it came to the fundamental basis of her work. She could no more overstate the political content of a novel to please Communist critics, than omit political views which she believed to be a real part of her subject to meet the wishes of Australian and British critics, even those like Louis Esson, whose judgments she valued in most literary matters.

Louis believed that "form of society, doctrines of religion, wars and revolutions all pass away; only art remains".[89] He insisted that Katharine's dialectic had damaged her work, but Katharine had no patience with Louis' aestheticism. Art could not exist for its own sake in a world where people suffered injustice and poverty, she believed. To have deliberately excluded her vision of "a new and better world" from her work for the sake of literary reputation was impossible. It was equally impossible for her to falsify the truth, as she saw it, for political favour. Repeatedly, Katharine insisted that propaganda alone was rarely successful as literature, but in its real sense, was always, inescapably, part of it. This was the view she took in a carefully considered reply to an American student at Ohio State University in 1938:

> The writer's approach to the people may be either by the direct statement of facts, or by the indirect method of attempting to recreate the cosmos in the lives of a group of people in a given place and time. The indirect method, in my opinion should be the method of writers of fiction who use the novel and short stories to stir and convince their readers of real value in life. But in doing so, I believe that writers must remain faithful to their material. It is their material, the stuff they present which must sway emotion and intelligence, not any preaching or obvious propaganda purpose.
>
> I agree that all great works of literature are propagandist in essence. They are so because they dominate the consciousness of the reader, through the mind of the writer and his interpretation of life and its values; but to obtrude a propaganda purpose is to make it ineffective . . . The objective of any serious writer should be to galvanize readers into an awareness of the causes which underlie frustration and tragedy, so that the comment arises: "Well, this is life. What do I think about it? What can be done about it?"
>
> What is propaganda? Here again the meaning of words has suffered a subtle change. Propaganda used to mean "the spreading of a certain set of ideas or principles". Certainly, I am propagandist, if that is so, and all writers of any consequence have been propagandist, whether they are conscious of it or not. It is impossible for the work of an individual brain not to bear the impression of that brain, either in its triviality or grandeur. But today, the word "propaganda" has acquired another significance, that is of a bald and blatant partisanship in relation to any particular set of ideas or principles.
>
> The question of propaganda, as it concerns the writer, it seems to me, is one of method. As an individual, as an essayist, as a public speaker, as a reporter, a writer may be baldly and blatantly partisan. He may use the direct approach to the emotion and intelligence of his audience. As a novelist

he sets out to show not his own, but the reactions of others to the experiences and circumstances of their lives and therefore his method should be indirect — providing circumstantial evidence, as it were, and leaving conclusions to the gentle reader. There is no doubt that in choosing the persons and theme of a novel, a writer selects those for which he has some predilection and that they move in accordance with his own interpretation of the realities of their environment.

It appears to me nonsense therefore to say as D. H. Lawrence does, that "Morality in the novel is the trembling instability of the balance. When the novelist puts his thumb in the scale to pull the balance down to his own predilection, that is immorality". Every novel worth anything bears the imprint of the potter's thumb. All the novels of D. H. Lawrence do.

"Art for Art's sake", I find a cliché, superficial and illogical. A work of art, I conceive to be some supreme expression of some beauty, truth, terror, or degradation in nature: a re-creation by the human agent of such a model or state of mind. Only in its capacity to reach the human objective is it of value. I cannot accept the thing created as of more importance than the creator or the human complex to which it must be referred.

Art for Art's sake becomes a mere rattle of words to soothe the vanity of ineffectual artisans who play with the tools of expression, but are too indolent or limited in faculty to fathom the sources of vital knowledge. Art to me is a revelation of human greatness in expression, and for humanity's sake.

Katharine's views on the place of social purpose in literature remained essentially unchanged. Although she placed greater emphasis upon the importance of political consciousness as her stated commitment grew more direct, she continued to despise the distortion of truth, either by the fabrication of events to suit a political purpose, or by concealment of conviction for the sake of conformity to accepted ideas. She could no more bring herself to invent a strike on the goldfields to give *Winged Seeds* a dramatic conclusion than she could ignore the historical truth of the abortive timber workers' strike in *Working Bullocks*. She insisted that, "if an artist is dealing with incidents and lives that are intimately bound up in the social forces that operate upon human beings he is justified, if not compelled, to reveal his attitude to those social forces". But she remembered great arguments in the old days with the IWW who had pressed her "to write in a narrow, propagandist way". She had been outraged by

J. B. Miles' suggestion that she might submit her manuscript of *The Real Russia* to the Communist Party of Australia; and flatly refused to do so.

Katharine recognized her tendency to idealize her characters, and rationalized an essentially instinctive inclination. In an interview with E. W. Irwin for *Masses and Mainstream,* she explained:

> I have always taken Gorky's advice, that art is a weapon, for or against, as a directive to intensify all that is fine in the characters who advance the purposes of humanity; and to intensify, too, those qualities which stand in the way of human advancement. Naturalism is not enough.[90]

Later, in the sixties, Katharine continued to deny that she wrote "as an agitator", but in an interview with Tony Thomas for *The Critic,* after the publication of her last novel, she agreed that she did seek to affect the attitudes of her readers:

> I write for the purpose of influencing people in the direction of ideas that I feel are important. Rodin said: "Art is the joy of the intelligence which sees the universe clearly and re-creates by illuminating the consciousness; Art seeks to understand the world, and make it understood. Art is the most sublime mission of man . . ." I write to reach people's common sense and intelligence, to show them that if they unite they can make a different world possible.[91]

Katharine's debate on the political role of literature was not confined to the West. Towards the end of 1950, *Novy Mir,* a Russian periodical, published a review of the work of Katharine Susannah Prichard suggesting that the role of the Communist Party in the industrial organization of the goldfields had not been sufficiently well presented in the first two volumes of the trilogy. Katharine flew to the defence of her position. "May I say, to begin with, if you please, that I do not believe a writer of socialist realism should falsify reality," Katharine wrote to Mikhail Apletin, Head of the Foreign Commission of the Union of Soviet Writers.

She explained that there was no Communist organization in Western Australia at the time with which *Golden Miles* dealt. Although, as the *Novy Mir* critic had said, the Australian Communist Party had been formed in Sydney in 1920, with Katharine herself among the foundation members, Sydney was as far from Western Australia as Moscow from Siberia. Katharine argued that it would have been quite unreal to claim any influence for the Communist Party on the goldfields at that time:

> It must be remembered that writers in a capitalist country cannot express themselves as freely on this subject, as Soviet writers. For a capitalist publisher to have accepted a novel sympathetic to Communism is something of a miracle, these days. It is only because I have won a reputation for artistry and literary craftsmanship that the publication of the goldfields trilogy has been possible. Yet *Novy Mir* finds fault with these qualities in my books! Even capitalist critics do not deny them. What they find fault with is the political content — which is too strong for them, although it is not strong enough for a Soviet critic.

After *Winged Seeds* was published, Katharine wrote again, thanking Apletin for his assurance that the critic had not understood the position of the Australian Communist Party in 1920 and warning him discreetly that its influence on the goldfields was not much greater in 1946, the period covered by the third novel of the trilogy. She contended that:

> The capitalist press says *Winged Seeds* is "too heavily weighted with political propaganda and has destroyed my reputation as a literary artist . . ." The political philosophy, I maintain, is integrated with the theme and the characters. I have chosen the types which express that philosophy — that is what the capitalist press does not like. But after all every creative writer does that.

The controversy died hard. Jack Beasley revived the suggestion that Katharine had failed to create a "vital revolutionary figure" in *Winged Seeds* when he published *The Rage for Life*,[92] an evaluation of her work from a Communist point of view. The Tom Gough of *Golden Miles* was not good enough, "a staid, uninspiring" figure, said Jack Beasley. More surprisingly in a Marxist critic, he found political analysis fundamentally opposed to imagination and emotion, "the true source of the timeless, never-ending magic of art".

Katharine wrote to the Australian Communist newspaper, *Tribune*, praising the "conscientious effort" made by Jack Beasley; but she could not accept his comments on the revolutionary hero. "Was I to falsify reality and produce one when the conditions did not?" she asked again. And as she had told the Soviet critics thirteen years earlier, she added, "I cannot believe this would have been ethically or artistically justifiable". The idealization which she had defended to *Masses and Mainstream* as a valid weapon in art's battle "for or against", Katharine now saw as a flaw consciously avoided in her characterization: "It has always been difficult for me not to idealize communists: to forget that they have weaknesses, bad habits and temptations like other men and women," she explained in a private letter to Jack Beasley.

Frank Hardy, savouring *Tribune*'s taste for ideological debate since the liberalizing promises of the 20th Congress of the Communist Party of the Soviet Union, also took issue with Jack Beasley's dogmatism. "Historical perspective measuring by now almost twenty years, has already vindicated Katharine Susannah Prichard and her trilogy," he wrote.

The Australian critics did not see it like that. The chorus of professional men-of-letters polished their spectacles and for those twenty years measured, weighed, probed and poked, analysed, dissected, and pronounced upon the life, work, character, motives and value of Katharine Susannah Prichard.

Australian literature was not regarded by the universities as a fit subject for academic study until 1954, when Tom Inglis Moore's course was introduced at the Canberra University College, initially without recognition for a degree. Professional literary criticism of a high standing, too, was confined to a few, like Nettie Palmer, Louis Esson and H. M. Green, who, since the passing of A. G. Stephens and the old *Bulletin*, were left with the columns of the daily press, women's journals and come-and-go literary magazines, before *Southerly* and *Meanjin* grew long-lived and learned. None could find a livelihood in literary criticism, any more than a novelist could live by his trade. None could quite match up to the ideal standards suggested by Hartley Grattan in the *New York Times:*

> A living, breathing critic is now urgently needed. The three literary quarterlies that started during the war cannot possibly deal with the new books soon enough to help the person who wants to keep up to date. Newspaper reviewing in Australia is decidedly not good. The new *Book News* monthly of Sydney will help one keep track of the books published — hitherto a difficult chore in itself — but it does not yet promise to solve the critical problem. So Australia unquestionably needs a live and functioning critic who knows a hawk from a handsaw, who isn't involved in one or another of the cliques, and who has the income and leisure to do his job properly.[93]

A young tutor in English and Education at the Technical Correspondence School of the Perth Technical College and postgraduate student at the University of Western Australia, was not the paragon of critical virtue whom Hartley Grattan suggested.

He was, however, the first person to tackle a full-length study of Katharine's life and work. In March 1950, he wrote to tell her the University had accepted a critical examination of her work as his topic for a Master of Arts thesis.[94]

Katharine, with some fifty years of creative writing to her score, twelve major novels, translations at that time in some six European languages, the distinction of Hartley Grattan's recent recognition as the most important fiction writer of Australia, and the Fellowship of Australian Writers' nomination for the Nobel Prize,[95] was pleased, and not a little flattered, to find herself the subject of scholarly study. "Had quite an interesting talk to a bloke who came to see me yesterday," she told me:

> He's writing a thesis for his M.A. degree on the works of your K.S. and wanted some information. Introduced himself by saying: "You don't remember me. But we've met before." And where do you think, darl? At Dunsborough! He was a lad who used to pass our shack on the beach — and sometimes ask whether he could bring you anything from the store, some distance away. You were six then! After all those years, here he was, wanting to make a study of the literary craftsmanship of K.S.

He called several times in search of information. Katharine provided him with dozens of photographs, biographical details, notebooks and extracts from her manuscripts to reproduce in his study. "I feel responsible somehow, for his getting through — would hate him to lose because he had chosen your K.S. for a subject," she said.

Katharine read the drafts of the biographical chapters of the thesis, and suggested improvements in his own literary expression. "I couldn't have believed a man who teaches English could write in such a school-boyish way", she complained. She was even more astonished to find that he had worked out a "marvellous theory" that she had "some sort of complex":

> He argues that, because Nigel was the elder brother, it was natural for me to feel "abnormally deprived" of my parents' affection, and that naturally, I bestowed all my tenderness on Alan, as the younger brother. Of course his whole elaborate theory falls to the ground, because Alan was the elder brother. It's very comical, isn't it? Particularly, as I'm sure there were no complexes in the relations of my brothers and me. We were too much the same age, and boon companions as children. I'm not conscious of ever feeling the slightest jealousy or antagonism between us. It wasn't until

we were grown man and woman, our lives and interests had gone different ways, that Nigel and I developed different points of view, and even they have not altered the basic affection between us.

Another quaint point in the thesis is that I'm supposed to have a maternal complex, because I fell in love with your father "when he was ill and in hospital"! So remote from the truth! He used to say he fell in love with me the first time he saw me, walking along the terrace of the Automobile Club: that I walked right into his heart. He knew I was the girl he had been looking for. He got sick leave and followed me to Australia. It wasn't until he made love to me then, that I was swept off my feet, and knew I was in love with him. But he did work hard to capture your K.S., darling. It was his tempestuous wooing, physical strength and beauty, I adored at first. Then as we grew to know each other better, his sweet nature, all the fine qualities of his great character held me so fast that no man ever again had any chance with me. There was nobody comparable with my Jimmy. Nobody, I felt could ever take his place — although of course, there were candidates. This attempt at giving biographical details, so out of tune with the facts, has made me realize that I ought to write my own biography, in order to prevent such queer versions being concocted.

Katharine believed that she had convinced her self-appointed biographer that there was no basis for his psychological analysis; but when the thesis was presented, he could not resist a Freudian pass: the thesis was composed of a conglomeration of specious psychological theorizing, contradiction and apologetic praise for his thoroughly infuriated subject. Katharine exploded:

Also this week, the young man writing his thesis for an M.A. called and left the M.S. for me to read . . . And what do you think his conclusions are? That the trilogy is not a work of "creative art, or literature". K.S. depicts herself in all her heroines, the heroes are "defective males" grouped round the central figure, and because of her political philosophy said K.S. is a propagandist not a literary artist. It's funny really! This is all described as "Narcissism". Do you see me in the Deb of *Working Bullocks* or Gina of *Haxby's* or Deidre of *The Pioneers* or Sophie of *Black Opal*? The characters are all different, and separate. He imagines that I am Elodie of *Intimate Strangers* — who of course was Rose A. and recognized herself. How is Elodie like Deb or Gene? Yet, this bloke says all my women characters are uniform! And as for the men, did you consider Michael in

> "B.O." a "defective male" or Dinny, or Tom Gough and Billy — or Farrell in *The Pioneers,* or Red Bourke in *Working Bullocks*? You've no idea what the Freudian obsessions of this lad have plastered on to me. But his nerve is what amazes me. To take all the information I could give him — which is the only valuable part of the thesis, and then set out to debunk the idea that my work is of any particular value, quoting all the adverse criticism, and not one critic who has given it high marks — from the materials I gave him! An amazing performance! However, what does it matter? The work stands, for what it is worth — and I am content to abide by the interpretation of life to which I have given all my qualifications as a writer — all the truth and knowledge I've been able to glean in my life's wandering. I was so sorry for the young man, and his inadequacy that I tried to help him all I could. Isn't it comical? He does allow me a capacity to write landscape poetically, but that's about all.

Katharine did not understand the importance attached by the universities, after Leavis, to an analytical approach to literature, as if criticism, too, could be scientific. The serious scholar was required to define the essence of his subject's philosophy (or have a go at a plausible invention), analyse creative method, expose the psyche, give evidence of original thought. A theory was needed, carefully wrapped in abstractions, against which the work could be measured, and when it failed to comply, condemned for its inconsistency. Microscopic vivisection was the rule — far better for the subject to be alive and kicking than a cadaver of the literary past: find an anachronism or hunt out a recurring image; dissect stylistic curiosities. Comparisons, invaluable! How did D. H. Lawrence do it? Quotations, in and out of context. Sources by the yard. Far easier to rip it to pieces, although a little innocuous praise was advisable to demonstrate a sound, balanced judgment. Emotional involvement was to be avoided at all costs: the detached approach; scientific, statistical, antiseptic. Feeling, it would seem, had no part in the academic critics' view of literature. It was a recipe Katharine learned. Found herself tagged and labelled: "realist", "romantic", "socialist realist", "romantic naturalist".

The universities' discovery of Australian literature could not have been expected to produce overnight the new attitude to literary criticism that Hartley Grattan envisaged. Revisiting Australia in 1965, he explained more carefully:

> I was aiming to say it was absolutely vital that Australian literature be generally acknowledged as of the highest signi-

> ficance to Australians. A nation without a literature is a nation naked in a censorious world. I tried to say that there were in existence at the time writings which gave substance to Australian literature historically and these should be precisely identified, carefully evaluated and a "canon" agreed upon.[96]

But instead of an eagle, the faculties of English hatched a flock of fledgling peewits: instead of vision, chirrupings in the grass.

G. A. Wilkes, at that time a lecturer in English at the University of Sydney, set the tone for the more serious "reappraisal" of the work of Katharine Susannah Prichard.[97] He bestowed rare praise upon *Intimate Strangers,* in which he found something of the delicacy of her verse; conceded that the trilogy might have succeeded in giving the story of an industry, but as far as telling something of the lives of the people was concerned, he found it a "monument of lost opportunities". His complaint was that the characters of the trilogy were presented by assumption. "She has not displayed them — she has displayed her admiration instead," he asserted. "Rarely have a novelist's obligations to her characters been so signally neglected."

Wilkes took up the propagandist cry against the books of the trilogy, clothing the journalists' naked accusations in decent academic dress:

> It is bewildering that so experienced a novelist should pose so intolerably about conscription, profiteering and trade unionism without taking care to embody the issues in the psychological process of action, making them the conditions under which these processes are worked out.

But Wilkes' statements, *ex cathedra,* for all their sonority, were less persuasive than that Western Australian MA student's groping explanation of his objections to the political material of the novels, differentiating carefully between points of view introduced in a way he considered aesthetically acceptable, and the occasions on which he found the novelist commenting directly on political questions.

Katharine took Wilkes to be a youthful critic "who doesn't know the first thing about criticism".[98] "The thing doesn't really affect me," she assured her friends.

But it did. She was hurt and discouraged by Wilkes' view of her work. "The debunking of K.S. seems to be a favourite pastime of Sydney University," she grieved. And later, in the same letter, showed something of the pain that her pose of defiant resignation was usually intended to hide:

> Seems, after all, my life's work doesn't amount to much! Just when one's ready to put all experience and technique into the job, the power's cut off. No matter! "She did what she could" — That's a good enough epitaph for your K.S.

Misconceptions about her attitude to D. H. Lawrence and supposed similarities in some of their work disturbed Katharine. She was anxious, too, to see justice done to Molly Skinner's collaboration with Lawrence in *The Boy in the Bush.* Katharine coaxed Molly Skinner to complete her autobiography, *The Fifth Sparrow,* in which the strange collaboration between this uncertain, harelipped Quaker and the erratic genius of literary, sexual liberation played an important part. But Katharine found herself expected to be both proof-reader and sub-editor. Quite exasperated with the carelessness of Molly Skinner's writing and determined not to become her "ghost", Katharine chose to make her point in her own way.

Her first admiration for the intoxicating freedom of Lawrence's language was a memory of the past, an old love almost forgotten, when Katharine wrote her article on "Lawrence in Australia" for *Meanjin:*

> My flat in London was perched high over the roof tops and trees of Chelsea Embankment. After reading *Sons and Lovers* there, soon after it was published, I felt as if a comet had swung into my ken.

Rereading *Kangaroo,* Katharine was struck by the superficiality of Lawrence's view of Australia and Australians, "infuriated by comments and conclusions drawn from so slight a knowledge of Australian history, character and conditions". The *Meanjin* article made it clear that she returned the gifts that *Sons and Lovers* once promised, coolly, with thanks. She concluded:

> Perhaps we all have a sub-conscious inferno to wrestle with. But Lawrence tore himself to pieces in a literary experiment, and gave us the pieces to study. Unfortunately, though, he transferred his psychological vagaries to many of the characters of his novels. He did not submit himself to other people as a medium for the inflection of their essential quality: he made them in his own image.[99]

Even Ellen Malos, one of the most enthusiastic participants in the "reappraisal" of Katharine Susannah Prichard, scorned the suggestion of a Western Australian student-journalist[100] that Katharine's story "The Grey Horse" was derived from Lawrence's "St

Mawr". "The Grey Horse" was published in 1924, she pointed out, and "St Mawr" not until 1925.

In its concluding chapter, Ellen Malos described her thesis on "Some Major Themes and Problems in the Novels of K. S. Prichard"[101] as "a work of demolition"; admitted that she had not attempted "to give a balanced assessment of Prichard's work"; had attempted "an understanding of weaknesses rather than successes". She had not explained her intention when she wrote seeking Katharine's assistance, nor when Katharine wrote to warn her that her university supervisor did not approve of K.S.P. and was not likely to be pleased with her choice of subject. "I have reached the stage where I am very tired of attempting to coat the pill in sugar so that it will be acceptable to sensitive academic stomachs," Mrs Malos replied, promising to present her view of the truth unvarnished, as far as her own "natural cowardice" would allow.

The truth, as she found it, was that the failure of Katharine Susannah Prichard as a writer was "inherent in Prichard's very conception of life" — her "romantic attachment to the land", and "idealisation of the outback community"; her failure to "reconcile the great passion and the demands of social reality"; her failure to "assimilate Marxism to her personal view of life"; her failure to "penetrate into the consciousness" of her characters; her carelessness. She was described as being "prepared to dash off something that is 'near enough' while she goes on with her real job of becoming involved in elaborating an image from nature instead of drawing out its truth", Those who took another view of Katharine Susannah Prichard's work, Jack Lindsay, Muir Holburn, Aileen Palmer, were accused of anxiety to find "a complete, consistent materialist dialectic in the novels".

"I know, very well, that some criticism of my writing is justified, but not sweeping condemnation of its essential value," Katharine wrote, consoling herself that her work could not have reached the minds and hearts of millions of people all over the world if it were worthless.

Katharine's advice to me, at a time when I had the first scent of a passing success in the theatre, suggested that she was more vulnerable to adverse criticism than she pretended when her public armour was on. She urged me not to become "self-conscious" in my writing:

> I know how I have been affected unwillingly, and almost subconsciously. Letting other people's opinions interfere with my individual expression. More lately than before there is

> a reputation at stake. A sort of reluctance to write below standard — when the important thing is to write what one wants to, how one wants.
>
> There's the need, too, to insulate against hostile criticism — which is just hostile for the sake of being hostile. Honest helpful criticism one can think over and accept. But sometimes, the hostility acts as a blight, if we don't just make up our minds not to let it — and do our damndest in our own way.

All the same, Katharine felt a little as though she had been given the same treatment by her cultured critics as that bestowed on her by the neighbour's dog: "George the Murray's dog has just called — but as I can't find a bone for him, he has lifted a leg at the bookcase and departed. Not exactly a compliment!"

Katharine had her own "sweetly reasonable" words to say on critics and criticism in an address to the Fellowship of Australian Writers in Melbourne in March 1953. She appealed for "an imaginative enthusiasm", discrimination, knowledge and utter honesty; contrasted Hartley Grattan's attitude to Australian literature with the position adopted by "sundry visiting English and American professors, who with little knowledge of the work of Australian writers, and less understanding of the life and thought of our people, have assumed there is no such thing as an Australian literature". She challenged the tendency to underestimate Australian writers:

> We find very little "imaginative enthusiasm" in the reviews of contemporary critics. Too often a critic seems to consider his functions to be chiefly fault finding. He "picks and pores over little inexactitudes" in a work of art, like a barnyard fowl, George Meredith used to say . . .
>
> I think, with Keats, that a writer should be the most severe critic of his or her own work. Make a study of craftsmanship: know the subject written about more intimately than any critic can, and take the utmost pains to present a story fearlessly, with vigour and simplicity.
>
> Despite all the talk, recently, of the need for criticism of Australian literature, I think we have had enough, if not too much, of negative criticism. There must be some destructive criticism — criticism of what is slovenly, false and vicious; but the emphasis should be on constructive criticism. What we need — what our young writers, particularly, need is criticism with an imaginative enthusiasm for what is best in their work — in its relation to truth, the realities of life in their own country, the beauty of an intelligence which

> sees beyond the debris and decadence of our time in crime and barbarous wars, seeking always to understand what are the real values in life, helping others to understand them, and so fulfil as the great writers of all ages have done that "sublime mission" of which Rodin spoke.

Perhaps Katharine expected even more of a critic than Hartley Grattan had hoped for; but there were two who, from quite opposite approaches, discovered the insight necessary to arrive at a valid understanding of her intentions, and her achievement in literature.

When Katharine first learned that Henrietta Drake-Brockman was to do a monograph for the "Australian Writers and Their Work" series, she was far from enthusiastic. "Lansdowne Press is advertising a book on your K.S. by Henrietta D.B. Help!" she wailed.

Katharine and Henrietta had long been reserved, uncertain friends. Politically at opposite poles, they were brought together by a cautious admiration for each other's strength of character and tenacity. Henrietta put political differences aside, gained Katharine's confidence and learned more of the influence of personal tragedy on her life and work than any other fellow writer. Her monograph[102] was a carefully constructed and correct account of Katharine's life and work, distinguished by a sincere search for personal understanding and mature critical judgment. "Henrietta's monograph is quite pleasing isn't it, though she can't see any merit in my awareness of the trend in social evolution?" Katharine wrote, surprised and grateful to be let off lightly. "She probably will join the chorus of disapproval when she reads *Subtle Flame,*" she added.

But Henrietta died suddenly within a few months and Katharine was shocked to find an unexpected loneliness and grief in her death. She wrote:

> I was really shattered by the news of Henrietta. She had been to see me only a fortnight before — looking so well, and still beautiful with a scarlet straw hat which was most becoming . . . It was an intimate friendship, despite political differences. She confided in me as I'm sure she didn't to anyone else — and actually that last day she came to see me asked: "What's the difference between socialism and communism"? The first time she had ever broached the subject or made any inquiry about the basis of my ideas.

To fellow writers in Perth, Katharine gave her tribute to Henrietta Drake-Brockman. It was the yearning grief of an old woman for a friend she still thought young, to whom all differences could be forgiven:

> The Fellowship without Henrietta! It seems incredible. We who are grieving can't think of her yet without tears welling. Never to see her come into a room, with her radiant vitality and beautiful eyes smiling! I have an inexpressible sense of loss.
>
> She was such a lovely girl when we first met before she was married. We were close friends over the years. Our friendship survived political differences of opinion: the indefinable bonds of love and admiration were stronger.
>
> Henrietta's strength of character, uncompromising appreciation of noblesse oblige, her generosity and the charm of her personality made her a fascinating companion . . .
>
> Henrietta has left us in the full bloom of her intellectual prowess. She will never be old in our memory. We will remember her as she was, always alive and sensitive in her perception of literary or art values.
>
> Dear Henrietta, I have loved you, and pay tribute to your warm sympathies with the comedy and tragedy of human existence.[103]

The political basis of Katharine's writing had been unknown ground to Henrietta Drake-Brockman. To Jack Lindsay there was no mystery in Marxist philosophy. He was at home with the complexities of dialectical materialism as he was with the history of ancient Rome, Greece and Egypt, or the culture of the Renaissance. Classicist, philosopher, historian, novelist, poet, playwright, critic, biographer and linguist, he brought immense erudition and scholarship to his study of the novels of Katharine Susannah Prichard. More than that, with the humility that marks creative genius' view of creativity, he set out to illumine his subject, not to expose it; to seek understanding of the work by its own lights, not to impose alien standards or direct judgment upon it.

Several years later, he explained his view of the critics' role in a personal letter to Katharine:

> In my opinion, if critical writing succeeds in finding the creative heart of a real writer and thereby helps to confirm him or her in purpose and conviction, it has done the most important thing it can do — and one page that does this is more important than a thousand pages which show off the cleverness of the critic.

When C. B. Christesen, Editor of *Meanjin*, commissioned the article on Katharine Susannah Prichard in 1961, Jack Lindsay had been living in England for many years. He was at that time the author of an astounding one hundred and thirty books. Within the scope of twenty pages, he satisfactorily unravelled for the first time the paradox of her realism and poetry, her lyricism and her materialism and found in them "a clear system of revelatory meaning":

> K.S.P. shows her commonfolk in all the grime and the constricting pressures of their environment; she endows them with no virtues that do not spring from their hardy, adventurous, yet extremely limited way of life. If there were no other factors in her representations, the result would be a pedestrian and documentary record. But other factors are strongly present as a leaven; and these, which saturate her realist account with poetic values, derive from her grasp of the social essence of work. In the pioneering conditions both the individual contribution and the social essence are plain, understood intuitively by the workers themselves and gathered without contradiction in the philosophy of mateship. But the social essence includes more than the cooperative and communal elements in thought and feeling which go to make up that philosophy. It involves also the living relationship to nature, the ultimate unity of labour-process and natural process. And it is by her deep comprehension of all this that K.S.P. achieves her full artistic force, her human richness, her transformation of realism into poetry. She is enabled to make working companions of a sober matter-of-fact statement and a lyrical impetus.[104]

He found the goldfields trilogy the peak of her literary achievement:

> The deploying of the enormous mass of material so that a clear pattern is kept, is itself a literary feat of a high order. The work is a social history, a record of the mines, and an epical novel. Inevitably there are points where the first two aspects threaten to swamp the third; but, taken as a whole, the plan comes off. The story of the mines is told in human terms. The endlessly crisscrossing lines of narrative fall into an easily recognisable pattern, so that a clear significance and an impression of swarming complexity are simultaneously conveyed.
>
> *The Roaring Nineties* is the most artistically satisfying section. For here K.S.P. deals with the pioneering world she knows and loves so well . . . Her triadic movement of people-work-nature is able to express itself with a magnificent fullness; and because she feels so entirely at home, she

> controls the intricate design of comings and goings, prospecting and rushes, failures and successes, without the least fall into confusion . . .
>
> The goldmining is not the background to Sally's life; the dialectical triad of people-work-nature ensures that the old manipulations of "private life" against a back-canvas, a social setting or a landscape, simply have no relevance to the creative method.

Jack Lindsay pointed out that Katharine's early work showed that she had arrived at an essentially Marxist approach in her writing before she knew anything of theoretical Marxism: it was an intuitive association of the work of man's hands with the soil and with growth; a heart-cry of protest against that which destroys man. "Her work can in no sense be described as an intelligent application of Marxism; only in its lesser sense could that description be used," Jack Lindsay concluded.

> Rather it is a creative development of the Marxist concepts of what humanises and what alienates, born out of an artist's deep sympathy for, and understanding of, her fellow men. Such a development could only occur in a country like Australia, at the time of K.S.P.'s early years of growth and maturing, for only in such a country would it be possible to observe and live through the rapid change from a pioneering man-to-man world into a world of capitalist monopoly. And thus it is that her work becomes an important contribution to world-literature as well as to the literature of her homeland.

"You should be proud," Clem Christesen told Katharine when he sent her the proofs of Jack Lindsay's article. She was, of course; found it "a wonderfully thoughtful and clear sighted thing", but wondered whether it was too analytical. "I feel I'm an instinctive story writer," Katharine said.

Jack Lindsay's own message to her, after Ellen Malos had challenged his interpretation of her work, was more precious to Katharine: "Your work has greatness, don't doubt that," he wrote in August 1962.

> I am arrogant in thinking that I can tell genius from talent and talent from mediocrity, and that I can tell significant structure and image from the insignificant — at least in other people's work.

"I felt on top of the world reading this," Katharine wrote. It gave her confidence, somehow, to forget the long winter of the fifties.

CHAPTER 18

CHILD OF THE HURRICANE

On a stray slip of paper, Katharine first scribbled the idea for a novel based on her own life. Among her notes for *The Pioneers* on Celtic legends, fragments of Erse, quotations from Sir John Rhys' *Celtic Folk Lore* and Raftery, the poet, "playing music to empty pockets", I found the story of a girl born during a Pacific gale "the child of the hurricane".

Katharine did not write that novel of a young woman facing the world's tempests, but she turned again to the name her Fijian nurse had given her for the title of her autobiography.

She had toyed before with the idea of an autobiography. The title and chapter headings for the sequel to the story of her childhood were listed on the back of a letter from the Editor of *Woman's World* asking for a special short story for the 1928 Christmas number; but "Cuckoo Oats" also waited among the pages of her notebooks for some unfulfilled spring.

As each new year began, Katharine looked back at what had been achieved in the year before, and made her plans for the year to come:

> I mark my years by the work done in them — and 1950 has gone without any record of achievement. Not that I've been idle. Every half hour has been filled — though I did have three lazy months by doctor's orders. But I've done practically no creative writing. Am facing the New Year with half a dozen designs brewing. Have sketched three. The Deakin play, novel — with half caste problem as subject to be called "Boronia". dramatic saga built on aboriginal legends, biography of K.S. and several short stories. I'd like to do also a monograph on my father — How much of the lot will get done, I wonder.

Katharine could arouse no enthusiasm for writing her memoirs: duty, more than anything else persuaded her to make a start. "Even in the rough they should be done — to counteract the stupidities and misrepresentations of callow commentators," she fumed, after reading the final version of the Western Australian post-graduate treatise on her life and work.

"I've started work on the Memoirs," Katharine wrote to tell me on 5 August 1951. Twelve years later, *Child of the Hurricane* was published; twelve years of frustration and indecision, when she doubted the wisdom of spending time on the thing at all, and longed to take up the more important creative work that she felt should be done.

Making the decision to start on the memoirs was difficult enough. It was harder for Katharine to put her mind to the job. More and more, she felt the absence of "her little family" in Brazil:

> I seem to live for your letters, lovey. Feel well fed, after reading my weekly word from you. You'd laugh though, if you saw me when a letter comes from Rio. I look at it, and feel like a cat with a mouse . Came home from town very tired on Friday and there was my bonne bouche in the letter box. I took off my town-going frock, got into a comfortable gown, lit the fire, put out my sherry and biscuits. Then sat down in an easy chair, and read my letter. Such a luxury and joy to read and re-read it — something I can have with an easy conscience, knowing I'm not depriving anybody of anything, and feeling all purry and quite satisfied with life for the moment. The rest of the world presses in, with other mail perhaps, and the evening news. Horrors of Korea, and conflicts everywhere; but I still can't believe that another war will be forced on this generation. The forces of peace grow amazingly. Even in the U.S.A., I understand, there's a struggle to maintain the present foreign policy against the growing dissatisfaction of the people.

Our three years in Brazil had ended by January 1952, and the family was ready to sail for home. All Katharine's thoughts were centred on our return. She visited the shipping agents in Perth, fossicked out sailing dates from Rio to Australia and planned the routes that we might be taking. Anticipating our departure, Katharine wrote:

> Now you will be on the sea! Every chug of the ship's engines bringing you nearer home. I can see all those miles of ocean and the waves rising and falling — hoping they won't be stormy, and you comfortable in your cabin.

Her imagination took her with us. "You will be getting your sea legs, now, I tell myself," she wrote to Cape Town to greet us on the way home.

> My heart beats go with the chugging of your ship's engines. Thank my stars that it isn't in the days of sailing ships you are making this long journey. At least you're not likely to be becalmed in the Sargasso Sea.

Not the Sargasso, but Rio de Janeiro! Poor Katharine, for once her imagination had deceived her. At the last moment our departure had been cancelled. There was no new work done during the long months of waiting for the family's return. "Perhaps I've been tired, and to finish the trilogy was enough", Katharine explained to herself.

The six weeks of our leave in Greenmount were a moment of special happiness to Katharine, after the years alone and the long months of waiting. The old house had been primped and plastered for our coming. Cupboards were laden with jars of her jams and preserves; but she admitted that "it wouldn't seem like home if every room wasn't oozing books and papers". Katharine was at once recaptured by her grand-daughter: she laughed at her quaint mixture of English and Portuguese, sang her Furnley Maurice's "Bay and Pady" songs, joined in her games and fiercely resented her own weakness when her blood pressure soared and she was forced to rest and be waited on herself for a few days.

Loneliness flooded over Katharine when we had gone. Neither the kindness of friends, nor her work, nor the simple pleasures of her wild garden which so often gave her comfort, could console her. "So quiet the house has been all day!" she wrote, finding what little consolation there was in the letters which had for so long been her only way of reaching us:

> For the first time the old place has failed to comfort me. The empty rooms — which still hold something of the presence of my beloveds — but not their solid forms, the sound of their voices — the comings and goings of their footsteps. I'm just full of tears — but not weeping, much — though the sight of a doll's hat with a yellow feather sends a few drops coursing. And then I scold myself: say how lucky I am to have had you: to know you are real: not just creatures of my imagination like Sally and Dinny, but my own Ric and Dodie and the precious poppet.

The sense of desolation would not leave her: "Nothing seems to matter and I'm not interested in anything. Everything seems so flat without you, my darlings . . . I do miss you so dreffully."

As the first devastating loneliness passed, Katharine scolded herself for her frailty:

> I'm still feeling so bereft. As if the light had gone out of my world — and yet I do tell myself I mustn't mope and be "melancholique". One shouldn't indulge these personal emotions, but I haven't allowed myself any personal emotion for so long . . . Never realized before what an old crock your K.S. is — like a broken down old Lizzie that simply can't take all the grades on the road without snuffing and spluttering and coming to a standstill.

Katharine could not bear to distress me, and by the end of the letter reassured me that she was feeling much better, "started to write and smoke yesterday. So all's well." But weeks later the memory of her family around her returned:

> It seems like a dream, darling! I keep seeing you — everywhere and the house still feels so empty: my heart "a deserted bird's nest filled with snow" . . . My only other visitors have been a flock of black cockatoos, who knocked down some pine cones for me and complained vociferously about the almond tree being so bare. There's something very weird and wild about their shrieking. They only come when storms have driven them this way: but I like them. Wish I could shriek like that when I feel storm driven.

Slowly, the peace and contentment of Greenmount returned. Katharine could still not find the strength to tackle any major work, but she did begin a short story. She was pleased to discover satisfaction in creative work again:

> It's nothing much but I'm like a dog with a bone. Can't leave it when there's something to gnaw at . . . Too conscientious about the use of words, perhaps — and now am more exacting with myself than ever, to get precisely the right values and reactions to every damned one. I'd rather be more slapdash, really. Sprawl and pile up adjectives like D. H. Lawrence. Why not? The meticulous method is quite wrong, I think. One ought to have space to say easily and naturally what is on the carpet. I seem to have been disciplined too much in my writing.

Two more short stories were finished, within the next month; but before the elusive creative impulse could be firmly re-established, Katharine found herself caught up in futile and exhausting litigation which dragged on for two years, destroying all possibility of concentrated work and straining her physical strength and nervous energy.

Mr W. C. Wentworth, then a Government back-bencher in the Commonwealth Parliament, wrote to the *Sydney Morning Herald* on 10 September 1952, replying to Tom Inglis Moore's criticism of his attack on the Commonwealth Literary Fund's award of fellowships to Communist writers. "Now Katherine [*sic*] Susannah Prichard (alias Mrs. Thorsell [*sic*]) is not only a member of the Communist Party in the most exact sense, she is also one of its leading operatives," Mr Wentworth wrote.

Katharine's solicitor, Christian Jollie-Smith, advised her that to imply that her married name was an assumed one, cast doubt on the validity of her marriage and was clearly actionable. Reluctant though she was to face the legal fracas, Katharine thought it necessary to stand up to Wentworth. Christian Jollie-Smith was instructed to issue a writ for libel against him and the *Sydney Morning Herald*.

Miles Franklin responded to the news as only Miles could:

> Katharine me jool,
> What a mess that poor Wentworth has got himself into with the C.L.F. and then to attack you in the S.M.H., you the sacred white cow of all of us (no disrespect but only the highest respect intended), but you must excuse the levity—can't help it in the face of such an ass. I've got to lie low, for Wentworth has me on his roll as a Communist stooge . . . and with *my* alleged *aliases*.

Miles' own suggestion was that I should confront the gentleman on the steps of Parliament House in Canberra, "punch his jaw and tell him to *alias* his mother as Mrs Thorsell!" And another good friend helpfully suggested that if Mrs Throssell was an alias, Ric Throssell was a bastard!

The *Sydney Morning Herald* declined the usual invitation to apologize and the case proceeded. Katharine hesitated to visit Canberra for fear that her presence would be embarrassing. But, case or no case, Katharine had Christmas in Canberra that year, and after the long law vacations, went on to Sydney to discuss the proceedings with Christian Jollie-Smith. She knew it would be foolish to make the trip back to Perth again, so she retreated to her sister's home, "Kirinaran", in Frankston to wait for definite news of the proceedings, travelling, she discovered, under another "alias" as "a first class ladye, with sleeper". Her friends in Sydney had filched her train ticket to make a new booking.

It hardly seemed worthwhile to begin any new work at "Kirinaran", although Katharine had her own room in a wing of the big, white weatherboard house overlooking Port Phillip Bay, surrounded by scrubby bushland with a sweep of open country falling away to the flats and the distant sprawl of suburban Melbourne. All the loving care that Katharine had missed for so long was lavished upon her at "Kirinaran". Bee was determined, that, for once, she must be allowed to spoil her big sister; and Pack, generous, kind-hearted, curmudgeon that he was, was proud to add this celebrated black sheep to the responsibilities of his retirement, over which he delighted in grumbling incessantly. There was a warm affection between such unlikely in-laws as Katharine and Packie. She teased him about his flirtations with the widows and wives of fellow retired gentlemen in Frankston. He solemnly counselled her on the state of tea and rubber shares; baited her with profound political pronouncements: "Great feller, Bob Menzies. Don't know where we'd be without him." And coughing and spluttering with the first roll-your-own cigarette of the morning stuck to his lip, an old pork-pie felt hat on his head and a dressing gown wrapped over his pyjamas, he religiously brought her an early morning mug of stone-cold tea.

As soon as her friends knew she was in Victoria, Katharine was besieged with invitations. She shuttled backwards and forwards between Melbourne and Frankston, for meetings of the Fellowship of Australian Writers and the Peace Council, escaped from "Kirinaran" bridge parties to stay with friends in Melbourne and was touched to find that a reception had been arranged in her honour:

> A reception to your K.S. The place packed, many old friends — writers mostly . . . You've no idea the complimentary things said! Two or three people spoke of your mother's reputation in Europe — how people asked in France and Germany and Poland and Czechoslovakia: "Do you know K.S.?" Frank Hardy told of driving in a peasant cart, about 400 miles from Moscow, and talking about books with the driver. Asked him who he thought was the greatest English writer and he said "Katharine Susannah Prichard". "Who's next?" asked Frank. "Aldridge who wrote *The Diplomat*," said the bloke. And then Frank read a message from Vance. Really most generous and moving, as Vance was to have been chief speaker, and had to go to hospital with another go of coronary trouble.

Katharine managed to do a film synopsis of *The Roaring Nineties;* made some revisions of her play on Deakin; spoke to the Fellowship, and sat for Noel Counihan. Counihan's portrait was a fine character study, full of suffering and visionary distances. But Miles Franklin teased Katharine delightedly when the portrait was exhibited for the Archibald Prize competition. "I'm glad I had the foresight to refuse Dobell's desire to make a taty bogle of me . . . you look as if you had been struggling in the desert among dilly bags for eighty years . . ." she told Katharine gleefully.

Still there was no news of the hearing from Sydney. Katharine fretted at the thought that time was leaving her behind. New books from Vance Palmer, Eleanor Dark, Kylie Tennant, Dymphna Cusack and John K. Ewers in the bookshops reminded her how long it was since there had been anything from Katharine Susannah Prichard, on sale. "I feel I'm wasting so much time," she complained:

> Ordinarily work all day and have letters and reading in the evening. But these days get a little time in the morning and have to spend almost every evening listening to radio serials. Blood and thunder and all sorts of rubbish: in self-defence have learnt to knit! And also made myself a pair of suede gloves. But it's infuriating to lose so much time.

Winter came without any news of the promised hearing. Katharine, accustomed to the mild Western Australian winters, froze. "I try to get a little work done," she wrote, "but it's difficult here. So cold in my room at the end of the house — though I get a hot bottle for my feet and rug-up. Still my fingers freeze, and then my brain seems to freeze also."

Hilda Esson died that winter. Katharine visited her in hospital and felt it was their last meeting:

> Poor darling, so wasted, and knowing now that there is no hope. Tonight they say she is very low, and her doctor thinks it may not be long. You will understand how distressed I am, and yet, for her, there is so little to live for. She felt, I think, that we were seeing each other for the last time. She may not be conscious when I see her again. She said — "Fifty years, it's a long time we've been so close to each other — and you've always been with me in a crisis." It has been a wonderful friendship — so intimate in sympathy, and yet not neurotic or erotic, as so many people imagine friendship between women must be.

They had been friends since their school days, Hilda and Katharine; shared each other's hopes and sorrows; poured out their hearts to each other in long, loving letters. "All the week I have felt the heaviness within, which comes of what I call 'drinking tears'," Katharine grieved when Hilda died a few days after her visit.

Nothing more was heard of the libel case until a year later, when Clive Evatt QC accepted the brief and a preliminary hearing determined that the case would be heard early in 1955. At that time the newspaper won a claim for security of £2500 against costs. By then I had learned a sharp lesson and with empty pockets and a bruised appreciation of the processes of law, advised Katharine to drop the case. "I daresay I'll take your advice," she agreed. "Am just fed up with all the dithering and waste of time."

On 11 February 1956, W. C. Wentworth wrote again to the Editor of the *Sydney Morning Herald:*

> Let me state, therefore, that at no time have I questioned the validity of her marriage to the late Captain Hugo Throssell V.C. I do not intend to qualify or in any way modify the statement I made at the same time that Mrs. Throssell has long been a member of the Communist Party in the most exact sense of the words.

Katharine herself would have been the first to confirm the authenticity of Mr Wentworth's revelation.

The legal wrangles were disposed of when Katharine at last took up again the long-neglected memoirs in January 1956, in the middle of Western Australia's annual, record-breaking heatwave:

> Two days of relief from the terrific heat — though still in the 90's, but with a cool breeze. More promised! It really has been the longest and worst on record. 110^0 and 116^0 in the shade at Greenmount some days — and nearly a fortnight of centuries with nights over 90^0. I took to the bath frequently and managed to write every day. Have made some progress with the "Memoirs", diving chiefly into the history of father's time in Fiji. V. interesting but rather interfering with the straight narrative . . . I'm still not very interested in writing about myself. Dislike the personal pronoun — the "I . . . I . . ." constantly creeping in. It all seems quite puerile and useless! I'd much rather be doing the novel — with "a purpose" I had in mind. Peace, and something really vital about the present situation. But now these wretched biographical notes have been begun, must finish them first, I suppose. It's a bad habit to get into — starting and not finishing things.

Often Katharine was tempted to abandon the memoirs when the physical strength necessary for concentrated creative effort failed her; or when her work for world peace drained her reserves of energy in a never-ending procession of committees and conferences. Again and again, she gave up the attempt to recall that naive young woman who, half a century ago, had set out to become a writer. Time after time, returned to the unfinished work to "clear decks" before tackling the novel which even as she began the autobiography was whispering in her mind.

"Infuriating for the works to play up like this," Katharine complained after a heart attack forced her to stop work on the autobiography and postpone plans for a visit to Europe. She knew that her health and strength would not stand the stress of travel much longer. She wanted to meet the writers in England and Germany and the Soviet Union who had become her friends: Jack Lindsay, Stefan Heym, Boris Polevoi, people who could share her ideals, who knew themselves the solitary world of a writer alone with the creatures of his imagination; friends known only through their letters, who seemed sometimes as unreal as her own characters. Greenmount seemed a very remote backwater when Katharine's mind went out to the world she had known in London and Paris and Moscow. She wanted to see it all again: to share in the excitement of the great peace congresses, where hundreds of men and women like herself who believed that they could put an end to war drew strength from each other's conviction, tasted the joy of working together, knowing that they were not alone in a hostile world.

If ever she travelled again, Katharine knew that it would be physically impossible to go alone. There would have to be someone to help with the frazzle of bookings and luggage. Someone to keep an eye on her if the "works played up". Someone who could share in the pleasure of revisiting old haunts and meeting new friends. Katharine asked Doon Stone if she would go with her to Europe. With translations of her work in Russia, Poland, Czechoslovakia, Rumania, China, Germany and France, Katharine was satisfied it could be done. "Seems as if the tide of my fortunes has changed, darl," she told me:

> £1,300 this week for royalties on the German translation of "R.N." (East Zone). A contract for "Black Opal" in the West Zone will work out at only £90 — which is a practical indication of how the wind is blowing.

Katharine felt rich:

> I'm feeling quite affluent. Such a relief to be able to take a taxi without feeling it and buy books when I want them, though so far I haven't had time, or been well enough to do

> any shopping. But it's been fun writing cheques for things I'm interested in.

Australian passports were invalidated for travel to Communist countries in Eastern Europe and Asia in those days — a defence measure in the ideological conflicts of the Cold War, the Government believed. Katharine decided that she would travel "on business in connection with my literary work". Once in London or Paris, she hoped that there would be no problem in crossing Europe to attend the Stockholm Assembly of the World Council for Peace. But almost as soon as the decision was made, the arrangements were cancelled. "Your lovely letter this week — so full of true understanding. But I do hate to disappoint you," Katharine explained to her friend.

> My doctor came yesterday — I've really had a very bad week — two nasty B.P. turns after the angina attack and in bed most of the time. He says it's out of the question to think of travelling just now for months. The danger, not only my stupid heart, but cerebral haemorrhage — which, of course, means a stroke and worse in the way of mental effects.

Katharine recovered steadily and "rested" by attending meetings of the Peace Council in Perth, and completing an account of her own political development, the only aspects of her past in which she could find sufficient significance to compete with the challenges of the present.

Why I am a Communist was published as a pamphlet later in 1956.[105] Katharine described the experiences of her childhood and youth which had led her to question why some people lived in poverty in the "filthy caves and dreary warrens" which she had seen in Melbourne as a young journalist, while others "whether they worked or not, could live easily and pleasantly squandering riches, and concerned only about their own pleasure and power".

She recalled her discovery of the Fabian Society, Guild Socialism, syndicalism and anarchism through reading and night lectures at the University of Melbourne; the voyages through religion and philosophy, "from Christianity to Rationalism, from Plato, Socrates and Epictetus to Buddhism, Theosophy and Christian Science":

> For ten years I studied these theories, taking each one in turn, discussing them with all manner of people, but committed to none, never a member of any organization; still

> not satisfied that I had found the answer to the questions my mind was asking: still not convinced that any of them offered logical solution to the problem of how the poverty and injustices suffered by so many innocent people could be prevented.

She had wept for the children of the London slums "playing with bits of wood and bone or an old bottle wrapped in dirty rags". Through the *Star* and the *Daily Chronicle,* she started an "Empty Stocking Fund" to bring a Christmas gift to every child of the slums in the years before the First World War. But there was no answer to her questions in charity.

> I talked to writers and politicians, millionaires and hunger marchers, attended lectures, went to meetings, almost despairing that there could ever be any change in a social system designed to preserve the power and privileges of the rich and to keep the working class in subjection.

Katharine told how she had met Russian political exiles in Paris in 1908 and learned of their struggles. "Poor things," she had thought, "how can they give their lives for such a hopeless dream?" Years later, the realization of those revolutionary dreams was an inspiration to her:

> Then crossing Prince's Bridge in Melbourne, one evening, I saw newspaper posters about the revolution in Russia. They were flaring against the sunset. In a moment I remembered those Russian friends I had met in 1908, and realized their dream had come true.

Until that time, Katharine had not heard of Karl Marx or Communism, despite all her "wanderings and searchings". In the writings of Marx and Engels she found the intellectual conviction for which her life had prepared her. Her visit to the Soviet Union confirmed her beliefs. This was her manifesto:

> After more than thirty-five years, my experiences and international affairs have strengthened my belief that Communist theory and practice — education and organization for true Socialism which is the next stage in social progress — can and will create a new era of peace, good living and happiness, not only for Australia, but for the peoples of all countries who unite to fulfil the highest destiny of mankind.

Even when *Child of the Hurricane* was finally completed, Katharine believed that all that was important went into *Why I am a Communist,* where she had spoken directly of the things that had formed her beliefs, without the personal reminiscences and "sweet nothings" she thought necessary to make her autobiography palatable to the general public. But the covering illustration to the pamphlet almost destroyed any pleasure she may have had in this direct statement of personal conviction. Someone had converted Enid Dickson's sensitive portrait into a crude line drawing with staring, empty eyes, a long upper lip and pouting mouth.

> That horrible face on the cover would put anybody off buying it. Do I really look like that? Don't know who did it. I sent a copy of Enid's portrait. Certain the artist had no photograph to go on, and I never sat for that face. My purpose in writing was to speak with sweet reasonableness of Communist theory, but if Coms. look like that hard-faced female, I don't wonder the dear public regards them with apprehension.

Twice more Katharine tried unsuccessfully to arrange the journey abroad. Her health would not allow her to accept an invitation to join the wives and widows of Australian winners of the Victoria Cross on a visit to London at Government expense for the 100th anniversary of the award. She was amused when reporters from the *West Australian* called to inquire why she was not going. Katharine told me:

> One of the reporter blokes asked:
> "Are you a writer Mrs. Throssell?"
> "Oh yes," says she.
> "What do you write?" says he.
> "Oh novels — and things," says she.
> "Do you write about Australia?" says he.
> So good for your K.S. to find she's not as "famous as might be".

With her strength at "one fly power", Katharine was forced to face the fact that she could not stand up to a long trip. "Always my will and mind are ready for much more than physically I can do. That's the worst of it," she apologized.

There were other opportunities, places on delegations to innumerable international conferences of the Left, warm invitations from Soviet writers to rest in their sanitoria, or to join the parties of Australians who each year travelled to the USSR as guests of the Soviet Government. Sometimes, Katharine was tempted to go, but now even a visit to Canberra was unwise. She knew that she would not travel abroad again.

Sorrows pursued her. So many of the small fraternity of Australian writers who were her friends had died: Henry Tate, Frank

Wilmot, Louis and Hilda, Miles Franklin—and now, Hugh McCrae. "Something of its joy has gone out of life with the death of Hugh McCrae," Katharine wrote in the tribute for *Overland,* that now so often seemed her duty.

Between Hugh and Katharine there had been a special understanding. They shared a romantic love of life and love itself. With him, Katharine could be a moth brushing wings; a distant lover in the gentle passion of letters filled with sweet endearments and soft words like kisses:

> There is a word magic in the slightest thing he wrote. Even letters to friends adorned with delicate, waspish drawings, as his thoughts flew to them, are little masterpieces . . . like the wild women of the woods, those of us who were Hugh's friends are burning rue and lamenting that he is dead.[106]

Katharine turned back to her memoirs. Perhaps, as she had found writing *The Wild Oats of Han,* there was some relief in the past from present sorrows, or perhaps the discipline which demanded the completion of work begun, again asserted itself. "Probably the 'memoirs', as much as I'll do of them, will be disposed of by the end of the year," she told me in December, 1958:

> But I'm too dissatisfied with them to think of publication, or even offering them to a publisher. The first person way of writing doesn't please me. I feel too self-conscious all the time, don't lose myself, as I usually do when I'm writing creatively—on an objective framework, at any rate. I'd love to do a new novel next year. It's been germinating a long time, but am afraid to begin something new, when there's so much I ought to tidy up and put in order.

In three months, the first part of the autobiography was completed; but Katharine was still doubtful whether the book would be submitted for publication. "Should get some disinterested opinion, I suppose," she said:

> The only importance of the screed, to give some ideas as to biographical facts . . . As a piece of literature, I feel it is not worthy of K.S. and too personal and unimportant to be of any use, really.

There the memoirs rested for another year.

The Congress for International Peace and Disarmament in Melbourne in November 1959, gave Katharine the inspirational spark that set her mind blazing with the new novel she had dreamed of — and landed her unfortunate memoirs firmly in the discard for another long and uneasy gestation. "Such a wonderful week it's been," she wrote from Melbourne:

> I've enjoyed every minute of it, and been quite well. Meeting old friends, and making some new ones — among them Mulk Raj Anand and Madame Isabella Blume — Mrs. Pauling too, though I wasn't able to attend meetings the Professor addressed, having to be on sessions of the writers' conference. However the Congress has been a splendid success, despite attempts to discredit it. You had only to hear the prolonged cheers and applause on the last night to realize that — besides the fact that there were 1,244 delegates representing 500 organizations.

Katharine began work on the new novel as soon as she returned to Greenmount. It was as if she had flung off the depression of the fifties and found fresh resolution in the beginning of a new decade. She worked regularly throughout 1960 and by the end of the year had even found time to tidy up some of the autobiography.

The first part of *Child of the Hurricane* was despatched towards the end of 1961 and Katharine was more dismayed than pleased to find that Angus and Robertson wanted her to complete the work. "Lorna[107] has typed Part II of the 'Memoirs'," Katharine wrote to tell me in April, 1962:

> She says she found them "fascinating". When I said I felt like burning the lot, she was quite hot and bothered on the 'phone. "Don't you dare," she said, which I suppose is a compliment, though I'm not at all sure I'll leave them for posterity. Think I'll write and ask Beatrice to return m.s. and photos if there's no definite proposition about publication.

She was relieved, all the same, when Beatrice Davis wrote to assure her that Angus and Robertson did want to publish the *Child*. The typescript was packed up and posted in sheer desperation, I suspect, to get it finally off her hands:

> I'm thoroughly disgusted and fed up with this m.s. I'll be glad to get rid of it — only wish I'd never started on the document. It tells too much and not enough of your K.S. Ending with marriage, and not giving the more important and mature development of my life. Don't suppose I'll ever have time to write — the end. Do forgive me darl, if it disappoints you. It's true enough as far as it goes — but doesn't go far enough, I feel.

> I'm much more interested to get on with *Subtle Flame* — the novel I embarked on a year ago — and which would be more vital with relation to life today, and the things that matter.

Never before had Katharine written "finis" to a work with which she was so dissatisfied; never had she been so relieved to be free of the thing. But when the familiar incubus of the last twelve years had been despatched, something seemed to be missing:

> I've been feeling quite lonely without *Child of the Hurricane* but gave myself some lazy days this week. As if to console me, some "kind friend" dropped a kitten, which I didn't want, over the gate. It's the umpteenth that's been donated in this way.

Katharine was not quite free of her unwanted "Child". She welcomed the careful, detached, editorial comments of Beatrice Davis and Douglas Stewart: rearranged chapters; gladly accepted the suggestion that a fuller description of the winning of the Victoria Cross be included; rewrote the brief introductory remarks on the days of her married life in Greenmount for the concluding pages of the book, and even acknowledged meekly enough Douglas Stewart's discreet suggestion that "raw whisky" might not be an appropriate description of the colour of her first love's eyes. "Delete raw," Katharine replied. "I meant whisky before water is added. Didn't know the raw spirit isn't brown."

Child of the Hurricane was in the bookshops before Katharine's eightieth birthday. She was as surprised and delighted as if it had been her first novel when strangers stopped her in the streets of Midland Junction, the small railway town at the foot of the Darling Ranges, to say "well done"; overwhelmed by a reception in Perth for the opening of Australian Book Week, "with the Lord Mayor presiding and herself, guest of honour, saying a few words". "A really exciting occasion," Katharine told me:

> Cables from all my publishers in congratulation, and presentation of a lovely red morocco letter case adorned with gardenias . . . I paid tribute to all the other writers in the West today, with special mention of Prof. Murdoch who had come to the gathering — looking rather frail, but pleased to hear my remarks as to his inspiration to young writers of his day.

Since she was herself so dissatisfied with the book, Katharine could hardly have been surprised when the reviewers generally found *Child of the Hurricane* disappointing; but now that her once-despised infant faced the "dear public", she took it, tentatively, to her heart. "Of course, if I had introduced a few obscene incidents the critics would have been better pleased!" Katharine responded, and was a little bewildered to find that *Child of the Hurricane* was more popular in Australia than any of her books except *Coonardoo.*

"I suppose she does seem 'sadly old fashioned', when you compare the K.S. biography with Hal Porter . . . However I couldn't write with a snarl about my early days . . ." Katharine concluded when she read Dorothy Hewett's tribute to "The Girl in the White Muslin Dress":

> This book, refracted through the mind of an eighty year old woman, has all the luminous, ardent glow, the exaltation of the young in the great morning of life, the great adventure when there were strange affinities between man and woman, even a girl and a horse.
>
> She dares to write tenderly, romantically, from the heart, when this kind of tenderness is considered sadly old fashioned.
>
> This is what gives her book its warmth, its translucent quality, and its rich simplicity. It is a great affirmation of life, but we are conscious of the transience of youth and loveliness, and the golden boys and girls of that far off Victorian summer of the heart have a deeper sweetness because we know they have gone forever.[108]

CHAPTER 19

NO WREATH IS WORTHY

Peace was Katharine's Promethean flame. She was seventy-seven years old when inspiration gathered into the determination to write her last novel. She had been thirty-three when she joined the anti-conscription cause during the second referendum in 1917. She, too, had been torn by the doubts and indecision which divided the Australian people when, in 1916, the Government first sought a mandate to conscript men for service in the Great War.

Katharine voted in favour of conscription in the first referendum. Both her brothers were on active service: Alan was in France; Nigel had not been heard of since the retreat from Serbia. "If recruits were needed, I thought, they would help to bring the war to an end", Katharine recalled. In her notebook, she described impressions of an anti-conscription meeting in the streets of Fitzroy:

> The crowd had gathered round an up-turned cart. A lantern was hanging from one of the shafts. There was a table for speakers to stand on. The entrance to Bird Street was thronged even when we arrived ten minutes before the speakers were timed to talk . . .
>
> Then the anti-conscription fellowship speaker arrived. The sweat poured down his face. A slight, mean-faced man, with the air of a racing tipster, he talked in a husky voice with an earnestness that shook his meagre frame in its shop-made, gingery brown clothes. And his breath, reaching across the crowd as he talked, in great gusts, blew a breath of beer with it and a shower of spray like fine rain.
>
> > "Friends," he said . . . "It's the first time in the history of the whole world that a people have been asked to vote themselves into conscription. In every other country it has been forced on the workers. But this — the passing of the Referendum will mean that democracy will put the shackles on itself. It's like breaking into Hell — and staying there."

> And over all the clear night sky, thick with stars. The warm still night. A pittosporum in blossom was scenting the air. Those same stars gazing down on the battle-fields of the Marne and Somme. What battles were blazing there — and here?

Letters from Alan describing the blunders that sent men needlessly to be torn apart in the filth of the Ypres battlefield, and the promise of her editor's son to "put on the gloves" with him when he came home if his father voted for conscription, persuaded Katharine that the soldiers themselves were opposed to it. The casual remark of a politician promising to get rid of unionists to the front-line trenches convinced her that her Socialist friends were right in believing that conscription would be used as a political device to break the trade unions. Censorship of anti-conscription views and the prosecution of anti-conscriptionists roused her. Katharine's doubts were over. She offered her services to the anti-conscription campaign. It was the first step in a lifetime's commitment to militant political action. "People of Australia, think for yourselves! . . ." her statement submitted to the Censor's Office in Melbourne proclaimed:

> Conscription, at this period of the war, I believe, is anti-Australian whatever else it may or may not be. It is . . . the last hope of desperate politicians of the conservative party . . . Their aims are political; they are seeking, ultimately, cheap labour and a spiritless working class; they are out after the bones of our industrial organizations, although they wear the sheep's clothing of patriotism dyed the Imperial purple.

The statement was passed by the Censor with a cautionary endorsement rubber stamped across the page warning that "the Censorship takes no responsibility for the publication of any political matter contained in these proofs". Katharine wryly added the comment, "The Press said 'No' ".

When Alan was killed, the steel entered Katharine's own heart:

> I hated the war bitterly and furiously . . . I could never forgive, or forget, intrigues which led to the armaments firms acquiring profits Lloyd George described as "of astronomical proportions" while the war brought disastrous hardships to the men fighting and nothing but sorrow to millions of their families.

The necessity to act was as much a part of her as love of beauty and life. A wrong recognized must be opposed, combated to the end and defeated. There could be no meek acceptance, no submissive martyrdom, no futile acknowledgement of inevitable evil.

The victory of the anti-conscription campaign was not enough. Fervently, Katharine searched for answers to the horrifying madness of war:

> I realized that my brother was only one of over ten million men killed in the war, and that many millions of men had been maimed, blinded, disabled as a result of war injuries. I was only one of millions of men and women who with rage and grief began to ask themselves: What are the causes of war?

She found her answers in socialism:

> Most of us who made a serious study of war, its causes and effects, emerged with the conviction that, as Professor Laski of the London School of Economics affirmed "its main causes lie in the economic field".
>
> It is no longer denied that the causes of war in modern times are to be found in the struggle for sources of wealth, spheres of influence and markets. The seeds of war, therefore, are contained in the economic system under which we live.[109]

Hugo Throssell VC, her own Jim, was her first and most devoted convert. Among the press cuttings describing the exploits of Western Australia's first VC, I found in the *Northam Advertiser* of 23 July 1919, the account of his statement to the startled people of Northam:

> Captain Throssell, V.C., who received an enthusiastic reception, in thanking the people for the warm welcome, said it was good to be back in old Northam again and receive dozens of warm-hearted hand shakes. He made humorous references to his exploits on the football ground and in the arena of the ring and, then becoming intensely earnest, said during the past five years he had seen much of the world. They had known him as a sort of irresponsible lad, but he claimed now to be a man. Nearly five years ago he had ridden through the streets of Northam in charge of eighteen men, who were amongst the first to enlist. With him were the late Harry Eaton and the speaker's brother Eric. Of that eighteen, seven were lying either in Gallipoli, Palestine or France. His hearers would realise the feeling within him when greeted by happy faces on his welcome home. War had made him a Socialist . . . He had seen enough of the horrors of war and wanted peace.

Katharine knew what would happen. She went around all her young nieces and nephews before the parade. "Remember to give Uncle Jim a big cheer when he makes his speech," she told them. It seemed a bit funny to the youngsters. Of course they would clap like mad for Uncle Jim, anyway. They did — while the good people of Northam listened in shocked silence.

No one could believe then that the insanity of the Great War could ever be repeated. It was not until the rise of Fascism in Europe that world peace again became Katharine's primary political concern. "Jim attended with me the first meeting of a Peace Council formed in Perth," Katharine wrote in ***Child of the Hurricane***:

> When Henri Barbusse and Romain Rolland wrote asking me to help with organization, in Australia, of the Movement against War and Fascism which had been inaugurated at Amsterdam, Jim supported the movement.

But only in her memory was he there, rising from his seat to glare at interjectors when she spoke during the appeals for Spanish Relief. By that time he had died, destroyed, Katharine believed, by a system that had trained him only for war. Katharine fought on without him, unrelenting in the pressures she placed upon herself, insistent in her demands on others.

Fascism she now saw as the threat to peace. Katharine quoted Mussolini's boast, "Fascism is War, and War is Fascism", to an audience of miners in Boulder in 1937; taunted them with Hitler's glib assurance, "Who ever really desires the victory of pacifist thought must give his whole hearted support to the German conquest of the world". "Are you afraid to fight for yourselves?" she challenged them:

> It is said men like a fight. Well, this is the greatest fight in all history we're involved in now. The fight for the right of humanity to grow and to progress; a fight against fascism and reaction. If ever there was a worth while fight it is this one, and every man and every woman ought to be into it, doing their utmost to out-wit fascism at every turn.

Armed aggression by Italy, Japan and Germany and the failure of the League of Nations gave new urgency to her pleas for "practical and resolute action":

> To indulge in sentimental theorizing will lead us nowhere. Pacifism, pure and simple, offers no obstacle to fascist aggression. It would not have helped the people of Abyssinia, China, Austria, Spain or Czechoslovakia. The policy of

> appeasement has been tried and proved a failure . . . To be sure, the amiable suggestion of an English archbishop that it would be a friendly gesture to offer the north of Australia to Japan, has not been acted upon; but if other peoples have been offered as sops to Cerberus why should we complain about being digested at leisure.

On the brink of war, Katharine poured all her passion into the effort to stir the Australian people into realizing that they could no longer watch placidly while Fascism overwhelmed them:

> If we have to fight, let it be for all that makes life worth living. For those who would serve the progress of humanity, to those who are opposed to war, for those who know that the preservation and development of democratic rights is the people's first line of defence in the struggle for peace, for those who value all that is most lovely in blossoming of the mind and spirit, there is no way but the defeat of fascism . . .
>
> It is false to say that war calls forth the highest energy of the human spirit. The struggle for peace and the defence of the living rights of the people calls for much greater integrity, self-sacrifice, physical and intellectual heroism. It demands an everyday, consistent, life-long activity against ignorance, apathy, and that "honest obliquity of understanding" which obstructs social advancement.
>
> The worm's way, of course, is to feed and breed; not bother about historic crises which determine the fate of mankind. But all of us who are in any way sensitive instruments for expression of the people's joys and sorrows, all of us who value our right of expression, knowledge, sanity and service, must realize the great need there is for us, today, to work for the preservation and development of democracy and international organization to ensure effective bases for world peace.[110]

Through all the shifts and turns in international affairs before the outbreak of World War II, and during the so-called "phoney war", Katharine held to two principles: Fascism must be destroyed; socialism in Russia must not be defeated. She followed the contortions and manoeuvres of Soviet foreign policy and was able to accept them on the basis of those two principles, believing that, out of the chaos and confusion of war, the ultimate hope of peace lay in socialism.

Katharine's enemies accused her of slavishly following the Moscow line, cynically betraying the ideals of peace, which she had herself pretended, by supporting aggression against Finland, Poland and the Baltic States in the Communist interest. "Do not think, as someone said recently, my spiritual home is the Soviet Union," Katharine told an Australia-Soviet Friendship Rally. "It is not. My spiritual home is the land I love, Australia, among my own people."

Victory over the Axis powers and the glowing gift of the Four Freedoms enshrined in the Atlantic Charter promised the peace that a war-weary world yearned for. Russian and American soldiers shook hands at the Rhine. Allied forces together occupied Berlin. Japan fell to the atomic bomb. But even while the stench of death was still in the air, the old animosities stirred again. From the bomb-shattered ruins of Berlin, I wrote in 1945 describing how one of my travelling companions in the occupation hostel, a Baroness rejoining her husband at an allied embassy in Moscow, had told me that the British and American Armies should have pushed on from the Rhine, defeated the Russians, still weakened by war, and destroyed Communism while there was time. That noblewoman, with her rings and her *real politik*, amid the desert of rubble that had been Berlin, with the millions of dead around her, was not alone in believing that the war had ended too soon.

Katharine realized that her own battles would go on after the last bomb had fallen. Fascism had been defeated. The Preamble to the Charter of the United Nations proclaimed the determination of the people "to save succeeding generations from the scourge of war"; but peace, she believed, would depend upon making that determination real. When an Australian poet wrote pleading that the "soldiers must return to the simple things, in the warm, work-aday world that once they knew", Katharine replied:

> Let us have done
> with simple things
> and dare to soar into the future
> on strenuous wings,
> made strong with their example:
> match their most gallant deeds
> with ours,
> to win a way of life
> for peace and justice,
> for joy and beauty,
> all may share . . .
>
> No wreath
> is worthy of our dead,
> or those heroic men
> who go through hell

across the starry skies,
upon the sea,
through jungle slime
and desert sand,
to battle now,
that we may live—
No wreath is worthy, I believe,
but this, the vow we give:
to work and fight
for the new world we promised them.[111]

Peace had never been a mere abstraction to Katharine, a word, an idea tossed about for a political purpose. To her, peace meant all those things she loved in life, "all the great things of loving and working"; the beauty she had found in this land, Australia: "the broad and quiet river, mirroring trees—those great white stanchions of the karri, like organ pipes for winds to blow their storm themes on—and shadowy backwaters where wild swans breed . . . the fertile distances of pasture lands, over which the shadows of clouds march, sapphire and indigo, after rain . . . the blue backs of hills like prehistoric monsters: red earth of the goldfields, torn by the shimmering wraiths of salt lakes and dead rivers . . . sand plains in springtime woven with wildflowers pink, yellow, saffron, purple, blue and scarlet . . ."[112]

Peace meant the joy she had known in living: Jim shouting the "Appassionata" against the wind; the memory of loquat blossom and his love; a small head against her breast, "the little V.C. of her bosom"; the contentment of work well done, the satisfaction of "doing your damndest"—and knowing it was good. The simple things, too: wine, good talk, laughter, the perfume of flowers in the garden; the song of birds in the morning; music to shout with; music to die to; the comradeship of friends striving together for a world in which the good things of life could be shared by all people.

Just four years after the most destructive war in human history, Katharine again put on the harness of the peace campaign. "Nothing can be more worthwhile for those of us who realize the barbarism of war than to give all our energy to avert the danger now threatening humanity," Katharine told the Congress of Writers for Peace in Melbourne in November 1949.

The icy fires of the Cold War were like a fever in those days; the annihilation of humanity by nuclear war a possibility so real to many that fear became part of their lives. War was unthinkable —and peace, the seditious slogan of the Communist front. To others the atomic bomb was a spur to active protest. Men and women who had been content to stand aside, joined the peace movement, prepared to risk the "Red" label rather than see the world drift into the agony of atomic warfare without raising their voices against it.

The Peace Conference held in Melbourne in April 1950 drew thousands of delegates, when Dr Hewlett Johnson, the Dean of Canterbury, spoke. "The work has been strenuous, but thrilling . . ." Katharine told me.

> Talking to ten thousand with the Dean and an American professor who is the most accomplished speaker I've ever heard. The old boy v. charming and gentle, sacerdotal, but valiant, and adored by all who heard him. The American, forceful but speaking quietly, with delightful dry humour. My little bit went over the air quite clearly, and t'is said, was not unworthy of the distinguished company in which it found itself . . . But I've been talking nearly every night this week and was very glad to flop into bed when I could. Today is to be one heavenly day of do nothing.

Stirring the enthusiasms of her own people in the West was a tougher proposition. Katharine gathered those few to whom peace had meaning greater than the risk of dismissal or the name of "fellow-traveller". Together they assailed the kindly, comfortable people of Perth. Katharine reported:

> Presiding at the Peace Conference on Sunday. Don't feel equal to the job—but there's nobody else, so I've got to make an effort. Am really fitter now, though—and at any rate can't endure the thought of rusting out.

From the Chair she explained the difficulty of organizing in Western Australia, because people were "scared to work for peace". She taunted, pleaded, begged for their help. Tried to convince them that there was something they could do, that they were not helpless to drift in the war tides of the world:

> Imagine it, scared to work for peace? What have they to be more terrified and horrified by than the threat of another war? . . .
>
> I do beg of you to realize what it means to be a stooge . . . Help us . . . and you can do that. You can talk to your friends . . . Nothing matters so much as for you to work to save yourselves, Australia and the Australian people from the horrors, from the crime against humanity which another world war would be.[113]

Unremittingly, year after year, through the endless ebb and flux in world affairs, in the face of the disaster of the Korean War, the hideous threat of the hydrogen bomb, the interminable negotiations of Panmunjom, Katharine poured her energy into the movement for peace, though she "dreaded the strain of long meetings". She spent her own strength ruthlessly. Despite promises to treat herself "as a cracked egg-shell", she tramped the streets of Fremantle canvassing signatures for the Peace Appeal:

> Found the people mostly willing to sign after a few sweet words. Only 15 of us did an hour in the morning and 3 an hour in the afternoon — and we got 260 signatures. A hot day, and I got very tired: heart began to jab, so I had to stop. But the thousands of names must impress a Government. Nearly 600 million now, is the world figure . . . There were a few snags of course! And I left them to their snagginess if they were very. Though usually, even they responded when I said, "My husband was Hugo Throssell V.C. and he said no man who had ever seen his mates killed, dying in agony would ever want to let anyone he cared for, son or brothers or friends suffer in the same way."

The end of the Korean War, Kruschev's amiable advances to the West and the conclusion of the Geneva Agreement on Indochina brought a brief glimpse of peace to the world. "What a joy it is to be in such harness!" Hewlett Johnson wrote to Katharine on 12 March 1955. "Personally I believe we are on the brink of a new era . . . God's cause always triumphs nor does he ever forget those who fall by the way: with him is no loss."

In September 1955, the National Organizing Secretary of the Australian Peace Council, Stephen Murray-Smith, wrote to say that Katharine had been accepted as the seventh Australian member of the World Council for Peace. It was both recognition and challenge to her. But the Anglo-French seizure of the Suez Canal and Russian intervention in Hungary blighted the hopes of 1955: the rapprochement in Europe dissolved, and the world saw again the shape of steel behind the mirage of peace. "Until this Canal business blew up, I thought we were making good way for prohibition of the atom bomb. Now goodness knows what madness may be cooking," Katharine mourned.

Her own plans to visit Europe cancelled, Katharine prepared for another desperate journey. A fleet of small ships prepared to sail from Japan into the Christmas Island atom bomb test area, as a gesture of protest. A British Quaker couple, Mr and Mrs Steele, announced their intention of joining the "peace fleet". Katharine decided that she, too, should go, even though she believed that the gesture was ill-advised. "Nothing can be more important than peace," she had told her audiences. To let others offer their lives while she stood aside would discredit her sincerity, make a mockery of the sacrifices she had demanded. Aileen Palmer's announcement that she was joining the peace fleet resolved Katharine's doubts. In a press statement explaining her decision she declared:

> I feel that it is my duty to support any effort to stop further tests of atom and hydrogen bombs . . . Already the injurious effects of radio-active material on the life of men, animals and fish have been recorded . . . This appalling danger confronts not only living people, but the generations unborn — if we fail to stop the criminal madness of these tests. They constitute a crime against humanity.[114]

She had no illusions of merciful incineration in the flash of the bomb. Slow death from radiation sickness was the purgatory the peace fleet invited — and Katharine was afraid:

> So far not a word about what's happening re the trip to Christmas Island. Needless to say I'm not looking forward to it and hope it doesn't happen. But I feel I had to offer to go — expected there would be some arrangements and organization. But nothing is being done about the affair, it seems. I don't really feel equal to the ordeal, but was prepared for it — even as a last gesture for peace.

It made more sense to Katharine to live for peace than to die for it. She was relieved when the whole proposition was abandoned and she was free to continue the search for peace in the way she had chosen: the long, hard way; the way of words and persuasion; the way lit by the conviction that some day there would be no more war.

The World Council's silver medallion for services to peace was awarded to Katharine at the Congress on International Co-operation and Disarmament in Melbourne, in 1959. She had herself chaired the writers' committee, and surprised former comrades with her firmness in countering moves to make the meeting a platform for attacks on Soviet intervention in Hungary. "You forget my Communist steel," Katharine reminded them. She agreed to have the Peace Medal "presented" again at a dinner in Perth six months later, to raise funds for the Peace Council in Western Australia, though she said that she would "just as soon not have to face the event".

But Katharine loved those occasions during the last ten years of her life when friends gathered to show her their affection and admiration, heaped bouquets of flowers upon her, showered her with the gracious compliments of public tribute to her work for literature and peace, made her the centre of their attention. Always she dressed for the part, although an evening dress was expected to last for five or six years. A new one was bought, or made to her own design by friends, at the cost of great persuasion: black or brown velvet, closely fitted, with a spray of red roses pinned at the shoulder, and the black fur cape that Annette Aarons had given her, accepted only on the understanding that it was to be used "by any young comrade who might need it for a special night out".

Katharine glowed like a girl in the excitement and pleasure of her friends' attention: gay, laughing, almost coquettish, in her response to their courtesies. And when the causes she cherished could benefit too, she accepted their generosity with good conscience and endured the ordeal of a speech, always quite unrepentantly "putting in a few words for peace". "It really was a wonderful evening," Katharine wrote when Professor Walter Murdoch presented the Peace Medal:

> Everybody seemed to enjoy the gathering and the meal. Including "the Murdoch buddy" as students used to call him in my days at the Melbourne University. He was very charming, said all sorts of nice things about your K.S. and so did Hew Roberts . . . Me in my glamour robes — the brown velvet I wore when I was speaking in Canberra — with roses and huge presentation bouquet. Afterwards various folk assured me I spoke well. "It was the speech of the evening" several people said. So at least, I didn't disgrace you, darl. Murdoch was in good vein, his easy manner and natural whimsical way with an audience, I do envy. I'm always too serious, I think. Financially the party was a success too — which is a comfort. Clem[115] worked terrifically hard to make it so — among other things, cadged, plucked and cleaned 40 chickens for the event. How's that as a gesture for Peace?

She was less directly involved in organizational work in the later years, but still attended the meetings of the Peace Council in Perth for as long as her physical strength allowed, discussed plans and activities over sherry on the veranda at Greenmount, or by the open fire in the lounge-room on wintry Sundays, when members of the Committee called to seek her advice or support. She told a meeting of young people:

> Those of us who have grown old in the struggle for peace, and who have worked strenuously for years to safeguard the young people of our country from the dangers of atomic war plead with you now to help us.
>
> I love youth. I love the beauty and strength of young lives, and to see them growing to maturity with courage and intelligence. Not standing aside, and trying to escape thought about serious matters which affect their lives, but giving their energy and enthusiasm to a great purpose.

Katharine herself stood outside the cinemas in Perth distributing "Ban the Bomb" leaflets to the crowds after the screening of *On the Beach;* at seventy-eight rode on the Peace Council float in the Labour Day procession through Perth; joined the tail-end of the Committee for Nuclear Disarmament march from Fremantle to Perth; collected signatures for a petition for a nuclear-free zone in the southern hemisphere; wrote inexhaustibly to the correspondence columns of the daily press condemning nuclear tests; met the international celebrities of the world peace movement, Priestley, Pauling, Sybil Thorndike, Paul Robeson, and to some gave the devotion of a comrade-in-arms: "I went down to the airport for arrival of the plane on Wednesday night," she explained, describing Robeson's arrival.

> There was a tremendous crowd to greet him, the biggest ever seen there — with banners and bouquets. I was supposed to make a speech of welcome on behalf of the Peace Council. And it was so funny, at the exact moment when I started on my remarks with a milling crowd all round, a huge female dashed between me and Paul, and hurled herself against Mrs. Robeson in a frantic embrace. I was so agitated that I couldn't continue; but he just removed the large female and said in the gentlest kindest way imaginable: "She's trying to make a speech of welcome". After which I was able to go on with my remarks. He really is a wonderful person, darl. No man I've ever met has so impressed me with his personal greatness. He's so simple and unaffected in manner, so dignified, yet straightforward and uncompromising in what he says. The voice — even when he speaks is deeply moving, but it's the man himself, I think, who demonstrates the greatness of the human spirit. He has overcome so much to become what he is, but remains sweet natured: a powerful intelligence and passion in the songs and speeches which require them.

Growing old gracefully was not part of Katharine's plan. She detested the limitations that the years imposed upon her activities. After her eightieth birthday she wrote:

> Awful to think of being such an antique, but I can't believe I've really accumulated so many years. If only I didn't get so tired and have to rest so much, I'd feel somebody'd made a mistake in their arithmetic. I can't actually be so old! But when I saw that awful photo in "Forty-two Faces", I realized it must be true, though don't often look so famine-stricken. Hetherington must have got a snap shot at a party, I think.

Even when the weight of the years and sorrows pressed upon her and she began to feel "as old as the great-grandmother of Methuselah"; when she doubted the worth of anything she had written and knew again the desolation of loneliness after the brief joy of my visits to Greenmount with the children — even then the flame of her dedication remained, flickering perhaps in the reluctant tears of her weariness:

> When I weigh up the values, that seems the most important — to have had a taste of personal happiness with people we love. Fame, for what it is worth, doesn't give it. I suppose it means something to have achieved what you set out to do, but, my own, what there is of it, seems flat and stale now. Service of the great ideals remains something which cannot be ignored. There'd be no self-respect if it were; but I sometimes wonder whether I've been stupidly idealistic — for such a confirmed materialist. Though the materialism of Marxism does not mean a rejection of great ideals, rather an intensification of service to them.

Her private assessment of the impact of the peace movement in Australia, in fact, was more soberly realistic than she admitted in public; but the knowledge that little could be expected in immediate results did not shake her belief that, in the long run, people could be roused; nor did she allow her own realization that there would be no changes in Australian Government policy to dampen the determination of others. "Clem will be going to Canberra for presentation of the petition to Parliament," she wrote in 1962:

> But I can't hope that it will make much difference to the official position. In the end, resistance of the people to the testing and use of nuclear weapons will be effective, I believe. But a lot more pressure is needed for the desired result. In Great Britain, at least, the movement is having some effect; and politicians are beginning to consider public opposition.

The triumphs, few though they were, became her own triumphs. She was elated by the signing of the Test Ban Treaty by Great

Britain, America and the USSR, but remained apprehensive of "measures which may be taken to frustrate the detente it promises". Each reverse to the causes she supported was a personal disaster. As Labor was defeated again and again in the Federal elections, she grieved for the dashed hopes of men she admired, and the failure of the electorate to understand the choices offered to them. Dr H. V. Evatt personified for her the fall of the Australian Labor Party's hopes in the twenty years that she knew of its political exile between 1949 and 1969. "I feel so distressed for Dr. Evatt," she wrote, when for the last time, he led his Party to electoral defeat. "He put up such a good fight, and it's deplorable to realize that his great qualities have not been appreciated."

A few years later, when Evatt died in retirement, his brilliant mind destroyed by a stroke, she regretted that she had not written to him in his decline to tell him how she honoured him for his influence in the Labor movement. Earlier, when he had faced enemies within his own Party and the screaming hostility of the press, she had sent him the last lines of Shelley's "Prometheus Unbound", acknowledging his courage and integrity:

> To suffer woes which Hope thinks infinite;
> To forgive wrongs darker than death or night;
> To defy Power, which seems omnipotent;
> To love and bear; to Hope till Hope creates
> From its own wreak the thing it contemplates,
> Neither to change, nor falter, nor repent;
> This, like thy glory, Titan, is to be good,
> Great and joyous, beautiful and free;
> This is alone life, Joy, Empire and Victory.

Katharine gave her homage to a great Australian, a man whose moral courage raised him, in her mind, above their political differences:

> As a last tribute, I like to think I hailed him as a Titan who had bestowed the largesse of his mind and spirit on the Australian people. He had enhanced their prestige and authority in national and international affairs. It is seldom that a statesman of Evatt's stature has been accorded such scant honour in his own country. He was imbued with the same practical idealism as Deakin and defeated by the failure of his generation to realize it.[116]

Labor's defeat in the 1966 election, fought largely on the issue of conscription for the war in Vietnam, shocked and dismayed her. She told me:

> So many people have just been stunned with the verdict of the people. It's difficult to believe "Vox Dei — Vox Populi".
>
> The Australia I knew and loved, is passing away — if it hasn't already passed. The Australia the men of the 90's fought for — and Eureka resistance to oppression symbolized. The traditional Australian refusal to accept methods of coercion — the struggle for adult suffrage, trade union organization, democratic rights — all seem to have been forgotten by the present generation of voters, who vote for the conscription of youth and seem satisfied for a greater number of Australian young men to be the victims of this criminal war in Vietnam —
>
> Sorry darl, I can't think of anything but the shame and disappointment I feel at the moment.

But Katharine continued to believe that the voice of the people could change events. She insisted that the mobilization of popular opinion for peace could become effective. In a statement on the war in Vietnam issued not long before her death, Katharine said:

> Ultimately, maybe, the voice of humanity, men and women of every nation, united in a roar from millions of throats thundering condemnation, will force the Government of the U.S.A., and its allies, to end the agony of the Vietnamese people.

It was in this belief that she wrote *Subtle Flame:*

> to make the masses of kindly, inert people, understand what is at stake for their homes and children — if they do not exert themselves in the interests of organization for international disarmament and peace.

CHAPTER 20

SUBTLE FLAME

Dark Power lurking in my life
Be thou my glory or my shame
Come thou with flowers or with the knife
O smite my life to subtle flame.

— Christopher Brennan

"You'll be pleased to hear I've started on the new novel . . . have been writing in my sleep even," Katharine wrote to me in May 1960. She did not expect to inspire a peace revolution with her words, as Tom Paine had once fired the imagination and hearts of the American revolutionaries, but perhaps to stir some spark of understanding in the "masses of kindly, inert people", to share with them some of her "passionate faith in the grail of world peace". Distasteful though she found the propagandist label with which she had been tagged by press and university critics in the fifties, she would not be deterred from tackling the subject of peace; but she knew that peace must be in the heart of her characters: it must grow in their minds as it had in her own. She did not mean to preach to the converted, but to woo the uncommitted, and kindle their spirits with her own fire.

True to the method she had developed in earlier work, Katharine found her fictional characters in real-life models. Her central situation was based upon actual events, although both people and events were re-created in new moulds, fashioned to the form of her life-design. Some, I knew. I could trace the threads of reality in the make-believe life Katharine gave them. Others were might-have-been wraiths of old friends.

> This man is a very complex character, a man in his own time, suddenly awake to a life he has lived automatically, without considering its deeper issues. Don't know whether I will be able to re-create him satisfactorily. Feel it's the biggest subject I've tackled, and not likely to be popular. But I can't consider that. It's a thing I want to do — if only I

> have strength enough and sufficient literary ability. It's an exhausting job — and obsessing me, damn it!

There were in fact three models for the character of David Evans, I learnt later; and, I suspect, some memories of her own father.

It would have been impossible for her to explore a new setting. There would be no time for her usual painstaking research. She could not afford now the slow process of absorbing the feel and sound of the parliamentary circle she had touched on in her play on the life of Alfred Deakin[117]; or the steel industry, womb of war and of the tools of peace, which had once intrigued her in Sydney. She must work from existing knowledge; draw on the store of life's experience.

Katharine found her setting in the familiar world of journalism: her father's world; the world which had left him without work, broken and disillusioned, haunted by the emptiness of his mind; the world in which she had herself learned the "rush and clamour" of the newspaper offices, the rattle of typewriters and "the cross currents" of telephones, the "musty, fusty breath" of the reporters' room, the "chirring and clicking of teletypes as they carried on their incessant gossip from overseas".

From these memories Katharine could create her journalist hero with intimate knowledge of the man, his work and the city in which he lived: the familiar triad of her creative method, with the new dimension a conscious search for the significance of life.

Her story required the close-packed space of the city, the hurrying tempo of the presses, the alleyways and back-streets of life's "struggle for existence". It was a scene out of place in the quiet seclusion of Perth, and Katharine explained:

> I have left the West spiritually and returned to Melbourne and the Dandenong Ranges, for the time, surroundings in which I grew up and which were familiar to me as a girl.

The central figure of her story, David Delane Evans, was to be a man whose life had already been set in the contemporary mould of success: comfortably middle-aged, at the peak of his profession, respected by his colleagues, absorbed in his control of the complex machine of a daily newspaper; loved and admired by his children, accepting the undemanding companionship of his wife; unconcerned by the forsaken ideals of his youth. In this man's mind, Katharine determined to kindle the flames of conscience, consuming all that his life had been. His was not the innate, unformed philosophy of Michael Brady, leader of the opal miners of

Fallen Star Ridge; the conviction of Mark Smith, strike organizer of the timber workers; the patient, lifelong search of the working miner, Tom Gough, nor the inherited purpose of his adopted son, Bill. To David Evans, commitment was to come with the cataclysmic, emotional violence of conversion.

The Korean War was Katharine's catalyst of disaster and redemption. The story opens with the death of David's son in Korea. Under the impact of tragedy, he looks again at his life; takes upon himself the guilt of public apathy and ignorance and his son's unthinking enlistment in a foreign war. David Evans resigns from the editorship of the *Daily Despatch,* disgusted with the compromises his success has led him to, dissatisfied with being the "faithful servant of the company" and determined to "write the truth as he found it". Through David Evans' pilgrimage in search of a way to reach the hearts of his fellow men, Katharine told her story of a man who became a torchbearer of peace, as she had been.

Two streams of Katharine's life joined in *Subtle Flame,* logically, inevitably: her writing, the craft that had given her livelihood, reputation and fulfilment, and her quest for peace, the unyielding labour toward "a world without war". Both flowed together in the story of the successful journalist who became a "worker in the cause of peace".

Katharine was fond of quoting Sean O'Faolain's saying: "It is not the subject that a man writes. It is himself." *Subtle Flame* was not autobiographical. Katharine's own political awakening and her career as a writer were completely different from those of her character, David Evans. But in a situation which was so close a parallel to her own most vital interests in life, it was not surprising that, as in the case of *Intimate Strangers,* she drew upon her own experience more directly than in novels set in surroundings which she knew only fleetingly; nor that she allowed her characters to speak her own hopes and fears.

David Evans expressed Katharine's own aspirations, when he explained to his daughter:

> I want to reach the people. I want to know them better, in order to talk to them: write for them. Stimulate their courage, so that they won't allow themselves to be driven like sheep to the slaughter. There, you see, I'm talking like a demagogue — and that's not the way I want to talk. Not ranting and exaggerating; but on the basis of facts, simply, in their own language.

"It is with logic and lucidity we writers should appeal to the common-sense of our people, and with the passion which will move them to act for peace — and the glorious future of a world without wars,"[118] Katharine herself had told the Literary Conference of the Congress of International Co-operation and Disarmament in Melbourne.

The audience David sought was Katharine's own target:

> I want to know how to reach all sorts of people. Not only the militant workers . . . or the men who build sky-scrapers, dig coal, run factories and trains; but men in politics and finance, the misfits, ne'er-do-wells, criminals — and fools like yourselves who dream of building a new world.

And Katharine shared David Evans' labour to present the ideas of peace with the irresistible, white heat of a thermal lance which would pierce the complacency of his readers, set their imagination aflame:

> Ideas and phrases beset him. They swarmed through his brain like a flock of midges, to be brushed away, and returning buzzed infuriatingly, until he was nervously exhausted by their fretting persistence. His impotence to deal with this subject effectively exasperated him. He took his pencil, scribbled a few lines to see how they would go as an opening, impatiently crushed the paper and threw it away. Over and over again, he attempted a brilliant and startling line of approach; and scrawled through it, because it was neither brilliant nor startling. Yielding to a sickening sense of frustration, he wondered whether his ability to write as he wished had forsaken him. Was he losing confidence in himself as a writer?

The first five chapters of *Subtle Flame* were completed and the initial enthusiasm had dissipated when Katharine wrote wearily of her own struggle for effective expression:

> Don't seem to have done anything but try to write all week — at least for the 3 or 4 hours I can get in the morning. But, somehow, it doesn't go well. My head feels tired and I slog at things that ought to run freely. I think, too, as one get older all the old ways of saying things don't seem vital and vigorous enough. So I revise and revise — every line seeming better another way. So it's slow going and exasperating to feel time flying and so little done.

In other moods she mocked her own mysticism and yearning to escape into nature and the beauty of things through her characters' self-criticisms: "Metaphysical meanderings; ecstasies over things whose only instinct was to live and propagate." "Perhaps I can't help idealizing, although I like to think I'm a realist," she confessed through another of her people. She castigated her own lapses into the language of political agitation: "It is not the wisdom of the serpent, or the cooing of the dove I object to, but the screeching of a cockatoo."

As if to remind herself of the resolution to speak simply in the language of the people, Katharine gave David for his familiar a caged parrot, Percy, cursing and shrieking from the perch on the veranda of the rooming-house where he began his assault on the mills of the press:

> As he passed an old house, crouching on the edge of the pavement, at the end of a terrace of two storey brick houses with narrow balconies, torn canvas blinds, and shabby coloured boards screening verandah beds, a harsh voice hailed him.
>
> "Hullo! Hullo there, rotten bastard! How about a drink?"
>
> David glanced about him to see where the voice came from. There was no one in sight but a grey parrot hung in a cage outside the old house. Its plumage was dull and dirty, its head nearly bald, a formidable black beak hooked out from it: beady black eyes winked from the circles of chalk-white lids.
>
> The parrot rocked on its perch and squawked hilariously: "Rotten bastard! Rotten bastard! How about a drink?"

The symbol of a caged society, shrieking its incoherent protest against fortune. How different from the flocks of white cockatoos which wheeled crying eerily over the deserted Wytaliba homestead when Coonardoo had gone!

The drug traffic, too, was employed both as sub-plot for a contrasting study of evil and brutality in the heart of man, and as an analogy for society, doped with violence, conditioned to murder, accepting subconsciously the inevitability of war. In rescuing the boy, Tony, from the bashing of a gang of drug pushers, David recognizes him as a surrogate for his son; and, in turning aside to help one boy, symbolically he continues his campaign to awaken a numbed and doped society.

Katharine was proud to have exposed the drug problem, then latent in Sydney and Melbourne, before it became a recognized issue of national importance. Her interest had been aroused almost by accident. She had met a former addict, who swore that he found the courage to break the drug habit through the inspiration of Coonardoo's devotion and fidelity. The book had been a revelation to him of the quality of the human spirit. He read it again and again, and somehow drew from it the determination to succeed in his own rehabilitation. Katharine based her account of the growing grip of the drug traffickers on Australian youth and the intimidation of young men on the fringe of the criminal underworld upon that man's experiences. Tony was a fictitious character, though Katharine herself rescued more than one "lame dog", including a young man who, like Tony in the novel, stowed away on one of the coastal ships travelling to Perth.

Subtle Flame, for all its wholehearted commitment to a cause, bears evidence that Katharine did not forget the lessons that the academics had attempted to teach her. David Evans was no ready-made character. The challenges he faced were the real demands of his own body and spirit: the defeat of his pride; the need for self-respect; the reassurance of sexual love; the ties of family responsibility; the necessity of friendship and the essential, inescapable needs of life: food and money and shelter. David Evans' pilgrimage took him from power to blind depair and, with renewed understanding, to the humility of acceptance that he was but "a mote in the world's woe". They were no men made of straw who barred his way, but the giants of a modern mythology: apathy, ignorance, prejudice and fear. Katharine painted her picture of the people of the city from life. She had met those same attitudes among the workers and housewives, shop girls and pensioners. She reported them with implacable accuracy:

> "There's always been war. There always will be war."
> "You can't change human nature . . ."
> "I've never thought about it . . ."
> "I'm not interested in politics . . ."
> "It will be God's will . . ."
> "War is a punishment for man's sins . . ."
> "Go home and pray . . ."
> "Are you a commo?"

It was no heroic, poster portrait of "the masses" Katharine drew. She showed her people in all their primitive savagery as they barracked and booed at a knock-down, drag-out boxing match at the stadium:

> David watched the faces in the gallery about him, cruel and rapacious as they followed the fight. Eyes glittered, mouths gaped and twisted with lunatic frenzy as men and women stamped, hooted, cat called, or howled their exultation.

Unshaken in his belief in the "fundamental qualities" of the human spirit, Katharine's David struggled with the undeniable reality of evil in man, concluding that kindness was "the common denominator" in all men, if it could be found through the corruption and decay of the struggle for existence, which he was himself to suffer when confidence failed and his purpose was forgotten.

The first part of the novel, tracing David's failure as a free-lance in the crusade for peace was almost completed by July 1961:

> Part I of the new novel is nearly finished — though I'm not pleased with it. Doesn't seem to be going the way I want. Too big a subject I've tackled perhaps — a sort of modern Don Quixote in the struggle for peace. But, my touch isn't light enough — I'm too much in earnest to make him a figure of fun. Knight of "the rueful countenance", he may be, and after all he's not tilting at windmills which don't exist. However, I can't let my bloke go until I've done my damndest by him. He's already got an existence of his own, and insists on being delivered from K.S.

It was a long and difficult labour. Work on *Subtle Flame* stopped after the completion of Part I. Perhaps Katharine's dissatisfaction with what she had written compelled her to put it aside for the time being. Not until the proofs of *Child of the Hurricane* had been disposed of, did she return to continuous work on the novel; but she remained dissatisfied with her treatment of the theme, overawed by the importance of the subject and conscious of the difficulty of escaping from the jargon of the Left. "The new novel goes slowly," she wrote in March 1964:

> Not at all well, really — though it nags at me all the time. Such a difficult and vast subject, and to make vital something so clogged with clichés and mundane associations!

Only Katharine's refusal to give up an unfinished job kept her going. Her vital energy was close to the point of exhaustion:

> Monday morn — showered and breakfasted, and facing the day with a jar of pink tea-tree on my table Bert[119] brought yesterday. The hills green again, and Alec[120] due for his usual visit. He likes a yarn and a cuppa, as well as doing his medical inspection of my B.P. and giving me the heparin injection which seems to stabilize it.
>
> I do keep well, darl, so don't worry about the regular visits — and much relieved not to have to go to the surgery. Only get v. tired if I do too much, so mostly don't. No steel in the backbone, these days, I'm afraid, my darling.

> Just keep going from sheer cussedness, and because life's still so full of interest to me.

Katharine was still "cracking hardy" when John Gilchrist, one of the devoted friends who did so much to care for her, wrote to warn me that she had had "a very bad turn" and was "generally much weaker than she had been for a while". Katharine herself insisted that she was better: "Don't worry about me, darl. I'll be all right by the time you get this," she wrote.

Within a few days, a telegram from Dr Jolly advised me to come at once to the west. Katharine had suffered a stroke and was in a critical condition. She was conscious when I reached the hospital. Her eyes filled with tears. Her left hand fluttered towards me: "My darling . . . I'm so sorry . . ." She was unable to speak more than a few confused words. Her right hand was paralysed.

Later, Katharine told the story of that nightmare:

> I am haunted by the memory of a night of horror. Not that any sinister images were associated with it. It was just that I had lost control of my mental processes. They whirled turbulently in utter disorder — the spate of thought disconnected, and flying in all directions, without rhyme or reason, and I had always imagined I possessed a centre of inner serenity.
>
> It was the confusion and rout of the power to control my mind that troubled me most. I could not sleep: was alarmed by the cataclysmic disturbance, but not afraid. There was no pain — no stabbing angina pains that might have been expected — only — the aching of my head, which I thought was due to high blood pressure and sleeplessness . . .
>
> Friends told me that Ric had been sent for. I felt that they thought I was dying, and was satisfied that it should be so. Lying in the "valley of the shadows" it seemed, a dark apathy encompassed me. Then doctor's voice, speaking rather sternly, came to me from far away: "You've got to exert the will to live," he said. I was unwilling to exert myself: did not want to live: dreaded the long climb back to health and normality. But doctor put it to me as an obligation, something requiring spiritual strength and courage. My speech regained clarity. I began to try to recover the use of my hand and take an interest in the thought of still living and again being able to write.

Slowly, as her will to live returned, Katharine's courage and determination led her along the way to recovery. Her devoted comrade, Annette, visited her each day and wrote telling me of her progress:

> The news today seems very good — although your mother was sad because of missing you, she again seemed to have made progress . . .
>
> We talked about the news and what she had listened to on the radio — she dictated a letter to Gwen Meredith about *Blue Hills* which I thought was a real step forward — she spoke of how the serial was an authentic piece of Australiana in a very appreciative way, as usual thinking about how she could encourage Australian writers.
>
> Katharine could lift her right arm up and move her thumb independently.

Loss of the use of her right hand was a terrible handicap to Katharine. It was almost as though her mind had become dependent upon the pen from which the words of beauty and anguish and exultation had poured for almost seventy years since, as a young girl, she first determined to become a writer. She could not bear to see her own hand white and useless, a thing, part of her, to be picked up and put away under the bed covers.

Later, Annette wrote for Katharine:

> Getting well; everyone is very kind — Annette scolds me. I had an amusing visitor yesterday who wanted to save my soul — I told him it took 5 clerymen to prepare me for confirmation. But he is a very nice bloke and President of the Peace Council so I have a lot of time for him. He said does it tire you to talk — I said yes, so he went promptly. He kissed me, and he said "Bless you — may I say that?" I said yes, but he has no hope of saving my soul. I told him immortality was an impermissible belief. He said: "What about personality when you die," and I said "Yes, personality lives on in the effect of what you do on others."

And then, letter by letter, Katharine began to teach herself to write with her left hand. It was heartbreaking to see the sprawling, wavering letters with which she managed to print her signature to Annette's gently, reassuring words: a page of coarse, yellowed, scribble-block with the words laboriously practised stroke by stroke: "KATYA . . . KATYA . . . KATYA . . ." And later, triumphantly: "KATHARINE THROSSELL . . .HIS KATYA . . . MOP . . ." (It had been my baby name for her which Katharine herself adopted: Mop — Moppingarra, the songman and magic-maker of the aborigines.)

For all of those long, anxious weeks in hospital, Annette visited her each day, comforting, encouraging, looking after the letters and telegrams from friends and well-wishers which poured in from all over Australia and abroad, writing the replies that Katharine dictated, arranging for a friend to look after her at home.

Greenmount was balm to Katharine. "The sweet peace of home enfolding me again," she wrote in a large, irregular, schoolgirl's hand:

> Amy[121] like a fussy mother bird, looking after me. So kind and thoughtful . . ."
>
> Here I am reclining on the verandah with the garden looking its beautifullest — lavender, cerise pelargonium and Christmas lilies, pink honeysuckle and nasturtiums all mixed up and growing wild together. A golden-breasted whistler pouring out his song, too! I'm so grateful for the peace and loveliness.

As her strength returned, Katharine became impatient with the inactivity that her illness had imposed on her:

> It seems as if I will never get back the creative impulse that has been my raison d'être hitherto. Not only that, but my secret joy also — the very act of expression, finding words to tell the world of some discovery of human worth in a life-story, or the conflict of ideas. Not that it matters, I suppose. One scribbler less, when there are so many jostling for a place in the lists. And I feel such a back number in this age of the machine and cybernetics. All the same I would not change my values for the cerebration and obscurity of the so-called avant garde writers.

She confided her fears to Stefan Heym, whose work she admired, and who, she believed, shared some of her own attitude to the "sublime mission" of literature. Writing from a world away in Berlin, Stefan Heym gave her sympathy and encouragement, understanding her tremulous pursuit of confidence as only another writer could; although even he could not fully appreciate the devastating impact of that "cerebro-vascular accident", as it was called in the innocent euphemism of medical science. "I know your mood so well," he wrote.

> Most of the days when I close my typewriter, I go into a tail-spin telling myself "You're no writer at all, how could you turn out such tripe — wordy, repetitious; not a new idea from beginning to end!" And it takes working over, and pruning, and re-writing (and also help and encouragement from Gertrude) and some days or weeks distance to find that, maybe, some of the stuff will stand up under criticism. I envy at such times the young writers who just blurt it out and think

> they're great; once upon a time I was just as naive; the older one gets, the more one doubts.
>
> All this only to encourage you to go on and do that book.

Katharine could not remain long in the slough of despair. Six months after her illness, she wrote:

> Naturally at 80 perhaps one should be content to count blessings and watch the world go by; not be concerned to shove and push any longer. But as Lawson said: "I've been at the Front all the years of my life!" And it's difficult to enjoy being a mollusc.

By the end of June 1965, Katharine was hard at work again, dictating to Annette once or twice a week from rough, handwritten notes. She had always suspected dictation because "the thought that should go into every sentence can't be poured out. It must be chewed over and weighed — given its right place for lucidity and beauty". There was no alternative, now. And having set her mind to it, Katharine dictated fluently and rapidly with little amendment to the typescript.

By the end of the year the last chapter of *Subtle Flame* had been written:

> Now begins the long job of revision — and it means a long m.s. to revise. I shouldn't be surprised if nobody wants to publish it—though the socialist countries will translate—if ever it does achieve publication in English.

In the last chapters Katharine returned to the painful memories of her own illness, with fragments of Dr Alec Jolly's theories on the part of the autonomic nervous system in cardio-vascular diseases[122] to bring the authenticity of fact and experience to her description of David's collapse, when a peace meeting on the Yarra Bank is broken up by a bodgie gang:

> His brain whirled: drove him helplessly into an exhausted lethargy . . . tumultuous emotions rushed through him in a swirling torrent of delirium . . . he sank into a state of suspended animation . . . resigned to a cessation of vitality, feeling death was hovering near him.

She remembered, too, the young woman who had watched by her own bedside:

> Sometimes Sharn's eyes had reached him through the turmoil and darkness of subconscious strife. Eyes of anguish, that implored and held him from slipping away from them. She

> had been sitting beside him, her hand on his arm. Every day, during visiting hours, she had been sitting there though he did not know.

And, perhaps, in her "Sharn's" own love for a comrade no longer young, Katharine found truth in the romantic conclusion to David Evans' lonely quest[123]: it was to her, to Annette, that *Subtle Flame* was dedicated.

Finding a publisher for *Subtle Flame* was more difficult than it had been for any one of the nineteen novels and collections of short stories which Katharine had written over fifty years since *The Pioneers* first brought her literary recognition. She knew that the book was too long and too controversial for Angus and Robertson. Jonathan Cape was dead. Without him, she feared her old publishers, too, would be less tolerant. "At present I'm putting the finishing touches to my 170,000 word swan song in novel form, *Subtle Flame*." Katharine told Beatrice Davis in February 1966. "I must offer it under the terms of contract to Jonathan Cape Ltd., but I fear they will find it too Australian and too controversial to publish. (I'm not suggesting that it's suitable for A. & R.)"

Her fears on this occasion were only too well founded. Cape's apologized discreetly that they were "somewhat disinclined in present circumstances, to make any offer to publish". The Russians had already offered to translate the book. Katharine preferred to await its publication in English. The Australasian Book Society reported that, although it contained "excellent writing and brilliant story telling" and was "a fitting reply to Pasternak's *Dr Zhivago*", the manuscript would have to be cut by 30,000 words.

Katharine despaired:

> I've got my own big job on hand, and it's heart breaking — cutting *Subtle Flame*. I think A.B.S. is the only possibility for publishing — because of its theme — otherwise I wouldn't cut — but it seems the price I must pay for publication. Les[124] says that if I can reduce to 120,000 words A.B.S. will publish in May 1967. So it must be done! If only the Russian translation will give the full text.

Katharine drove herself to the distasteful task: cutting, reorganizing, rewriting. Annette patiently typed and retyped, page after page. The manuscript was stacked in piles on Katharine's working table, over the sofa and on the floor, spilling out along corridors like lines of wounded, white-bandaged and bloodied.

"The mutilation of 'S.F.' is taking all my writing time," Katharine grieved.

By the end of the year she believed she had done all she could. " 'S.F.' has gone to its fate . . . I feel, now, I'd just as soon have burnt the m.s.," she wrote, exhausted and discouraged.

Even in its truncated form, *Subtle Flame* was a long novel. Faced with a financial crisis which threatened its existence, the Secretary of the Australasian Book Society wrote pointing out that they stood to lose $700 on the publication and shamefacedly appealed to Katharine for some help in the matter of royalties.

The ABS, a co-operative publishing company, devoted to the publication of Australian books on significant social themes, had been a favourite cause of Katharine's. She had been prepared to offer ABS 20 per cent of her cherished foreign rights; had helped with the publication of other writers' work, and had willingly made a gift of royalties on a deluxe edition of *N'Goola.* Katharine felt she could not refuse to help ABS; but she resented bitterly the implication that her work would not sell. She had very firm ideas about her own professional principles and stood up to any publisher, capitalist or Communist, who offered royalties on terms less favourable than "the accepted rates". It was hard to accept that years of work would mean nothing. Katharine replied to ABS putting her position directly:

> Needless to say I was very depressed by your letter of May 30th. I am not a wealthy woman: have lived for years on a fraction of the basic wage. Only when there has been an occasional cheque for foreign rights have I been able to pay, as I did, for the publication of Vic Williams' poems and Bert Vickers' first novel. And never has a publisher incurred a loss by the publication of one of my books. Now, it looks as if, in order to prevent A.B.S. facing a substantial loss, I would have to forgo royalties up to at least £300. (I can't think in dollars, or wrestle with financial statements.)
>
> If I do this, and in any case, I must retain the rights to foreign translations. Apparently, the only funds I am likely to receive after five years' work, will be from foreign translations — if any . . .
>
> All good wishes, and so sorry to be downcast about the prospects of *Subtle Flame* — which I expect the critics will bash anyhow with their heaviest beetle-crushers.

ABS decided to do everything possible to honour their royalty obligations; discovered, to Katharine's relief, that they would cover the direct costs of *Subtle Flame* and did, in fact, year by year, pay off the deferred royalties.

Subtle Flame was now widely known to be Katharine's last novel. "A writer never retires", Katharine told an ABC interviewer. "While I live, I'll write — though probably not another long novel." To Stefan Heym, she explained:

> I'm not conscious of any diminution of mental energy, but physically I feel that a long distance novel is more than I'd have staying power for these days — though I've still got novels in my mind which will be still born.

At receptions in Perth, Melbourne and Sydney, fellow writers and friends gathered to honour what most knew must be the end of her long career. Katharine was heartened by the generous tributes of other writers who wrote or spoke acknowledging her achievement. Stefan Heym, who had shared the book's birth pains with her and given her the heart to see it through, recognized the quality of the work, and left deeper criticism to others less keenly aware of its cost. "I think it is a powerful, deep and deeply felt story," he wrote:

> I would call it a modern, realistic *Pilgrim's Progress;* your Evans in his search for peace and humanity typifies some of the best people of our time . . . At times, I found myself wishing that your political discussions were shorter. But I suffer from the same malaise. We feel that what we have to say on peace, socialism, freedom etc. etc. is so important that we say it, forgetting that we don't own a newspaper but only a one-man novel-writing shop.
>
> I don't want to go into the commonplace praise of, "Look, and she did it all at about eighty and after a grave illness." That's neither an excuse nor a merit, and I don't consider you aged, anyhow; you have a young, contemporary mind and the spirit that goes with it.

With few exceptions, the Australian press critics refrained from using their "beetle-crushers"; but Katharine saw only kindness in their admiration for the courage of a woman of eighty-four. She knew that she had failed to achieve the impossible objective of arousing "the masses of kindly, inert people".

The events of the Korean War and the peace campaigns of the fifties seemed forgotten causes, overwhelmed by the passions of Vietnam. "History has leapt beyond my time of writing," she admitted to Jack Lindsay. Making her own assessment, Katharine concluded, sadly:

> All my Welsh guile, literary expertise and passionate faith in the grail of world peace, went into this book to make the

story interesting, contemporary and convincing. But I'm afraid it had no effect on the people I had hoped to reach . . . The Promethean spark which lies dormant in everybody, and has triumphed over so many savage instincts and customs, in the past, had not been fanned by this book to the subtle flame which ultimately, I am sure, will burn out from human affairs the corrupt and cruel business of war.[125]

CHAPTER 21

WHEREON MY EYES HAVE RESTED

Oh thou lovely landscape,
Down and sea,
Whereon my eyes have rested,
Lovingly,
Good-bye.

I will not sigh
That I must go,
But blest and refreshed pass on
To yoke my spirit
To the things that are —
Hitch my frail waggon
To the lonely star.
— Katharine Susannah Prichard, 1913

The old house was sinking in a sea of trees when I brought my son, Jim, to stay for a while with Katharine at Greenmount, in those last years. Honeysuckle and currants tangled over the open veranda, jasmine was a fragrant jungle of vines; wattles and red gums showered roofs and veranda with a spray of fringed, white blossom and the weather-stained flotsam of dead flowers. There were great cracks in the stone walls of the veranda where the foundations of the house had shifted, easing the weight of the years. The jarrah beams of the pergola were careened on their pillars of moss-stained rock. The black, oiled weatherboards of the old house hid their age under a rusty bloom of the red, hills' dust. Jim solemnly inspected the verandas where I had played as a child, and promised Katharine that he would come back with his hammer when he was a big boy and fix it for her.

Katharine liked to think that the place could grow old with her:

> I feel it would be a mistake to try to keep the place as a memorial — or museum — anything of that sort . . . We must not be sentimental about the old place.

The house and its two acres of abandoned orchard, Katharine regarded as my patrimony. Astounded by the substantial estate that Miles Franklin had left, and highly critical of the way in which the annual literary awards were administered under the terms of Miles' will, Katharine had long determined to leave no bequests. She preferred to make her gifts to the causes she believed in while she lived.

She cared little about keeping the place in good order, although she was grateful when friends took on the job of replacing rusted guttering and essential repairs. A house should not become a "shell for your back", Katharine warned me. She saw no good purpose in modernizing and redecorating. She preferred the high, unstained jarrah cupboards which lined the kitchen, the deal shelves, bare, uncurtained windows and straight-backed, wooden chairs to chrome and plastic.

For years she had made do with a wood stove. Even after a small electric oven was installed, she still liked to do her "gin cooking" over the open fire in the sitting-room on winter evenings when there was only herself to cook for. The gadgets which had become domestic necessities in most Australian homes had no appeal to her. "I don't want anything the workers can't have in their homes," Katharine told Annette. She could not believe that with the affluent society's gift of hire purchase, most workers' homes were stocked with all of the goods and graces of the commercial world.

She had loved wandering through the home paddocks at the end of the day's work, gathering bundles of dry twigs, gum-leaves and pine-cones for the chip heater that snuffled and snorted to produce a trickle of tepid bath water, or threatened to explode in a sudden geyser of scalding steam. It was a carefully schemed operation to get a hot-water service, a radiogram or an electric heater into the house and installed surreptitiously before Katharine could object. But as she became less able to rely on herself, and the simple ways of doing things were no longer simple, she accepted gratefully some of the comforts of modern living.

When foreign royalties gave her the illusion of an affluence which she had never before known, Katharine found more pleasure in writing a cheque for the *Tribune*, the Australian-Soviet Friendship Society, the Peace Council, the Realist Writers' Group or Arts Vietnam, than in her own comfort. It was a pleasure to her to meet travelling expenses for a friend; to finance the publication of a new writer's work; to sponsor a private edition of one of my own plays, or pay for music and ballet lessons for the children. Only when it was to help the kindly, devoted, Yugoslav woman who called each week to wash and clean for her, did Katharine find it worthwhile to buy electric gadgets because "she couldn't bear to see Mrs Klaritch down on her knees" polishing the rough jarrah floors, or sweating over the wood-fired copper in clouds of smoke which poured from the cracked masonry, threatening to set the whole place on fire.

Television was utterly out of the question. "Such a waste of time," she told neighbours, who thought it would keep her company. Some radio programmes she loved; always listened to the news and the Sunday music sessions and often tuned in her ancient cabinet model to an Australian play. Katharine was so distressed when a broadcast play of mine could not be heard for static on her archaic contraption, that friends took up a collection to give her a transistor radio for her eightieth birthday. Katharine thought it far too expensive a gift. She was embarrassed that friends from other States had been approached for contributions and was mollified to learn that the balance of the funds collected had paid the deposit for a local candidate standing for election to Parliament.

That little radio was a great joy to Katharine. On hot summer nights she would lie on the veranda at Greenmount "looking up to the stars", listening to her favourite Beethoven in the hot stillness, letting the music "soak through" her: the Ninth Symphony:

> That adagio, I think, is the most divine thing in music. I feel I could die to it, so completely it expresses the inexpressible, all that one thinks and feels about the sadness and sweetness of life.

Or the "Eroica", when she "could have got up and shouted with the music". "I sit and am soothed by lovely cadences and harmonies," Katharine wrote:

> Only latterly, have I been able to indulge my feeling for music. Always before, I could not allow time or thought for it, except occasionally. But now, I listen as to a universal language.

Through her love for music, Katharine became interested in the work of a young Perth pianist, David Helfgott. Each week or so in the years before he left to take up a scholarship in London, David, an awkward, unassuming young man, caught the bus to Greenmount, ate the dinner that Katharine specially prepared for him and played to her for hours. "I had a wonderful night, this week," Katharine wrote.

> My young friend, David Helfgott came to dinner — and played to me all the evening . . . His technique is marvellous already — and he reduced me to tears as he played the Chopin nocturnes. To have so much glorious music — Chopin, Tchaikowsky, Liszt — all to myself. It was almost too much. I felt quite drunk with it.

A strange and touching friendship, this intimate understanding between a young man on the threshold of his all-absorbing vocation and an old woman in whose sympathy he found encouragement. Katharine missed his private recitals when David was in London, but tried to keep herself in touch with his progress. In April 1969, she wrote:

> I gave myself an Easter egg of the 3rd Concerto of Rachmaninov — which David is to play with orchestra, so I would like to know it quite well. Clem got it for me and I was so excited that I forgot my pot with an evening meal on the stove — 'till a horrible smell of burning assailed us. No matter! It was worth losing a dinner for the Rachmaninov. The most glorious music — which I regaled myself with when Clem had gone.

The fears and doubts that haunted Katharine after her illness lingered. She was not afraid to die. As Dymphna Cusack discovered, when she stayed in Greenmount, Katharine had no fear of death, "because she had never been afraid of life". To become incapable, dependent; to outlive her usefulness—that remained Katharine's dread. "I've come to the conclusion it's almost a crime to be old," she said.

But the shadow of apology, almost of shame, that there had been in her eyes when a word eluded her or some quite inappropriate phrase came to her tongue after her illness, had disappeared. (Though she had been able to laugh at the foolish things her lips would have her say, telling herself, "No, no. Not that"; perhaps finding the lost word in Russian or French.)

She could use her right hand freely to write. She had learned, reluctantly, to shepherd her strength. The cautious shuffling step of extreme age left her, as her confidence returned and her unyielding determination to live out her life fully and usefully reasserted itself.

"What a vintage year for K.S.P. 1967 has been," I told Katharine: *Subtle Flame, Happiness* and the children's story *Moggie and her Circus Pony,* illustrated by Elaine Haxton, and dedicated to her grandchildren, Querida and Jim, more work of Katharine

Susannah Prichard's than ever before released in any one year; but *Happiness* was a selection of earlier stories, and *Moggie* had first been written for the girls of Wirth's Circus, years before.

Katharine knew that her major work was finished. "I feel I owe you an apology," she told Dymphna Cusack:

> Years ago Prof. Walter Murdoch said of me, "In the Parliament of world literature she is the member for Australia"—because I had so many translations into foreign languages, but now, you have more than I have, so I'm resigning in your honour, dear.

Not satisfied to rest on the fading laurels of earlier days, Katharine continued to write: articles, reminiscences, short stories and, for *Southerly,* a long account of her "Perceptions and Aspirations" in literature.

In the challenge of the new school of Australian writing, Katharine found a cause to stir her faith in the democratic traditions of Australia into new life. She rebelled against "the canonization of the primal non-ethical energies" and was outraged by the suggestion that the greatest achievements of Australian literature were in the discovery of the "reality of madness". In a letter to me, Katharine protested:

> The tendency is towards sordid introspection—and an appreciation of instanity as revealing ethical and aesthetic truths. My work seems all to be vieux jeu, as far as these pundits, who regard "terror" as the basis of being, are concerned. I have exalted reason and sanity above all these maundering and bawdy fantasies—that does not mean I have not enjoyed with my characters some bawdy roistering, natural and healthy as may be. It's the nauseating, smelly evacuating of diseased emotions, I can't abide.

An assertion that the *naissance* of modern Australian literature dated from the period of Patrick White and Randolph Stow, provoked her to reply:

> Whatever the significance of White and Stow, I suggest the aesthetic and humane philosophy which animated a past decade of writers and poets should not be disregarded . . . It has been disturbing to note a trend in Australian literature which disparages environment . . .
>
> Australian writers may absorb international culture without imperilling their quality as Australians, whereas to deny an Australian spirit of the body of our literature, would be to foist a macabre dummy on the Australian people, and

> to offer soundless, scentless changeling to world literature.[126]

Some political battles still remained to be fought. The *Southerly* article was Katharine's last stand in defence of the literary pioneers who had given Australians national consciousness, pride and vision.

Mail continued to pour into number 11 Old York Road, Greenmount, from Europe, America, Asia and all over Australia: letters from school children who had read "Moggie" and "Han"; from teachers of English in Russia and Latvia; from scholars and research students in Texas, New York, Toronto; from fellow writers in Germany, England, Russia and France; from fans who had become Katharine's friends, and those, unknown, who paid her the compliment of their pleasure in her work; quaint, heartwarming letters glowing with admiration:

> Dear Katarine Susanne!
>
> I'm sorry,
>
> I beg your pardon and disturb my letter.
>
> But I very want to write to you.
>
> I'm sorry. I didn't read your works. I didn't know, what lives such Beautiful Woman, such talented Australian writer Katarine Susanne Prichard I'm sorry. I'm sorry.
>
> Now I have read our Soviet "Literary Newspaper" Boris Rurikov, the correspondent of the "Literary Newspaper" has written about you very good. His article has title "The Child of the Hurricane".
>
> I like this name. What is it a wonderful name! What is a wonderful life; The life one woman's who has name Katarine Susanne Prichard.
>
> I'm very glad. This great Woman lives on the Earth, on the nice planet, on our planet.
>
> No. Katarine is not old and weak. She is strong Woman with a Great Kind Heart.

Literary periodicals, information bulletins, and circulars, political pamphlets and glossy, propaganda magazines from North Korea, Cuba, the Soviet Union and North Vietnam, the despair of an overburdened postman, arrived in an unending flood. Sometimes it seemed that Katharine's name, in all its variations, must have been on every foreign distribution list throughout the Communist world. Some, like *Foreign Literature,* she enjoyed, relied on to keep her informed of new work published in other countries; others lay, a dusty monument to Socialist construction, in the corners of every veranda, cupboard and bedroom.

Usually, in those last years, there was a friend to keep house for Katharine at Greenmount, although she really preferred to do things for herself when she was able. She was an undemanding, but to some a difficult companion. She needed the solitude she had become accustomed to; had no patience with domestic gossip. Few of her housekeepers stayed for long. But each, in her own way, was attached to Katharine; and she made their problems her own.

Always when she was ill a friend could be relied on to look after her. But she was relieved when a succession of "universal aunts" had found Greenmount "too lonely", "too dark", or "bad for the asthma", and for a while she was once more alone:

> This is the way I like to live, and if someone can be found who likes this sort of life, well and good — if not, I'd just continue as here-to-fore, and count my blessings . . . I dread having to cope with another "person", however, much prefer my single blessedness — and little extravagances, which would have to be curbed if I had to pay more in wages.

For my peace of mind, she agreed there should be someone living with her permanently at Greenmount after she fell in the garden and bruised her face badly. She joked gamely:

> Wasn't a sight that you would have wanted to paint, green and purples Picasso would have loved; but my poor mug has gone back to normal now. And I don't expect to be falling about again. This time it happened at about 9.30 in the morning, so it wasn't due to one-over-the-odds of my favourite sherry.

Each day, when Dr Alec Jolly called to see Katharine on his way to the surgery in Midland Junction, she had a cup of tea ready for him. At the end of the week, he often came in for an evening drink on his way home. Katharine had the utmost faith in him as a doctor, admired the keen, searching mind that led him to explore new avenues of curative medicine, science, mathematics, anthropology and philosophy. He expounded at length, perched on the edge of his chair, his eyes creased with the intensity of a new enthusiasm. Katharine curled in her armchair, trying to look as if she could grasp the dimensions of time in space, theories of inherited immunity or the origins of aboriginal consanguinity taboos.

Writers visiting Western Australia usually made a point of calling on Katharine at Greenmount. She welcomed the all too rare opportunity of talking book-talk to Eleanor Dark, Alan Marshall, Hal Porter, Randolph Stow, Frank Hardy, Judah Waten, Max Harris, Stephen Murray-Smith, Florence James, Mary Durack, Leslie and Coralie Rees who found her at eighty-five "as clear-brained, gentle, kindly alert as ever, firmly anchored in her own convictions . . . certainly nothing of the old lady, as she sat slimly in her slacks and high heels".[127] It was a feast when Dymphna Cusack and Norman Freehill could stay with her in Greenmount bringing news of China, Russia and all the countries of Eastern Europe they had known. They talked for hours. In Dymphna Cusack's memory, impressions of Katharine remained like fragments of fallen crystal: "Her hair was grey — waving. It always seemed to be in a private wind, because you thought of Katharine in movement. She had the warmest brown eyes and a smile of such all embracing kindness." There were tears in Dymphna's eyes as she remembered:

> She saw people with great-heartedness. She took them for themselves. She didn't need them to reflect her in any way . . . She looked so fragile, and she was so fragile, but when you were talking to Katharine you were dealing with steel: this curious quality of integrity that went through all her thought and her mind.

Katharine was delighted, too, when some of the leading speakers at the writers' seminar of the 1967 Festival of Perth came to tell her about the proceedings. She told me:

> Such a lovely gathering after the seminar in connection with the Festival of Perth. Tom Inglis Moore came to see me, and Clem Christesen and Dr. Brissenden and Hew Roberts. Bert Vickers and Ossie Watson brought them. It was so hot in the lounge for afternoon tea, that as soon as the sun left the verandah we moved out there — and I had a review of the seminar . . . I was thrilled that the "boys" wanted to come and see me, and enjoyed the talk which consisted mostly of telling Clem what a rotten Chairman he had been. Bert led the attack. I was so sorry for Clem . . . However, it was what Ka would call a beaut' party — and I thoroughly enjoyed it.

Other friends, too, shared those last years with Katharine: fellow members of the Peace Council, young writers and poets whose work she had helped and encouraged, old friends from the goldfields, union leaders from Fremantle and Midland Junction, the neighbours who called to do her hair, bring her flowers or just to "see how she was getting on".

But looking back, Katharine sometimes felt cut off from the literary life she had known: "I've been so isolated here from contact with men whose literary standards I value," Katharine told me:

> Since the days when I could discuss literature with Louis and Hilda, Vance and Nettie, Hugh McCrae and Frank Wilmot, there has been nobody in the West — except Murdoch who I've seen, only rarely, and perhaps Henrietta.

With Walter Murdoch, Katharine maintained an affectionately railing correspondence, chiding him gently from time to time when his weekly essays in the *West Australian* were unkind to progressive points of view, paying him the tribute due to an old master in the sincerity and warmth of her acknowledgment of her debt to him. She wrote on his birthday sometimes, or in the New Year, or when some brief glimpse of recognition shone upon that gentle, modest man, content to serve Australian letters in quiet obscurity. He replied to Katharine's criticisms with gracious irony, joining her, perhaps, in the hope that the first sputnik would be a harbinger of peace, and pointing out that it was no more a "triumph for socialism" than Rutherford's splitting of the atom was a "triumph for capitalism". His letters were disarming in their simple acknowledgment of her achievements, the tenderness of their understanding and gratitude. "My dear Katharine Susannah," he wrote in August 1967:

> How disrespectful that sounds! It was far otherwise that I addressed Miss Prichard in the days when we boarded the same tram in Melbourne when the century was young, or when we met in London and couldn't visit the House of Commons and had to make do with the House of Lords! Thank you very much for your letter, which is, as usual, far too kind to me. You must have seen from the beginning how very far I was from being fit to be a university lecturer . . . I have, since those old days, learned to be at least aware of my own limitations — which is the beginning of wisdom, I am told — rather a late beginning in my case. I have always been proud to boast that, anyhow, you were one of my students. The only one who has become world-famous.

Books remained her lifeline to the world. She read widely and continuously, stirred by lucidity of expression as she had always been. After reading A. D. Hope's *The Cave and the Spring* she told me:

> I have a reverential admiration for Hope — his lucid and lovely prose, and the intensely realized imagery and melod-

ious rhythm of his verse. How different, thoughtful and scholarly A. D. Hope's methods of criticism are.

The thaw in Australian-Soviet relations was slow in penetrating to the remoteness of Western Australia. As the exchange of scientific and cultural visits began to flow once more between the two countries, Katharine's home in Greenmount became a regular stopping place for visitors: writers like Alexei Surkov, Anatoli Safronov, Editor of the Russian magazine *Ogonyok*; Danil Granin, author of *For those who Seek;* Boris Ryurikov, Editor of *Foreign Literature,* scholar and critic; Oksana Krugerskaya, Katharine's own friend and translator; Ludmilla Kasatkina, who was to become a Doctor of Literature and Professor of Australian Literary Studies at Moscow University with her thesis on the work of Katharine Susannah Prichard; the concert pianist, Tatania Nikolaevna; scientists from the Russian Antarctic expedition; sailors from the Russian ships *Orlik, Simferopol, Valdimir Myakovsky* and the ice-breaker *Ob;* dancers from the Bolshoi Ballet, the Osipov and Moiseyev companies; artists from the Moscow Circus and a party of Russian tourists: "The great event of my week was the visit of a group of Soviet tourists — 12 no less, at 10 o'clock in the morning," Katharine reported:

> Joan[128] came to help me with refreshments — just a fruit drink which I made with lemons, strawberries, apricots and passion fruit — in the garden. Joan brought a flagon of white burgundy, a local light wine, said to be v. good. Anyhow, they all fitted into the lounge and Professor Ivanov, leader of the group, made a little speech saying how readers throughout the republics of the U.S.S.R. were introduced to Australia by K.S. . . . and the Archbishop, a quiet young bloke gave me a charming little peasant woman presenting the traditional loaf and salt to a stranger.

Katharine took great pleasure in the warmth of her Soviet visitors' admiration, at a time when her reputation in Australia had faded. She was completely captivated by the courtesy of the baritone of the Moscow State Variety Theatre, Arkady Talmasov, when he sang a song dedicated to Katharine Susannah Prichard, "in recognition of the hours of happiness her creative powers have given me", and kissed her hand in an old-world gesture of homage. She was immensely proud, too, of the medal for distinguished artists presented to her by the Bolshoi Ballet Company. Leonid Zhdanov, a dancer of the company, wrote of the Bolshoi Ballet's visit to Greenmount in the Russian magazine *Culture and Life,* after his return to Moscow:

> Our hostess wearing casual clothes met us on the verandah, which was littered with the fallen leaves of wild vines that entwined it from top to bottom. We seemed to have come to a different world, a world of genuine beauty, peace and wisdom. In a small room a fire was burning in the grate, and on either side of the fireplace, stood deep armchairs. Paintings hung on the walls here and there and the photograph of a young man stood on the mantelpiece.

Her Soviet visitors would have been amused, and perhaps surprised, to know that Katharine jokingly referred to the family portraits as her "ikonostasis", and each day picked fresh flowers to put before "the beloved little family", her offering "to whatever powers may be" for our happiness and well-being.

Her own joy in the beauty of things sustained Katharine even when she fell into conflict with old friends. "I find pleasure in such simple things, these days," she told me:

> A vase I've just arranged as a poem to autumn, with yellow leaves, rose berries, scarlet geraniums, and there's jasmine and a peace rose for your photograph which smiles at me every morning, when I put a fresh flower for you, darl. The loquat is in bloom, the grass inches high, so beautiful before it becomes a menace, and the hills green overnight . . . Last Sunday, I had a row with Bert Vickers — so perhaps the V's will not come today . . . He thinks he can dominate me in an argument. And then gets annoyed when I say: "But you're so stupid, Bert". He doesn't know anything about Marxism, and presumes to criticize those who do know.

Bert Vickers did return. Aware of his debt to Katharine, although neither of them ever spoke of her support for the publication of his first novel, tirelessly thoughtful and considerate in other ways, he could not resist debating furiously all the issues of the day, from currency reform, freedom and democracy, to the Soviet invasion of Czechoslovakia. Katharine recorded their controversies in her letters to me, her hand shaking with agitation, her writing sprawling almost illegibly across the page:

> V. has just been and gone — after a furious argument. I said "Democracy is a camouflage for the autocracy of capital". You may not agree with me, darl. I suspect you won't — but I resent his attitude of apologizing for and defending the obvious failures of capitalism to recognize that there can be no democracy without economic equality for the exercise of political rights.

With some friends whose ideas diverged from her own, Katharine proposed peace. "Let us contend no more," she wrote to Bill and Dorothy Irwin — and to others in Western Australia who had chosen a different path. Those close to her knew that a second stroke could kill her and avoided provoking her pointlessly into arguments to which there could be no resolution.

Katharine forgave Bert Vickers, and was herself forgiven. Towards the end of her life she wrote:

> Bert has just rung to say he's cooked a meal to bring with him this evening. My boy friends are very kind to me, aren't they — though I don't treat them very well.

CHAPTER 22

WITH CLENCHED HANDS

Bury me with clenched hands
And eyes open wide,
For in storm and struggle I lived
And in storm and struggle I died.

— Francis Adams

All Katharine's political faith was centred in Communism. For fifty years her devotion to the Communist Party of Australia inspired her hopes; sustained her in the tragedies of her own life; exacted personal sacrifice without limit: filled her last days with torment.

News of the formation of the Communist Party of Australia had first reached Jim and Katharine at "Wandu". "I went to the West early in 1919," Katharine told Ian Turner. "That year, or early in 1920, I got a wire from Earsman to say: 'The Communist Party of Australia has been formed and you are a member.'"[129]

In love, barely able to believe in the fragile happiness her soldier husband had brought her, Katharine had no hesitation. If it were necessary, she was ready to sacrifice even this to "the great objective values" in which they could both now believe. "The most interesting part of our lives together has been reading and talking," Katharine wrote to Nettie Palmer:

> Jim has grown so to my point of view that he usually describes himself as a Bolshevik and certainly has done more explanation of what Bolshevism is than any man I know in this State. Can you see him explaining what the word means to the State Attorney General?

At times it must have seemed as if he was her only follower. She reported:

> The Party in this State is very small and weak as to effective membership. When the group was first formed, propaganda meetings were held in the Trades Hall . . . Usually only

> about ten or eleven people came and these were mostly fossils, but even these dwindled until there were only four of us one evening — the lecturer, the Secretary (then G. W. Whitbread), myself and my husband.[130]

It was apparent that different methods would have to be adopted to teach the workers of Western Australia the meaning of Marxism. A telegram from Earsman told her: "You are instructed by the Communist Party to form study circles in Western Australia"; her first political assignment. Katharine was determined that it should succeed. "I was petrified!" she remembered.

> I didn't feel that I was at all competent to form study circles. I decided I should study for three months before I could become competent. So I studied solidly all day for the three months. "Capital" and anything else that was available.[131]

A leaflet issued in the names of John Curtin, Katharine Susannah Prichard, George Ryce, a young fitter at the Midland Railway workshop, and Jack Hogarth, union secretary, was sent out inviting the workers to attend the Labor Study Circles. Katharine explained:

> The most advanced educationalists today agree that the best method of teaching is that which urges students to read and study for themselves, applying to sympathetic instructors only for help over difficult propositions and knotty problems. And this is a method the Labor Study Circles may apply with the greatest advantage to many thoughtful working men and women and to the movement of the workers . . .
>
> The Labor Study Circle in Perth meets on Wednesday evening, each week. One Wednesday is devoted to discussion and explanation of a book being read by members, the following Wednesday to a lecture dealing with principles of Marxism. This arrangement is intended to give an understanding of the principles of Marxism to a wider circle than is able to join the more enthusiastic students of the reading group.

The Study Circles were a limited success. Katharine gave most of the credit to her comrades, although she prepared most of the lecture notes, later published in a series of political pamphlets and, at Jim's suggestion, carried the message of socialism to the unlikely ears of the women of the Anglican synod at the conservative Karrakatta Club in Perth.[132] One passage stands out from those first political pamphlets of Katharine's. Of Marx, she said:

> He was one of the greatest thinkers of all time. And he was not only a great thinker. He did not only think and allow others to interpret his thoughts in the actions of every day life. Marx spent his living strength of brain and body for the workers.[133]

Her own life was dedicated to the same ideal.

For most of the fifty years of her association with the Communist Party, Katharine worked in close co-operation with her fellow Communists. No task was too menial for her. No demand too great. She had only contempt for the self-esteemed intellectuals who believed that they could bring a superior intelligence to discussion of policy and tactics and who drifted away when personal ambition was thwarted or the going got tough. It was not all comradely understanding, however, in her own relationship with her Communist Party comrades in the west. The very intensity of the idealism that gave strength to Katharine's dedication, proved to be one of the main causes of occasional conflict. Few of the local leaders could measure up to the ideal standards of political and personal behaviour which she expected of a true Communist. Within a few months of the formation of a branch of the Communist Party of Australia in Perth, Katharine had brushed with the nominal leader, when she presumed to correct his misunderstanding of the Soviet attitude to unions. Her direct personal contact with the leaders of the Party in Sydney was, no doubt, irksome to the local hierarchy. Earsman, as General Secretary of the Communist Party of Australia, instructed the Provisional Secretary of the Perth branch on 24 December 1920:

> I have worked with Mrs. Throssell for a number of years and I strongly recommend that the branch secures her active co-operation in all work. I know her as a good teacher and a good tactician and her knowledge of the revolutionary movement is based on a good experience and a very wide reading.

It was to Katharine the Party headquarters appealed when the Branch Secretary complained about other members. She replied defending the rank-and-file members from their local leader's criticism. She advised:

> What our movement needs more than anything, I think, is clear, long-sighted action, not the John Blunt rushing like a bull at a post that has characterized the revolutionary movement for so long.[134]

Concerned with the pressure of organizational work and the strain of factional in-fighting, there were times when Jim tried.

not very successfully, to put his foot down; but the arrival of a baby put an end to Katharine's work with the Labor Study Circle, which, without her enthusiasm, withered in a fashion expected of greater entities, and died. In *The First Furrow,* Joan Williams records:

> The arrival in Western Australia of Mrs. Throssell in 1919 had provided an individual of strength and purpose, well grounded in Marxist theory, around whom organization could crystallize. She could expound the principles of socialism with passion, conviction and simplicity. And what was most vital, she could see past the personality conflicts and crude theoretical errors that hampered formation of a united organization.

Katharine herself consistently avoided seeking, or accepting, an official position in the Communist Party. She was content to exercise what influence she could in Western Australia through her membership of the State Executive. But there were times when she too felt the sting of Communist Party discipline; suffered the bitterness of misunderstanding and false accusation at the hands of her own comrades. "I remember seeing Katharine in tears," an old Party member told me:

> It was at the Party headquarters in Perth. Katharine was sitting at the end of the table. A comrade from the Control Commission accused her of a departure from the Party line in something she had written. He spoke from a typed sheet detailing her errors. He said that her bourgeois origins had separated her from the workers and led her to kow-tow to the bosses. I was there. I heard him . . . I saw the tears running down her face.

Personal differences of opinion had no effect either upon Katharine's beliefs or on her loyalty to the organization. A fellow Communist who had spent most of his life in the mines at Kalgoorlie, explained:

> Katharine understood the working-class movement. She told workers, "You shouldn't rely on me". But she knew the necessity of persons like herself to the working-class movement; like Lenin and Marx.

When Bill Mountjoy became Branch Secretary in the thirties, she was satisfied to back-stop his work, travelling to Perth each week to sub-edit his articles for the roneoed Party news-sheet, *The Red Star*. "Really, she taught him to write," his wife, Lindsay, remembered:

> She was a very special person to Bill and to me, and to our daughter, Rosa, too, who adored her as a small child. I can see her as clearly as though it was yesterday racing down the street, to welcome her, curls flying, calling out "Comrade Katharine! Comrade Katharine!"

There were times when she found herself unable to work with a particular individual and when others rebelled against her almost puritanical demand that a Communist leader's personal life should be beyond reproach. She objected strongly to excessive drinking and supported the removal of a Party leader, despite personal considerations, when he was found to be visiting the pub too frequently with a well-known police officer. But she argued for five years to vindicate a member expelled as a security agent, and subsequently cleared of suspicion.

After Jim died, Katharine found some consolation in her dedication to the hopes they had shared. Her conviction was an inspiration and an ideal to the young intellectuals of the Left. "For many of us Katharine was a saintly figure," Gordon Burgoyne remembered.

> I believe that by her character alone she did a great deal to bring young people of our kind into the Left movement . . . To people of my kind there was something a bit repellent about orthodox communism: its authoritarianism, the jargon. Then one thought of Katharine. She was so gentle. She talked like a human being.[135]

Katharine remained a member of the Western Australian State Executive of the Communist Party of Australia all through the period of its illegality, until she went to Sydney during the Second World War and became a member of the Central Committee.

She played relatively little part in the determination of policy. Her role in the Central Committee was primarily concerned with cultural affairs and relations with the USSR. She spoke rarely. Jack Hughes, one of her fellow members, recalled:

> Katharine was not one to participate in debates or discussions on the Committee as if it were a requirement of office to do so. She spoke only on questions she regarded as being of great principle and concern to the Party, and on those matters with which she was personally involved or had a deep attachment.[136]

She urged the most effective assistance to the Soviet Union in the war against Nazism; supported the Australian Party's position of independent equality with the Communist Party of Great Britain; opposed the adoption of the American Communists' policy of co-operation with capitalist post-war reconstruction; pressed for the inauguration of a people's choir. Ralph Gibson, the Communist Party's principal Marxist theoretician, respected her knowledge of theoretical Marxism, although she was not generally regarded as an expert in Marxist philosophy. R. Dixon, later President of the Communist Party of Australia, remembered:

> Katharine was a person whose views were sought because of her long experience, standing and knowledge. When important issues arose, she could always be relied upon to undertake a difficult task.[137]

"For Katharine Prichard there is no such thing as neutrality," Dixon told a meeting in Marx House to celebrate the Twenty-sixth Anniversary of the Party's foundation,[138] not long after Katharine stepped down from the Central Committee and returned to Perth.

She did not resume membership of the State Executive in Western Australia, but was regarded as an "honorary delegate" to the Communist Party's annual conference in Perth. Every year, until she was no longer able to travel, it was one comrade's honoured task to call for Katharine at Greenmount and take her in his old, open tourer to the conference in Perth, where a place was reserved for her among the presidium.

The sense of commitment remained when Katharine had long since ceased to have any role in the organs of the Communist Party. She felt herself personally involved in each one of the crises and conflicts that racked the Communist movement in the fifties and sixties. For her it was necessary to make her own decision, and when her view of the correct course of action differed from the "party line", to make it known to the hierarchy. There could be no easy game of "follow the leader", no "opting out" of a difficult situation. But, until the last weeks of her life, she made it a rigid and unvarying rule to accept party discipline and avoid public differences of opinion, once a decision had been adopted.

Constitutionally, Katharine was incapable of acting in a way which she herself believed would bring harm to Australia, though others frequently saw the views she held in a different light. At the time of the Cold War, the Communist Party was challenged with the question whether Australian Communists would support the Red Army if it were to invade Australia.[139] Incredibly, Katharine found herself faced with the issue by her own comrades.

She was addressing a public meeting when a piece of paper was passed to the speaker's stand instructing her that, if the question were asked, she was to reply that, as a Communist she would support an invading Red Army of liberation. Katharine flatly refused. She believed that the question was unreal, deliberately provocative and divisive. As a result, she found herself in dispute with the hot-heads of the Communist Party — not for the first time; nor the last.

Katharine was aware that she had substantial personal support, as much among the rank-and-file of the Communist Party and the working unionists as among the intellectuals, who later found the inflexibility of her interpretation of Marxist principles and her concepts of loyalty to "the first Socialist State" unacceptable. "Communism is really a religion of love and service to humanity," Katharine had once explained to Miles Franklin:

> Not sentimental and based on supernatural fantasies — but practical, courageously facing realities and through education and organization striving to bring people to a realization of their own divinity and power.

It was that kind of dedication to her political faith that had led one critic to describe her as "a sort of left-wing saint".[140]

For many years the Communist Party made use of her reputation, with Katharine's complete co-operation; joined, tardily, in praise of her literary achievements — and reaped the benefit of support among writers and intellectuals for causes with which she was personally associated. "The undeniable truth is that this gentle little woman has straddled like a giant the two modern epochs of Australian literature," Frank Hardy wrote in 1955, seeing her as the pioneer of a new militant trend in the Australian novel:

> Katharine Susannah Prichard has raised the banner, charted the course, it is for us Younger Communist writers to follow in dealing with themes from the struggle of the modern industrial workers.[141]

At the time of her eightieth birthday, and the publication of *Child of the Hurricane, Tribune* devoted a full page to greetings to Comrade Katharine. L. L. Sharkey wrote on behalf of the Central Committee and "all Australian communists":

> Your literary work alone is an indestructible monument, sufficient for more than one lifetime but you have also written your name into history for your political activity and indomitable courage.[142]

Edgar Ross wrote in the *Communist Review*,[143] unknowingly correcting an old injustice which had once brought tears to a Bolshevik's eyes:

> Katharine Prichard! What pictures the name conjures up of a physically rather frail but mentally robust agitator campaigning for trade union rights, organising the unemployed, pamphleteering for socialism, demonstrating for socialism, demonstrating for peace and freedom for the best part of half a century . . . a true daughter of the true nobility, the working class.

It was totally unthinkable to Katharine to contemplate using her influence among members to secure support for her own point of view, against a decision adopted by the Communist Party; to commit the deadliest of sins in the Communist calendar, the sin of "factionalism". She saw no error in putting forward a dissident view through the Communist Party's own press, when a more permissive policy encouraged open debate on important issues; nor in raising hell when her letters to the Party newspaper, *Tribune*, were politely refused publication.

Katharine could be unrelenting when she believed a matter of principle was involved and thoroughly intolerant of differences of opinion among some of her personal friends. When Guido Baracchi took the Trotsky line in the thirties, Katharine broke, without hesitation, a close friendship which had gone back to the days of the foundation of the Communist Party of Australia, and only relented after thirty years when he took up the banners of the Vietnam Moratorium. "I still recall with intense sorrow her visit to Sydney when she spoke at the Town Hall and how I rushed on to the platform after the meeting longing to just take her in my arms," he recalled as a man of eighty-five, "but she said she didn't want to speak to me, and I faded away."[144]

For others, with the tolerance of the years, Katharine retained a warm personal affection, even when political differences separated them. She was prepared to risk her own good standing to defend a friend who had incurred the Communist Party's displeasure. Stephen Murray-Smith, Editor of *Overland*, had been vigorously attacked in *Tribune* for a suggestion that the labour movement was hostile to the intellectual when Katharine wrote appealing for "sweet reasonableness", rather than "the sledgehammer of hostility", and suggested:

> Even if "revisionist" tendencies cause disappointment and bitterness, we must strive to unite all elements of the Labour

> Movement for a common objective: not widen the breach between us.[145]

Tribune withheld her letter from publication and Katharine appealed to the Communist Party Secretariat for reconsideration:

> Over the years, I have often been silent when I should have protested. Now, towards the end of my life, I have come to the conclusion that this is a weakness for which I should criticize myself. A good Bolshevik must fight for the honour and prestige of the Party — failing to do so is cowardice. After revelations of the 20th Congress, it was realized what members of the Executive Committee of the Party in the S.U. should have done to prevent errors of those last years of Stalin's life. We were told there must be more freedom of expression for rank and file members of the Party. This I think has led to many of the difficulties of the present time . . .
>
> I do not forgive Stephen or anybody for leaving the Party. But this "revisionist" bug seems to have struck so many people lately, that, in my opinion, the strength of the Party is indicated by the dignity and reasonableness with which we treat the afflicted . . .
>
> Needless to say, I will accept Party discipline if the decision is not to publish the letter — although I would be deeply hurt, and regret for the Party's sake, such a decision.[146]

Katharine's appeal for tolerance and "sweet reason" was published[147]; but she herself had no doubts about the question of intellectual freedom, in the Pasternak case, nor of the merits of *Dr Zhivago* which had been discussed in the offending edition of *Overland*. She told the Soviet writer Boris Polevoi:

> A story of tragic futility of an individual confronted by world shaking events beyond his sympathy and comprehension could have been powerful had the writer been inspired by "the vision splendid of the revolution" and "the realization of its triumph in his own time". But Pasternak could not rise above his egocentric, superstitious and puerile conceptions, even to recognize what gave strength to the Soviet peoples in their struggle against the Nazi invasion. That reference to it as a "purifying storm" etc., in the Epilogue seems to me one of the most indefensible sections of the book.[148]

Shaken by the terrible disorientation that had overwhelmed her consciousness at the time of her illness in 1964, and driven by the will to strive until the last ounce of her breath, Katharine's mind clung to the old truths. She sought reassurance of the worth of existence in her own terms and became intolerant of new ways and ideas; impatient of the concessions to change made by others. Doubt and despair were the siren songs that lured other spirits. She could not accept the sweet, soft, lotus-land promise of rest and graceful old age. At eighty-two, she fought on, against her own frailty and the slow, corroding rust of compromise; seeing the seeds of futile anarchy in the new, left liberalism which placed individual liberty and personal freedom above unity.

In 1966, when the Russian writers Daniel and Synyavsky were brought to trial before the Supreme Court of the USSR on charges of distributing anti-Soviet propaganda, Katharine opposed those who petitioned for their release. She found herself in opposition to the Central Committee of the Communist Party of Australia which had issued a statement finding "the arrest and sentence of these men to be unnecessary and wrong",[149] Katharine told the General Secretary, L. Aarons, that she was "not impressed by the dialectics which were responsible for the decision" and accused those who concurred of "supine opportunism". She insisted that "to defend the first Socialist State was more important than to placate writers and intellectuals with bourgeois leftist conceptions of freedom":

> I am still indignant that the Party of which I have been always so proud to be a member in this instance should have acted in a way which I disapprove of in joining the chorus of criticism aimed at a decision of the Supreme Court of the U.S.S.R.

She asked for permission to dissociate herself publically from the statement of the Central Committee through *Tribune*.[150]

Katharine remained unconvinced when the General Secretary wrote to her again explaining that:

> The real question is: what does a Socialist Australia mean in terms of democracy, of freedom of thought and expression? In this respect, it was an issue of principle, for this democracy and this freedom is not only an issue for writers, artists, scientists and intellectuals, but is a deep conviction among the people and first of all in the heart and mind of the working class.[151]

"Freedom — what for?" Katharine asked. "There's a lot of loose talk about 'freedom'. Absolute freedom is an illusion even in an anarchist society."[152]

The intransigence of her position, and the forthrightness of Katharine's criticism earned her the enmity of some of the leading

Communists in Western Australia. They rejected the inflexibility of her adherence to "the Moscow line" and resented her interference in policy decisions in which she no longer had any official role. Katharine was unaware of the whispered assaults upon her integrity: one of her comrades described her as "a self-opinionated old bitch"; some former Communists suspected that the extraordinary generosity of her financial support to Communist causes was an underhand attempt to buy favour for her own point of view; criticized her for failing to leave her entire estate to the Party; insinuated that she could not have been a "real Communist" since she had "put her son into the diplomatic service". Others became convinced that a "Cult of Katharine Susannah" had developed, which they saw as their duty to demolish.

Most Communists and writers of the Left ridiculed the idea. Dymphna Cusack said:

> There never was a cult of Katharine that I was aware of. There was general acceptance of her role as doyen of Australian writers and probably the most significant of them. But we're just not given to cults here, and Katharine would have been the first person to denounce it.[153]

In general, she was respected and revered by fellow Communists, even those who disagreed with her. There were others who continued to believe that Katharine was right: saw her view, not as the inevitable conservatism of age, nor as senile inability to understand change and adapt to it, but as sober reality based upon a correct interpretation of Marxism, deep understanding of the fallibility of human nature and hard-headed acceptance of the unpalatable truth that individual liberty must still be tempered in the common good, even after fifty years of socialism.

Her stand, naturally, was applauded in the Soviet Union. Boris Ryurikov wrote, in *Soviet Literature*:

> Above the frenzied dance of the bourgeois press and the anti-Soviet hullabaloo a wise and just woman raises her confident voice, speaking out against attempts to vilify socialism.

He found in her work the genuine humanism of our time — to see and study the whole of life, unafraid of any contradictions, not hesitating to portray what is repulsive and evil, yet seeing the grains of goodness and justice, the noble and kind feelings in people which nothing can destroy".[154]

Katharine herself was shaken, however, by Stefan Heym's revelation that he, too, had run into trouble in East Germany. He had refused, he said, to lie to the Party or the people; refused to admit his error and successfully sued the local publishers for breach of contract when publication of a new novel was forbidden. "I have seen a copy of the article which you sent to Dorothy[155] defining what should be the attitude of a writer in a Socialist country," Katharine told him:

> It seemed to me justifiable, and I could not see how any but doctrinaire fossils could find fault with it.
>
> It has always been understood in the S.U. as far as I know, that defects of administration should be criticized. This was recognized up to the period when Stalin resented criticism, I think. Your statement was intended, not to undermine a Socialist regime — the basis of Socialism — but to strengthen them, by pointing out a writer's duty to indicate errors of administrative tactics.
>
> This is quite different to the way Sinyavsky and Daniel wrote, speculating in anti-Soviet articles for foreign consumption.[156]

The Soviet invasion of Czechoslovakia in August 1968 was the last crisis in Katharine's conflict with her own party, the party that she had helped to build and in which she had placed her faith in the long fruitless struggle for Australian socialism and the world of which she dreamed.

Among the floods of paper which spilled from the segment of earthenware drain-pipe which served as a letter-box at Greenmount, Katharine had found newsletters from Prague and odd, avant garde literary magazines salted with esoteric poetry and incomprehensible satire. Uneasily, Katharine at first accepted them as straws in the wind of the liberal changes contemplated in Communist Czechoslovakia. Friends returning from Prague told her of plans discussed openly among intellectuals for a new liberation. Katharine declined to join the soul-searching debate among Communist liberals when those who supported the concept of a separate path to socialism and the ideas of Socialist democracy learnt that the Soviet Union had intervened to block the Czech Communist Party's programme of liberal reform: "They're having a debate at Dorothy Hewett's — Lilley's tonight on this subject. I haven't been invited, but couldn't go in any case," Katharine told me:

> Am out of favour with the reformist group in Party affairs. Am regarded as a "hard-liner": if that means abide by the principles of Marxism-Leninism, of course, I do. And have no patience with this "open door" policy for the sabotage of

> socialism as established in Czechoslovakia and the U.S.S.R. All this talk of freedom leaves me cold. Freedom for what I ask? Exploitation and war to which we are committed otherwise. But all the same the situation in the Party, at present, is so split by divergences of opinion that I could not recommend any young person to join it. Although the basic principles are, as they always have been, the basis for a sound reorganization of society.

Even when the Warsaw Pact was invoked and Soviet tanks entered Prague, it was not easy for Katharine to reach a decision, despite an announcement by the National Committee of the Communist Party of Australia protesting against the invasion.[157] She insisted upon waiting until the facts of the Czech situation were known from sources other than the daily press before finally making up her own mind. All her instincts and years of belief in the infallibility of the Communist Party of the Soviet Union predisposed her to believe that there must have been overwhelming reasons for action which would inevitably divide the Communist movement throughout the world; discredit the ideals of an international brotherhood of man and the possibility of universal peace in socialism. The probability of an irreconcilable difference with the Australian Communist Party was a deep, personal anguish to her; the prospect of being divided from those upon whose love she depended, unthinkable. "I've been having a nasty B.P.—along of arrgufying about the S.U. and Czech," Katharine wrote to me at the end of August 1968:

> It put me to bed for a day or so, but better now. I have confidence that the S.U. would not have acted—except when necessary in defence of socialism. A. agrees with me—but the A.C.P. does not and that's my grief. Of course you will have to agree with the P.M. and the Government so I don't expect you to see my point of view, darl. And we must not argue on this or any other matter.

By mid-September, Katharine was satisfied that her view had been correct, although few shared her conviction:

> The truth is beginning to come out re the counter-revolutionary coup in Czechoslovakia—anyhow the breaking down of the socialist control, of the State apparatus . . . I felt so sure that something inimical to the Socialist State was brewing—a door being opened for the revanchist policies of the F.G.R.

She took the opportunity of an hour-long interview with Ellis Blain for the Australian Broadcasting Commission to put her views on record. "I must tell you about the famous interview," she wrote:

> I'd agreed to it a week before my B.P. began to play up, and it was Alec's morning. He came at 9 o'clock — and talked until almost 10 — when the blokes were due to arrive. I was feeling a bit wonky — only recovering from the B.P. and it still high — and before I had time for my toast and coffee the mike team arrived followed by Ellis Blain, a tall, rather imposing figure. Then for an hour I went through a gruelling volley of questions. My voice sounded v. weak and frail, but the men (six of them) said it was alright. I suppose they would say so anyhow.

There was no hesitation, however, when she was asked whether she would like to see a system of Communism established in Australia. She replied, carefully choosing her words:

> Hardly Communism. I would like to see a socialist Australia on the terms that the people of Australia wanted and were willing to support. But I would not like to precipitate any action that would force a change too rapidly.

And when, at the end of the interview, she was challenged with the situation in Czechoslovakia, Katharine declared:

> I have every confidence in the Soviet Government to take every step that's necessary for the defence of Socialism. I am opposed to all the criticism against the Russian move in Czechoslovakia.

On 25 September 1968, a statement of her position disagreeing with the encyclical of the National Committee of the Communist Party on Czechoslovakia was printed in *Tribune*. Katharine, for the first time, was publicly in opposition to the leadership of the Communist Party of Australia. As the Russian tanks withdrew from Prague, and Czechoslovakia dropped from the headlines, Katharine was glad to escape to the simple pleasures of home.

And still there was work to do. She produced a short article on the Danish author Martin Anderson Nexo for a symposium on the centenary of his birth, and struggled with an article on Lenin for the celebration of the Fiftieth Anniversary of the Revolution. "I've had such a busy week, darl," she told me:

> An article to write on "Why is the name of Lenin dear to you?" I found it difficult to say, not to indulge in fatuous eulogy, condense the great achievements and at the same time give something original to what I had to say. Then there were two messages for international conferences, over-

> seas correspondence and books to autograph. Not what you'd call a busy week, darl — but enough for me these days.

Katharine could not continue to stand aside when she learned that the Australian representatives at the Conference of Communist and Workers' Parties in Moscow in June 1969 had been openly critical of Soviet policy, and had attempted to insist on discussion of the Czech situation. "I've written to 'Trib.'," Katharine told Norman Freehill on 2 September 1969, "after some reluctant conclusions that this statement had to be made. Whether the letter will be published — 'as writ' — remains to be seen." The letter was not published. Katharine had written: "I am no longer proud and happy to say I am a member of the Communist Party of Australia."

Her letters to me did not mention this last bitter breach with the Communist Party, but I found the handwritten draft among the papers on her worktable, scribbled on the coarse, yellowed pages of a writing-block; scratched through, corrected and rewritten in red. She accused members of the National Committee of deserting the principles of Marxism-Leninism; dissociated herself from the attitude of the Australian representatives at the June conference in Moscow and supported those who upheld the action of the Warsaw Pact countries in Czechoslovakia.

Tribune's request that she reduce the letter "to the stipulated 300 word limit" arrived in Greenmount too late for Katharine to reply.[158]

Katharine did not leave the Communist Party of Australia. Among fellow Communists who shared her concern, it was agreed to try to influence the Party's policy through the Party's own organs. Her last subscription to the Communist Party of Australia was paid three days before she died.

Years later, Frank Hardy, as a Communist writer who had himself taken a different path, looked back on Katharine's stand in those last years. Groping for understanding of the storms of conscience and conviction that had swept over so many Communists in the sixties, he found regret in her championship of old colours, and admiration for her unquenchable spirit:

> I think that Katharine, ideologically, belonged to an earlier period . . .
>
> I think she was terribly wrong. I think it is a great tragedy, but it was part of her . . . It was an error of hope, if it was an error. She still believed in the perspectives of the communist future, the brotherhood of man, and still believed that the Soviet Union was the main instrument of it.[159]

CHAPTER 23

TO NOURISH A WILD FLOWER

In September 1969, when I told her that I would be coming to a brief, official conference in Perth, Katharine wrote:

> Have just heard a chestnut-breasted whistler — and seen him in the garden — such a handsome fellow with his black waistcoat and white collar above the chestnut breast. And he warbles gloriously in the gum-tree at the end of the verandah. I've been asking him to come and sing for you, darl. Though you'll have hardly any sunny hours with me, and October usually a glorious month.

Greenmount in the spring was a joy to Katharine, although she could no longer walk over the paddocks to the place where the wildflowers grew. My "Yoirimba",[160] she called it, the scrub-covered hillside just beyond the barbed-wire fence and the cropped green slopes of Sugar Loaf Hill. They had dreamed once, Katharine and Jim, of the house they would build among the trees, with the plains of Perth before them.

There, after the day's work, Katharine had ridden Wyburn, leaving him to pick his way over the rough ground between the tangle of spiney hakea, where old-man blackboy bushes stood peaceful guard, time-forgotten, their spears tufted with tiny, white flowers.

Somewhere there she picked the first sprigs of leschenaultia for Tom Inglis Moore, racked with arthritis in the Canberra hospital:

> Caverned under the mushroom cloud,
> The doom towering to blackening strife
> I stared at the shadows, stricken numb
> As the cancered flesh awaiting the knife,
> Till out of the West from your hand there flew
> Ecstasy's flower, this burning blue.
>
> Handsel of sky fallen for warm
> Rememberance of heaven, token of sun,

This shadowless blaze, this miracle glow
Comes from eternal fires that run
Down the aeons uncoiling the bud,
Surging in mind and prodigal blood.

You and the leschenaultia glow
As a blue flame of hope, a fire
Smiting the darkness with double sign
Of skyward beauty and eager desire
Quick in the veins of man and earth,
Cascading in love to endless birth.[161]

Now, Katharine could only look from her veranda across the black border of the Great Eastern Highway to the hills where she had led the children of the Greenmount State School to find wild-flowers, "the shy bush people" she taught them to know, and perhaps to love a little, as she did. Stooping, she walked each evening along the overgrown paths of her own wild garden, careful to avoid the fallen gum-nuts rolling underfoot, pausing now and then to pick a handful of ripening strawberries, and frowning, to pull up a weed. "I don't like pulling them out. They are like the proletarians of the garden among all the flowers," Katharine explained, laughing at her own fantasy.

A dying flower touched her still, as it had the child Han, weeping for a bunch of withered wild orchids in the hills of Launceston:

> Sitting on the side verandah with the jasmine a shower of blossom and the bougainvillaea a blaze. But not a bud on the wistaria. I grieve for such beauty departed. Thirty years of loveliness which will never be the same again. Too much to grieve for these days, perhaps, to weep about a dead wistaria, but it's sad to see the vine all grey and lifeless where the lovely lavender lace used to fall beside my window.

Katharine was not unprepared for death. Even before her illness in 1964 brought her close to the end of life, her erratic heart made her aware that at any time she might die. Katharine was determined that she would not be caught in disarray. Quite without sentiment, she discussed the disposal of her personal treasures. Most of her belongings of any material value had long since been given away to special friends, or disposed of to raise funds for some good cause when money was scarce: the gold settings of a brooch paid the rent for the first Peace Council rooms in Perth; a ring was sold to raise a gaoled comrade's bail. There were to be small gifts for her grandchildren — Karen, Querida and Jim, when they were twenty-one — and for Annette. For Dodie, her "most valuable possession, the opal cameo ring of Pallas Athene, to pass on to Karen later", and her mother's Honiton lace; an amber necklace, a Russian shawl, a silver-mounted riding whip, some books and paintings, and the red-enamelled tea-kettle Karen gave her, for a friend who had always admired it.

Systematically Katharine went about putting her papers in some kind of order so that I "would not have the frazzle of dealing with them":

> I've been sorting papers diligently during the week — found one I'm sending you, from you, in Berlin. At first I couldn't remember how you ever got there, and then realized it must have been on the way to the Soviet Union. But it's so interesting to read now, I thought you'd like to see it again. Burnt a lot of my letters to you in New Guinea — haven't had the courage to burn yours! It made me sick to read, or glance through the files of Daddy's correspondence about the rodeo — with the bank, the Roads Board and other organizations he got into trouble with. To me a painful memory — all records of those affairs better be confined to the incinerator. Do you agree?

A dilapidated copy of the "Granny Peace" stories, which Katharine had written for the *New Idea* in 1917, was reprieved from the fire. The first episode of the series was so torn, so nibbled into fancy patterns by silverfish, that it was unreadable. Intrigued, Katharine wrote asking for a photocopy from the files of the magazine, and was pleased when the Editor replied asking permission to reprint the first episode.

Katharine had little time for reminiscences, although almost subconsciously it seems, her mind turned to the completion of unfinished business. One by one, she made a clean sweep of the things she had wanted to do: a cheque for Karen, anticipating the completion of her degree, "as a nest egg for the great adventure in travel when she's ready to make it"; copies of my play, *The Day Before Tomorrow,* sent with Katharine's own gentle commendation to publishers and friends in England, Germany, France, Czechoslovakia and the Soviet Union; her father's short stories prepared for publication; and a fourth article on Lenin. "Don't write so fluently these days — though I never did have the 'flowing pen' of my father. Mine has always been the mot juste — and seeking for exact expression, rather latterly it has been more so — and getting round slick clichés," Katharine explained, turning back to the days before she found matter more important than the way things were said:

> Although I don't altogether disapprove of clichés — they seem so much part of the modern way of speaking. To exclude them is to seem almost pedantic — too nice and "raffined". I feel guilty of saying a thing's "beaut" like the jumper Ka made for me, instead of "beautiful", for example.
>
> But about these articles, it's difficult to say the same things, over and over again, but to try to discover a new angle for each one.

The approval of friends meant as much to Katharine as any official honour could. In the last years of her life, when the University of Western Australia inquired discreetly whether she would accept an honorary doctorate, Katharine declined. It was too late, she said. Besides she disapproved of honorary degrees; and Sir Robert Menzies had just been made a PhD.

The last, and least expected, accolade came not from Australia, to which Katharine had devoted her heart for eighty-five years, nor from the Soviet Union, the centre of her ideals for half a century, but by one of the whimsicalities of chance, from the United States of America. She was astonished to receive a letter from the Editor of the *Mark Twain Journal* informing her solemnly that in honour of her outstanding contributions to literature she had been elected "A Daughter of Mark Twain". In a manner which might have been appreciated by Twain himself, Katharine replied: "I am honoured to be mentioned in the same breath as Mark Twain, of course; but I doubt whether he would have been honoured by so many illegitimate daughters."

Friends were indispensable to her. Katharine looked forward to dinner at Greenmount with good comrades like Vic and Joan Williams, the Western Australian poets, or Bill and Dorothy Irwin, once fellow journalists. To sit around a fire talking of poetry, books, union affairs, politics and peace was pure pleasure to Katharine. But even those most welcome for a casual yarn over sherry, understood that there were to be no visitors when they were warned that I was coming from Canberra. Katharine was jealous of the few days we could have together. She wanted to be sure that there would be time to talk; time to recover empty hours; to speak fears that never were spoken; to find the reassurance of belonging again.

Always when I came, Katharine waited for the sound of the plane sloping down over the ranges; the crunch of car wheels on gravel at the gate; the door's slam. Always, standing shadowy against the light in the doorway, waiting; doing her fluttering little dance of joy as she came towards me: "It is you, darling? Is it really you?"

"Ric is due tonight on the late plane from Canberra — and I'm aching to see him," Katharine wrote to her friend Doon Stone on 2 October 1969. "Such a strange, lonely life it is, these days . . ."

That night it was not Katharine who came to meet me under the broken arch of trellis.

"Alec?"

I could hardly see him in the darkness, silhouetted against the curtain of yellow light from the veranda.

"She's gone, Ric . . . Katharine died about an hour ago . . ." Alec Jolly crying out in his own grief: "God, who am I going to talk to now?"

"I would like the Australian Communist Party in W.A. to take charge of funeral arrangements," Katharine had written in 1961. Now, I believed, she would not have wished that instruction to stand. There seemed no alternative to making the arrangements myself. No orations, no eulogies, Victor Williams' poem to Katharine said what was to be said;

> The ridge of iron through our country's story;
> The fadeless flowering of our people's dreams
> Up slopes of labor, through the shocks of battle —
> The future gathers to your words and deeds.
> The hands you joined, no bombs can break apart,
> Writer and fighter in one human heart.[162]

It was a Communist funeral, as she wished: the coffin draped in the Red flag, symbol of the ideals her life had served. With tears, a neighbour brought an armful of leschenaultia: "ecstasy's flower", it blazed against the scarlet banner, a triumphant elegy of love and hope.

Her ashes were scattered on the slopes of Greenmount, in view of the old house where the happiest years of her life had been spent.

"Good to think of becoming part of the earth, and perhaps nourishing a wild flower", Katharine had written.

NOTES

References to sources are confined to published material, other than Katharine Susannah Prichard's own major works, where the origin is not stated in the text, and to correspondence between other persons.

1 "That Brown Boy", *The Sun and Society Courier*, 17 April 1899.

2 "Bush Fires", *The New Idea*, 5 December 1903.

3 *Southerly*, No. 1, 1953, p. 214.

4 *The Equinox*, Vol. 1, No. VII, March 1912, pp. 251-290.

5 *Every Lady's Journal*, 6 April 1915. Sumner Locke died in childbirth. Her son, Sumner Locke-Elliott, became a successful playwright and novelist (*Rusty Bugles*, etc.).

6 "Lavender", from *The Earth Lover*, Sunnybrook Press, Sydney, 1932.

7 *Daily Mail*, London, 27 October 1915; reprinted in the appendix to *For Valour* by Ric Throssell, Currency Press, Sydney, 1976.

8 *Triad*, 10 June 1918.

9 "For Alan", from *The Earth Lover*.

10 An unpublished poem from the Emerald notebooks.

11 "The Beloved", from *The Earth Lover*.

12 The *West Australian*, 27 June 1921.

13 Letter from Hilda Esson to Nettie Palmer, 10 July 1919. Palmer Collection, National Library. MS. 1174.

14 *Westralian Worker*, 10 December 1921.

15 The amendments were not included in an unsatisfactory reprint of *Black Opal* [*sic*] published by Caslon House, Sydney, in 1946, although it was likely that the revisions were made much earlier. The Angus and Robertson 1973 edition is taken from K.S.P.'s amendments to the original Heinemann edition.

16 *Australian Women's Mirror*, 28 April 1931.

17 *Louis Esson and the Australian Theatre* by Vance Palmer, Georgian House, Melbourne, 1948, p. 67.

18 *Fourteen Years* by Nettie Palmer, Meanjin Press, Melbourne, 1948, p. 24.

19 *Beckett's Budget,* 9 November 1928.
20 The contracts in fact provided for a royalty of 10 per cent on the first 3000 copies and 15 per cent on sales above 3000 copies at a price of six shillings.
21 Introduction to *N'Goola,* Australasian Book Society, Melbourne, 1959.
22 Bungarra — an aboriginal word for lizard.
23 Narloo — an evil spirit; featured in the corroboree of Act 1 of *Brumby Innes.*
24 One-act versions of *The Pioneers* and *The Great Man* were produced by the Pioneer Players, Melbourne, in 1923. *The Burglar,* a one-act comedy, was performed at the Australian Drama Night arranged by William Moore and Louis Esson in Melbourne in 1909.
25 Gregan McMahon's plans to produce the play for J. C. Williamson's in 1927 collapsed. *Brumby Innes* was not produced for forty-five years. It was first presented by the Australian Performing Group and the Nindethana Theatre, at the Pram Factory, Melbourne, under the direction of John Smythe, in November 1972, when it was greeted by *The Australian,* 11 November 1972, as "the great Australian play". A full account of the dramatic writing of Katharine Susannah Prichard is included in the 1975 edition of *Brumby Innes.*
26 Letter from Mary Gilmore to Nettie Palmer of 18 December 1928. Palmer Collection, National Library, MS. 1174.
27 *Bulletin,* 14 October 1929.
28 Letter from S. H. Prior to Vance Palmer, 9 May 1929. Palmer Collection, National Library, MS. 1174.
29 Letter from Katharine Susannah Prichard to Leon Brodsky (Spencer Brodney) of 25 May 1930, Latrobe Library, Melbourne, MS. 57859.
30 Letter from Katharine Susannah Prichard to Douglas Stewart, 28 December 1963.
31 From an unidentifiable press cutting.
32 *Louis Esson and the Australian Theatre,* pp. 87-88.
33 *Meanjin,* Vol. 24, No. 4, 1965, p. 412.
34 *Daily News* (Perth), 21 July 1930.
35 Palmer Collection, National Library. M.S. 1174.
36 Katharine Susannah Prichard and Cecilia Shelley, later Secretary of the Hotel, Club and Caterers' Union, formed the Unemployed Women and Girls' Association. (Interview with Joan Williams in *Our Women,* September 1963.)

37 Letter from Hilda Esson to Frank Dalby Davison, 22 April 1939. Davison Collection, National Library. MS. 764/994.

38 Letter from Nettie Palmer to Alan Marshall, 18 May 1937. Marshall Collection, National Library.

39 See also Chapter 19.

40 Article for *Aufbau Verlag,* Berlin, June 1954.

41 In a note to the unpublished poem Katharine explained: "We heard Moseiwitsch play the Appassionata, and next day, as he ploughed the orchard in a westerly gale, Jim was singing fragments from it, and full of the joy of life, breaking into the work-room where I was writing to embrace me".

42 The play, entitled *For Instance,* was reviewed by the Melbourne *Herald* on 11 August 1914: "In this work the writer showed a skill in compacting together romance, politics and social economics. For it was designedly a play with purpose." No text of the play survives.

43 The Workers' Art Guild was formed in the mid-thirties by K.S.P. and Keith George, its first director. The Guild revolutionized theatrical experience in Australia with Keith George's outstanding productions of Clifford Odets' *Till the Day I Die* and Irwin Shaw's *Bury the Dead.*

44 *Forward One* (1935); *Penalty Clause* (1940).

45 *Book News,* 20 September 1933.

46 *Australian Writers and Their Work: Katharine Susannah Prichard,* by Henrietta Drake-Brockman. Oxford University Press, Melbourne, 1967, p. 38.

47 *Southerly,* No. 4, 1968, p. 240.

48 Letter from K.S.P. to Nettie Palmer, of 1 September 1937. Palmer Collection, National Library, MS. 1174.

49 *Australian Writers and Their Work: Katharine Susannah Prichard,* pp. 39, 40.

50 *Who Wants War?*, Franklin Press, Perth, C. 1936.

51 R. Dixon, *Communist Review,* October 1939.

52 K.S.P. informed the University Historical and Economic Society: "I had an early morning visit from the police one day last year and they took all papers having reference to Communism." (*West Australian,* 19 April 1933.)

53 *The First Furrow* (Militancy and Communism in Western Australia: Prelude and History), by Joan Williams, Lone Hand Press, W.A., 1976, p. 176.

54 Letter from A. Edwards to R. Throssell of 6 March 1972.

55 K.S.P. became a Life Patron of the Fellowship of Australian Writers, as a founder of the Writers' League, following amalgamation of the two bodies in 1938. (*Fellowship,* Sydney, September 1944.) K.S.P. became an Honorary Life Member of WA section of the FAW when it was formed in 1938.

56 *Overland,* June 1958, p. 31.

57 *The Pioneers* was filmed by W. Franklyn Barrett in 1916, and in 1926 by Raymond Longford. Both productions failed financially. A pirated version of the story under another name was also discovered by Longford's company. No copies of the three films can now be traced.

58 *British Australasian,* 8 April 1915.

59 *Book News,* 20 September 1933.

60 From notes from a lecture by Professor Allan Edwards on K.S.P. at the University of Western Australia in September 1951.

61 *Sydney Morning Herald,* 11 April 1959.

62 ABC, Perth, 1941. Most of the stories of K.S.P.'s early days in London are retold in *Child of the Hurricane.*

63 Letter from Professor Walter Murdoch to Secretary, Commonwealth Literary Fund, 9 December 1940.

64 The ban on the Communist Party was not in fact lifted until December 1942, after the Government had received "satisfactory undertakings guaranteeing assistance in war production and in preventing stoppages and absenteeism", (*The Government and the People,* Hasluck, Australian War Memorial 1952, p. 591.)

65 *The Realist,* No. 30, 1968, p. 18.

66 *Communist Review,* July 1938.

67 *The Realist,* No. 30, 1968.

68 Ibid.

69 *Meanjin,* Vol. XII, No. 4, 1953, p. 418.

70 *The Communist Party of Australia* by Alistair Davidson, Hoover Stamford, California, 1969.

71 *A Short History of the Labor Movement* by Brian Fitzpatrick, Rawson, Melbourne, 1944, p. 213.

72 *Daily Telegraph,* Sydney, 10 March 1943.

73 Letter from Eleanor Dark to Ric Throssell of 15 July 1972.

74 *Meanjin,* No. 3, 1951; No. 4, 1961.

75 *A.B.C. Weekly,* 24 February 1945.

76 Thirra — Zest, spark. A word borrowed, I believe, from its inventor, E. J. Brady.

77 *New York Times Book Review,* 22 June 1947.

78 George Farwell, journalist, broadcaster, co-editor of *Australian New Writing.*

79 Nina Oks, Russian tutor and collaborator in K.S.P.'s Introduction to *Creative Labour and Culture,* by Maxim Gorky, Current Book Distributors, Sydney, March 1945.

80 Neé Elman Hague Gallacher.

81 Bob Saunders, a Kalgoorlie friend to whom *The Roaring Nineties* had been dedicated.

82 "To God from the Weary Nations", quoted on p. 136.

83 Keith George, formerly director of Workers' Art Guild, Perth, and Linley George (Wilson).

84 Mrs R. P. Throssell, nee Eileen Dorothy Jordan, also referred to as Dodie.

85 Sam Aarons, Secretary of Communist Party, Western Australia; and Annette Aarons.

86 K.S.P. founded the Modern Women's Club in Perth in 1938 in response to a decision of the WA State Executive of the ALP forbidding its women members to join the Council Against War and Fascism. The Modern Women's Club continued to function as a progressive social and cultural organization for twenty years. It was dissolved on 18 July 1958.

87 Clarice Dunstan, formerly secretary to H. V. H. Throssell.

88. *Meanjin,* No. 3, 1951.

89 Letter from Louis Esson to Frank Dalby Davison of 7 May 1952. Davison Collection, National Library.

90 Republished in Canada in *New Frontiers,* Vol. 5, No. 2 1956.

91 *The Critic,* December 1967.

92 *The Rage for Life,* by Jack Beasley. Current Book Distributors, Sydney, 1964.

93 *New York Times,* 22 June 1947.

94 Permission to quote the thesis or name its author was denied.

95 John K. Ewers suggested nomination of K.S.P. for the Nobel Prize for Literature in the *Australasian Post,* 8 December

1949. The proposal was adopted by the Fellowship of Australian Writers in March 1950. The Executive of the FAW in South Australia again nominated K.S.P. in 1961.

96 *Meanjin,* Vol. 24, No. 4, 1965.

97 "The Novels of Katharine Susannah Prichard", by G. A. Wilkes, *Southerly,* No. 1, 1953, p. 220 et seq.

98 G. A. Wilkes (Ph.D Oxford, MA, Dip.Ed., FAHA) had obtained his MA with first-class honours, and the University Medal in English in 1952. He became Professor of Australian Literature in 1962, and Challis Professor of English Literature in 1966.

99. *Meanjin,* Vol. 9, No. 4, 1950, p. 252.

100 R. Sadlier, *Westerly,* No. 3, 1961.

101 "Some Major Themes and Problems in the Novels of K. S. Prichard", MA Thesis by Ellen Malos (University of Melbourne, 1962).

102 *Australian Writers and Their Work: Katharine Susannah Prichard,* by Henrietta Drake-Brockman, Oxford University Press, Melbourne, 1967.

103 *Fellowship News,* April 1968.

104 *Meanjin,* No. 4, 1961, pp. 366-387.

105 *Why I am a Communist* by Katharine Susannah Prichard, Current Book Distributors, Sydney, 1956.

106 *Overland,* June 1958.

107 Lorna Roberts.

108 *Westerly,* December 1963.

109 From notes for an address by K.S.P. on Peace and War, 1938.

110 Ibid.

111 From *On Strenuous Wings : A half-century of selected writings from the works of Katharine Susannah Prichard,* edited by Joan Williams, Seven Seas, Berlin, 1965.

112 From "The Land I Love", by K.S.P., reprinted in *Overland,* June 1958.

113 From notes for an address by K.S.P. to Peace Conference, Perth, September 1950.

114 *The Guardian,* Melbourne, 24 April 1957.

115 John Clements, Secretary of the Peace Council in Perth.

116 *The Realist,* No. 30, 1968.

117 *Deakin,* a three-act play by K.S.P., was entered in the Commonwealth Jubilee Stage Play Competition in 1951. A play on the same subject, *Tether the Dragon,* by Kylie Tennant, won the competition. *Deakin* remains unpublished and unproduced.

118 From notes on an address by K.S.P. on "Clarity in Literature", Melbourne, November 1959.

119 Bert Vickers, Western Australian novelist.

120 Dr Alec Jolly, physician to K.S.P.

121 Amy Barrett, friend and occasional housekeeper to K.S.P.

122 See "Vaso Motor Disorder: The Third Factor in Cardio Vascular Disease", by A. T. Jolly, *Annals of General Practice,* December 1962.

123 There were two models for Sharn although Aileen Palmer, whose character K.S.P. had drawn on in the earlier stages, protested "even I wasn't nearly as badly dressed as Sharn".

124 Les Greenfield, formerly Secretary to Australasian Book Society.

125 *Southerly,* No. 4, 1968.

126 Ibid.

127 *Pen Newsletter* No. 10, June 1970.

128 Joan Williams, poet, journalist and Editor of *On Strenuous Wings.*

129 Record of interview between K.S.P. and Ian Turner, 29 February 1960 (Australian National University, Research School of Social Sciences.)

130 Letter from K.S.P. to H. L. Denford, Secretary of Communist Party of Australia, 16 February 1922.

131 Interview with Ian Turner, as above.

132 *The New Order: being an address on Socialism — with after thoughts,* by K.S.P., People's Printing and Publishing Co., Perth, 1919.

133 *Marx: the man and his work.* An address to the Labor Study Circle, by K.S.P., *Westralian Worker* Print, Perth, C. 1921.

134 Letter from K.S.P. to H. L. Denford, as above.

135 Letter from Gordon Burgoyne to Ric Throssell, May 1972.

136 Letter from Jack Hughes to Ric Throssell, 2 October 1972.

137 Interview between R. Dixon and Ric Throssell, Bankstown, 1 July 1972.

138 *Workers' Star*, Perth, 25 October 1946.

139 In July 1949, L. Sharkey, General Secretary of the Communist Party of Australia, was sentenced to three years gaol for sedition on the basis of a statement to the press that if Soviet forces entered Australia "in pursuit of aggressors", they would be welcomed by Australian workers.

140 James Gamble, *Sunday Mirror*, Sydney, 1 December 1963.

141 *Communist Review*, December 1955.

142 *Tribune*, 4 December 1963.

143 *Communist Review*, April 1964.

144 Letter from Guido Baracchi to Ric Throssell, 10 June 1972.

145 Letter from K.S.P. to Editor of *Tribune*, 18 May 1959.

146 Letter from K.S.P. to Communist Party Secretariat, 2 June 1959.

147 *Tribune*, 10 June 1959.

148 Letter from K.S.P. to Boris Polevoi, 23 December 1958.

149 *Tribune*, 23 February 1966.

150 Letter from K.S.P. to L. Aarons, 29 March 1966.

151 Letter from L. Aarons to K.S.P., 4 April 1966.

152 Letter from K.S.P. to L. Aarons, 29 March 1966.

153 Interview between Dymphna Cusack and Ric Throssell, 29 June 1972.

154 *Soviet Literature*, No. 4, 1969.

155 Dorothy Hewett, Western Australian poet and playwright.

156 Letter from K.S.P. to Stefan Heym, 25 April 1966.

157 *Tribune*, 28 August 1968.

158 The letter from *Tribune*, dated 2 October 1969, arrived in Greenmount after K.S.P.'s death.

159 Interview between Frank Hardy and Ric Throssell, 1 July 1972.

160 Yoirimba — aboriginal word meaning "how beautiful", used in K.S.P.'s short story "Yoirimba", included in the *N'Goola* collection.

161 From "Leschenaultia" by Tom Inglis Moore, dedicated to K.S.P., *Bulletin*, 28 August 1957.

162 From "Katharine Susannah Prichard" by Victor Williams, included in *Delegate*, Lautrec Studios, Melbourne. The poem was read by the author at K.S.P.'s funeral on 4 October 1969.

BIBLIOGRAPHY

This bibliography is confined to publications by or concerning Katharine Susannah Prichard.

The following list of the works of Katharine Susannah Prichard is based upon a check list originally compiled by Hugh Anderson (*Biblionews* Vol. 12, No. 3, March 1959 and July 1959). More recent publications have been added. Short stories published in magazines and subsequently included in collections have been deleted. Particulars of produced but unpublished plays have been added. A select list of articles has also been included. The list of novels and short stories published in translation is incomplete. In addition to those listed, *The Roaring Nineties* is believed to have been translated into Byelo-Russian, Rumanian, and Armenian; *Winged Seeds,* into German, Rumanian, Latvian and Chinese. Short stories are also believed to have been translated into Italian and Hungarian. A translation of *Coonardoo* into French by Helene Jacomard is in preparation by La Petite Maison.

NOVELS

The Pioneers. London, Hodder and Stoughton, 1915. Reprinted 1916; also at New York, 1917; Revised edition, Adelaide, Rigby, 1963. With this novel K.S.P. won the Australasian section of a competition conducted by Hodder and Stoughton in 1915. It was broadcast in Afrikaans but not published; and a film was produced by Franklyn Barrett in 1916, and by Raymond Longford for Australian Films Ltd during 1926.

Windlestraws. London, Holden and Hardingham, 1916.

The Black Opal. London, Heinemann, 1921; *(Black Opal)* Sydney, Caslon House, 1946; Angus and Robertson, 1973 (A&R Classics); Dusseldorf, Progress-Verlag, 1959. Trans. Joseph Kalmer.

Working Bullocks. London, Cape, 1926 (several impressions); New York, Viking, 1927; Sydney, Cape, 1944; London, Cape, 1946; Sydney Angus and Robertson, 1956, Angus and Robertson, paperback, 1972; Moscow, ZIF, 1928, trans. M. Volosov; Moscow, Khudozh. Lit., 1965, trans. S. Krugerskaya and T. Ozerskaya.

The Wild Oats of Han. Sydney, Angus & Robertson, 1928. Melbourne, Lansdowne Press, 1968. Prague, Ausatros, 1979 trans. Jamila Emmerova.

Coonardoo: The Well in the Shadow. (Bulletin Prize, 1928.) London, Cape, 1929; New York, Norton, 1930; Sydney Cape, 1943; Sydney, Angus and Robertson, 1956; Pacific Books, 1961, 1968, 1971; Sirius Books, 1964, 1965; A&R Classics edition, 1975; Moscow, 1959, I.L. Trans. T. Ozerskaya and E. Piterskaya; Prague, Klub Ctenaru, 1960, Trans. Jarmila Emmerova, Slovak Bratislava trans. Pavel Branko.

Haxby's Circus: The Lightest, Brightest, Little Show on Earth. London, Cape, 1930. Several impressions and included in Florin Books, 1932; (*Fay's Circus*) New York, Norton, 1931; Sydney, Angus and Robertson, 1945 (Australian Pocket Library), A&R Classics edition, 1973; Prague, Odeon, 1969, Trans. Zora Wolfova; there are no details available of an edition published in Hungarian c. 1933, Russian, 1985 trans. D. Kraminova.

Intimate Strangers. London, Cape, 1937. Sydney, A & R 1976.

Moon of Desire. London, Cape, 1941.

The Roaring Nineties. London, Cape, 1946; Sydney, Australasian Publishing Co., 1946; Moscow, Foreign Language Publishing House, 1955 (in English), Introduction L. Kasatkina. Foreign language editions: French, Paris, le Portulan, 1946, Trans. Edith Vincent; Russian, Trans. and abridged by T. Ozerskaya and V. Stanevitch, Moscow, I.L. 1949, 1958; Czech, Prague, Svoboda, 1949; Polish, Warsaw, Czytelnik, 1950, Trans. K. Szaniawski; Latvian, Riga, Latvian State Publishing House, 1951; Slovak, Bratislava, Matica Slovenska, 1952, Trans. A. Kuzmany-Bruothova; German, Trans. G. R. Leys, Berlin, Volk und Welt, 1954; Russian, Introduction V. Mikheev, Moscow, I.L., 1954; Chinese, Trans. P'eichin, Jen Min Wen Hsueh Ch'u Pan She, 1959; Ukrainian, Khudozh Lit'y, 1963, Trans. L. Solonko; Dnipro, 1973, Trans. L. Solonko (with note by A. Petrikovskaya).

Golden Miles. London, Cape, 1948; Sydney, Australasian Publishing Co., 1948. Foreign language editions: Russian, T. Kudryartseva and S. Serpinsky, Moscow, I.L., 1949, and 1958, retranslated by T. Ozerskaya and T. Kudryartseva; Czech, Prague, Svoboda, 1949, Trans. J. Pospisil; Latvian, Riga, Latvian State Publishing House, 1951; Polish, Warsaw, Czytelnik, 1951, Trans. J. Dehnel; Slovak, Bratislava, Matica Slovenska, 1952, Trans. A. Kuzmany-Bruothova; German, Berlin, Verlag, Volk and Welt, 1954, Trans. K. Heinrich; Rumanian, Bucharest, Editura de Stat Pentru Literatura si Arta, 1956, trans. M. Gheorghiu, Russian, 1985.

Winged Seeds. Sydney, Australasian Publishing Co., 1950; London, Cape, 1950. Foreign language editions: Polish, Warsaw, Czytelnik, 1951, Trans. J. Dehnel; Slovak, Bratislava, Matica Slovenska, 1952, Trans. A. Kuzmany-Bruothova; Russian, Moscow, I.L. 1953, 1958, Trans T. Kudryartseva and T. Ozerskaya.

Subtle Flame. Sydney, Australasian Book Society, 1967. Foreign language editions: Russian, Moscow, Foreign Literature, 1971; Czech, Prague, Svoboda, 1975, Trans. Jaroslav Stoklasa. Russian, 1986, trans. O. Petrikojskaya.

AUTOBIOGRAPHY

Child of the Hurricane. Sydney, Angus and Robertson, 1964; A&R Classics edition, 1974; Moscow, Progress, 1966, Trans. I. Poletavoi and B. Rostokina.

SHORT STORIES

COLLECTIONS:

Kiss on the Lips and Other Stories. London, Cape, 1932, including "The Grey Horse" (*Art in Australia* Prize 1924), "The Cooboo", "The Cow" and "The Curse", etc.

Potch and Colour. Sydney, Angus and Robertson, 1944, including "Jimble", "The Mayor of Bardie Creek", etc.

N'Goola. Melbourne, Australasian Book Society, 1959, including "Yoirimba", "The White Turkey", "A Devout Lover", "Buccaneers", "Josephina Anna Maria", etc.

On Strenuous Wings. Berlin, Seven Seas, 1965, Ed. Joan Williams.

Happiness. Sydney, Angus and Robertson, 1967, including stories from previous collections.

Tribute (edited by Ric Throssell) Brisbane, UQP, 1988.

SHORT STORIES IN MAGAZINES — CHRONOLOGICAL:

(Short stories subsequently included in collections are not listed.)

"That Brown Boy". *The Sun and Society Courier,* 7 April 1899.

"Bush Fires". *New Idea,* 5 December 1903.

"A City Girl in Central Australia: Her Adventures and Experiences at Back o' Beyond". (Serial in six parts), *New Idea,* May-October 1906.

"The Kid". *Bulletin,* 17 January 1907.

"Kit, The Wildcat". *Red Funnel,* June 1907.

"The Blue Gown". *Steele Rudd's Magazine,* October 1907.

"Diana of the Inlet". *Equinox,* London, March 1912.

"The Paper Lantern". *British Australian,* 24 July 1913.

"A Wanderin' One". *Australasian,* 25 March 1916.

"The Grandchild". *Australasian*, 12 August 1916.

"Earthenware". *Australasian*, 6 January 1917.

"Wild Honey". *Bulletin*, 16 August 1917.

"Granny Peace: Her Story". (Serial in six parts), *Every Lady's Journal*, October 1917-March 1918.

"Danny Neil". *Australasian*, 15 December 1917.

"Trenoon". *Australasian*, 18 January 1919.

"The Almond Tree". *Table Talk Annual*, 10 October 1932.

"The Apricot Tree" ("Sour Sap"). *Ogonyok* (USSR) No. 48, 1959; *The Tracks We Travel* (ABS), 1965.

"Mongalilli". *Ogonyok* (USSR) No. 40, 1968.

"The Woman With a Broom". *Realist Writer*, No. 6 May 1961.

SELECTED SHORT STORIES AND COLLECTIONS IN TRANSLATION:

Chinese: "Christmas Tree" (no details available).

Czech: "N'Goola", Berlin, Seven Seas, 1960, Trans. Eva Musilova (included in *Za Sluncem*).

German: "The Grey Horse", Zurich, Verlag Schweizer Kavallerist, 1960 (included in *Der alte Schimmel*); Walter-Verlag 1961 (included in *Australian Short Stories*).
"The Bride from Far-Away" and other short stories, Berlin, Verlag Volk und Welt, 1962, Trans. Gisela Petersen.
"The Swap", Das Magazine, 1978.

Polish: "Communists are Always Young", Warsaw, Czytelnik, 1955 (included in *I Drzewa Mowia*).

Russian: "Christmas Tree" and other stories, Moscow, Ogonyok Library No. 23, 1958.
"N'Goola" and other stories, Moscow, Khudozh. Lit., 1958.
"Christmas Day at Yienda" and other stories, Moscow, I.L., 1960, Trans. N. Vetoshkina and E. Piterskaya.
"Treason" and other stories, Moscow, Khudozh. Lit. 1962.
Japanese: "The Cooboo", c. 1987.

PLAYS

Brumby Innes. A play of three acts, Perth, Patterson's, 1940. (*Triad* Prize 1927.) Sydney, Currency-Methuen, 1975.

The Pioneers. A play in one act, was included in *Best Australian One Act Plays*, Angus and Robertson, 1937; reprinted in *Drama and the School* No. 34, 1967.

The Burglar.* One act, first produced by William Moore and Louis Esson, for the Australian Drama Night, Melbourne, 1909.

Her Place. One act, first produced by the Actresses' Franchise League, London, 1913.

For Instance. One act, first produced by the Actresses' Franchise League, London, 1914. (No copy traced.)

*The Great Man.** Three-act comedy, first produced by the Pioneer Players, Melbourne, 1923.

*Women of Spain.** One act, first produced by the Workers' Art Guild, Perth, 1937.

*Forward One.** One act, first produced by the Workers' Art Guild, Perth, 1935.

Penalty Clause. Three acts, first produced by the Workers' Art Guild, Perth, 1940.

*Good Morning.** One-act sketch, first produced by the New Theatre of WA at the Modern Women's Club, Perth, 1955.

*(Campbell Howard Collection, University of New England.)

Bid Me To Love (c. 1927). Published Sydney, Currency-Methuen, 1975. First produced by Canberra Repertory 1973.

Deakin (1951).

VERSE

Clovelly Verses. London, McAllan and Co., 1913.

The Earth Lover. Sydney, Sunnybrook Press, 1932.

REPORTAGE

The Real Russia. Sydney, Modern Publishers, 1934.

On Strenuous Wings (Ed. Joan Williams) Berlin, Seven Seas, 1967.

CHILDREN'S STORY

Moggie and Her Circus Pony. Melbourne, Cheshire, 1967.

PAMPHLETS

The New Order. Perth, People's Printing and Publishing Co., 1919.

Who Wants War? Perth, Franklin Press (c. 1936).

Marx, The Man And His Work. Perth, Labor Study Circle of WA (c. 1921).

The Materialist Conception of History (c. 1921).

Why I Am a Communist. Sydney, Current Books (c. 1957).

SELECTED ARTICLES

"Australia", *The Home Annual*, 1 October 1936. Reprinted "The Land I Love", *Overland* No. 12, 1958.

"How Has the Australian Writer Affected Australian Life", a discussion between K.S.P. and Gavin Casey. In *Australian Writers Speak*, Sydney, Angus and Robertson, 1942.

"Tribute to Henry Lawson", *Communist Review*, October 1943.

"Hoax Renders Service to Literature", *Communist Review*, March 1945.

"Monty Miller as I Knew Him", *Tribune*, 1 December 1945.

"Creative Labour and Culture", by Maxim Gorky, Introduction by Katharine Susannah Prichard, Sydney, Current Books, 1945.

"Koestler, the Irresponsible", *Meanjin*, Vol. IV, 1945, p. 176.

"Lawrence in Australia", *Meanjin*, Vol. IX, No. 4, 1950, p. 252.

"Bernard O'Dowd", *Meanjin*, Vol. XII, No. 4, 1953.

"Humour in the Short Story", *Etruscan*, March 1954.

"Henry Handel Richardson", *Overland*, No. 1, 1954.

"Flora Eldershaw", *Meanjin*, Vol. XV, No. 3, 1956.

"Hugh McCrae: a Tribute", *Overland*, No. 12, 1958.

"Dr Zhivago", *Overland*, No. 14, 1959.

"Contrasts: Meredith and Marchesi", *Meanjin*, Vol. XXI, No. 3,. 1962.

"Some Thoughts on Australian Literature", *The Realist Writer*, No. 15, June 1964.

"The Short Stories of Henry Lawson", *Realist*, No. 27, 1967.

"Some Perceptions and Aspirations", *Southerly* No. 4, 1968.

"*Straight Left: The Articles and Addresses of K.S.P.* (edited by Ric Throssell) Sydney, Wild & Woolley, 1982.

SELECTED COMMENTARIES

Beasley, Jack, *The Rage for Life*, Sydney, Current Books, 1964.

Cusack, Dymphna, "Katharine Susannah Prichard", *The Realist*, No. 14, March 1964.

Drake-Brockman, Henrietta, *Katharine Susannah Prichard*, "Australian Writers and Their Work", Melbourne, Oxford University Press, 1967.

Drake-Brockman, Henrietta, "K. S. Prichard: the Colour in her Work", *Southerly*, No. 4, 1953.

Eldershaw, M. Barnard, *Essays in Australian Fiction,* Melbourne, MUP, 1938.

Franklin, Miles, *Laughter Not for a Cage,* Sydney, Angus and Robertson, 1956.

Franklin, Miles, "Katharine Susannah Prichard", *The Modern Writer,* Vol. 2, No. 4, 1946.

Grattan, C. Hartley, "Recent Australian Books", *The New York Herald Tribune Books,* 15 May 1932.

Grattan, C. Hartley, "Readers and Writers Down Under", *The New York Times Book Review,* 22 June 1947.

Green, H. M., "Katharine Susannah Prichard: Her Place in Australian Literature", *The Australian Woman's Mirror,* 28 April 1931.

Green, H. M., *A History of Australian Literature,* Vol. 2, Sydney, Angus and Robertson, 1961.

Hardy, Frank, "Greetings to Katharine Susannah Prichard", *Communist Review,* December 1955.

Hardy, Frank, "Katharine Prichard and the Revolutionary Hero", *Tribune,* 3 March 1965.

Hardy, Frank, "Page from a Diary", *Australian Author,* No. 3.

Hetherington, John, "Katharine Susannah Prichard: Her Great Influence on Our Literature", *The Age,* 28 January 1961.

Hetherington, John, *42 Faces,* Melbourne, Cheshire, 1962.

Hewett, Dorothy, "Excess of Love", *Overland,* No. 43, 1969/70. (Comment *Overland* No. 44, 1970.)

Holburn, Muir, "Katharine Susannah Prichard", *Meanjin,* No. 3, 1951.

Irwin, E. W., "Australia's Katharine Susannah", Toronto, *New Frontiers,* Vol. 5, No. 2, 1956.

Lindsay, Jack, "The Novels of Katharine Susannah Prichard", *Meanjin,* No. 4, 1961.

Lindsay, Jack, "Reply to Ellen Malos", *Meanjin,* No. 1, 1963.

Malos, Ellen, "Some Major Themes in the Novels of Katharine Susannah Prichard", *Australian Literary Studies,* No. 1, 1963.

Malos, Ellen, "Jack Lindsay's Essay on Katharine Susannah Prichard's Novels", *Meanjin,* No. 1, 1963.

Miller, Morris, *Australian Literature to 1938,* Vol. II, MUP, 1940.

Miller, Morris and Macartney, F. T., *Australian Literature to 1950,* Sydney, Angus and Robertson, 1956.

Moore, T. Inglis, *Social Patterns in Australian Literature,* Sydney, Angus and Robertson, 1971.

Murray-Smith, S., "The Novel and Society", in *The Literature of Australia,* Ed. Geoffrey Dutton, Adelaide, Penguin, 1964.

Palmer, Aileen. "The Changing Face of Australia: Notes on the Creative Writing of Katharine Susannah Prichard", *Overland,* Nos 12 and 13, 1958.

Palmer, Nettie, "Katharine Susannah Prichard, Novelist and Enthusiast", *The Australian Women's Mirror,* 27 July 1926.

Palmer, Nettie, *Fourteen Years,* Melbourne, *Meanjin,* 1948.

Palmer, Vance, *Louis Esson and the Australian Theatre,* Melbourne, Georgian House, 1948.

Palmer, Vance, "Katharine Susannah Prichard : Her Novel on the Aborigines Greatly Shocked Australians", *The Age,* 14 March 1959.

Roderick, Colin, *The Australian Novel,* Sydney, Brooks, 1949.

Roderick, Colin, *An Introduction to Australian Fiction,* Sydney, Angus and Robertson, 1950.

Ross, Edgar, "Katharine Susannah Prichard", *Communist Review,* April 1964.

Rubin, Vladimir, "Katharine Susannah Prichard and Soviet Readers", *Soviet Literature,* No. 1, 1964.

Ryurikov, Boris, "Child of the Hurricane", *Soviet Literature,* No. 4, 1969.

Thomas, Tony, "Katharine Susannah Prichard Interviewed", *The Critic,* 22 December 1967.

Throssell, Ric, "My Father's Son", Melbourne, Heinemann, 1989.

Waten, Judah, "Katharine Susannah Prichard Reconsidered", *The Australian Socialist,* August 1970.

Wilkes, G. A., "The Novels of K. S. Prichard", *Southerly,* No. 4, 1953.

Williams, Joan, "Katharine Susannah Prichard", *Our Women,* September-December 1963.

Williams, Justina (Joan), "Rage that Engenders", *Southerly,* No. 1, 1972.

Williams, Joan, *The First Furrow*, Lone Hand Press, Perth 1976.

INDEX